The Indian Easements Act, 1882

(ACT NO. V OF 1882)
WITH EXHAUSTIVE COMMENTS

By

J.D. JAIN

Eighteenth Edition 2026

Allahabad Law Agency®
FARIDABAD (HARYANA)

Published by:
ALLAHABAD LAW AGENCY®
16/2, Karkhana Bagh, Plot No. 33,
Mathura Road, Faridabad (HARYANA)
Phone : 0129-4012541
Mobile : 9313703594
e-mail : allahabadlawagency@gmail.com

ISBN:- 978-93-7472-749-2

Eighteenth Edition : 2026

Price : ₹ 325/-

Typeset at : **Neo Software Consultants**, Prayagraj

Printed at : **Compudata Services, New Delhi - 20**

PREFACE TO THE EIGHTEENTH EDITION

The present edition has been thoroughly revised and recast and latest cases have been incorporated. Several new points have been discussed in detail, various Chapters and illustrations also have been made more exhaustive wherever possible.

This edition strives to keep up the quality of the preceding ones. The entire territory of law is covered with the use of Indian and English authorities, in clear language. Sole object has been kept in mind to present the reader with a correct, concise, clear and complete view of the provisions of each section of the Act and exposition of the principles involved therein.

It is hoped that the present edition will be found useful to the students appearing in law and competitive exams.

I am considerably indebted to the publishers, Allahabad Law Agency for bringing out the book in time.

Any suggestion for the improvement of the book will be thankfully received.

—AUTHOR

Ministry of Law and Justice

Central Government notifies replacement of old criminal laws with new:

S.O.2790(E).—In pursuance of section 8 of the General Clauses Act, 1897 (10 of 1897), the Central Government hereby notifies that where any reference of the Indian Penal Code (45 of 1860), or the Code of Criminal Procedure, 1973 (2 of 1974) or the Indian Evidence Act, 1872 (1 of 1872 or any provisions thereof is made in any—

(a) Act made by Parliament; or

(b) Act made by the Legislature of any State;

(c) Ordinance;

(d) Regulations made under article 240 of the Constitution;

(e) President's order;

(f) rules, regulations, order or notification made under any Act, Ordinance or Regulation,

for the time being in force, such reference shall respectively be read as the reference of the Bharatiya Nyaya Sanhita, 2023 (45 of 2023) (BNS), the Bharatiya Nagarik Suraksha Sanhita, 2023 (46 of 2023) (BNSS) or the Bharatiya Sakshya Adhiniyam, 2023 (47 of 2023) (BSA), and the corresponding provisions of such law shall be construed accordingly.

विधि एवं न्याय मंत्रालय

केंद्रीय सरकार पुराने आपराधिक कानूनों को नए से प्रतिस्थापित करने की अधिसूचना जारी करती हैः

एस.ओ.2790(ई).—जनरल क्लॉजेज अधिनियम, 1897 (10 ऑफ 1897) की धारा 8 के अनुपालन में, केंद्रीय सरकार एतद्द्वारा अधिसूचित करती है कि जहां भारतीय दंड संहिता (45 ऑफ 1860), या आपराधिक प्रक्रिया संहिता, 1973 (2 of 1974) या भारतीय साक्ष्य अधिनियम, 1872 (1 of 1872 या इसके किसी प्रावधान का कोई—

(क) संसद द्वारा बनाए गए अधिनियम में; या

(ख) किसी राज्य की विधानमंडल द्वारा बनाए गए अधिनियम में;

(ग) अध्यादेश में;

(घ) संविधान की धारा 240 के अंतर्गत बनाए गए विनियमों में कोई संदर्भ दिया गया है;

(ङ) राष्ट्रपति के आदेश;

(च) किसी अधिनियम, अध्यादेश या विनियम के अंतर्गत बनाए गए नियम, विनियम, आदेश या अधिसूचना,

जो तत्समय प्रवृत्त हैं, ऐसे प्रत्येक संदर्भ को क्रमशः भारतीय न्याय संहिता, 2023 (2023 का 45) (बीएनएस), भारतीय नागरिक सुरक्षा संहिता, 2023 (2023 का 46) (बीएनएसएस) या भारतीय साक्ष्य अधिनियम, 2023 (2023 का 47) (बीएसए), और ऐसे कानून के प्रासंगिक प्रावधानों के संदर्भ के रूप में पढ़ा जाएगा।

CONTENTS

CHAPTER VI
Licences

TABLE OF CASES

C

H

I

J

N

O

P

THE INDIAN EASEMENTS ACT, 1882

An Act to define and amend the law relating to Easements and Licences

Preamble. Whereas it is expedient to define and amend the law relating to easements and licences, it is hereby enacted as follows :

PRELIMINARY

1. Short title.—This Act may be called "The Indian Easements Act, 1882";

Local extent and commencement.—It extends to the territories respectively administered by the Governor of Madras in Council and the Chief Commissioners of the Central Provinces and Coorg and it shall come into force on the 1st day of July, 1882.[1]

NOTES

Origin of the right of easement.—The right of easement is a right as old as the day when human race first emerging from barbarism, adopted the custom of living together in towns or living as other's nighbours, or respecting each other's rights. It found it indispensable for common good to adopt the general principle that *an individual should enjoy his property, though fully and exclusively, yet so as not to interfere with neighbour's legitimate enjoyment of his own property rights*. This salutary principle appears to be the original foundation on which easements are based.

Local extent.—The Act as originally passed in 1882 applied to the territories administered by the Governor of Madras in Council, and the Chief Commissioner of the Central

1. Extended to the Union Territory of Jammu and Kashmir and Union Territory of Ladakh by Act No. 34 of 2019, Fifth Schedule, w.e.f. 31-10-2019.

Provinces (now Madhya Pradesh) the application of the Easements Act was extended to the Presidency of Bombay and the North Western Provinces and Oudh (now Uttar Pradesh). The Act does not apply to Bengal, Punjab, Assam, Bihar, Delhi and that part of the present State of Orissa which formed part of old Bengal.

Retrospective effect of Act.—It is a well-accepted principle of law that no presumption can be made about the retrospective effect of any Act or statute, unless it has been clearly stated in it to be retrospective. This Act is not retrospective. This Act does not affect rights acquired prior to 1891.[1]

This Act came into force in Madras, Coorg and Madhya Pradesh on July 1, 1882 and was extended to Uttar Pradesh, Bombay and Delhi from 1891.

The Act is not exhaustive.—The provision of the Indian Easement Act are of remedial nature. It is neither prohibitory nor exhaustive. But at the same time it does not interfere with the right of the others and modes of acquiring easement.[2]

The simplest form to understand the easement is to set out that it is merely a right annexed or appurtenant to land to utilize other land of different ownership in a particular manner or to prevent the true owner of such other land from utilizing his land in a particular manner or to do something or require something not to be done thereon. In other words, an easement is a prohibitive or restrictive right of enjoyment.[3]

In those parts of the country where Indian Easements Act is not in operation, there is no reason why the principles underlying the provisions of the Act should not be followed in so far as they embody the rules of equity, justice and good conscience. Where the Act does not rest upon equitable principles, reference to the rules of the English law will be legitimate.[4]

2. Savings.—Nothing herein contained shall be deemed to affect any law not hereby expressly repealed; or to derogate from—

(a) any right of the Government to regulate the collection, retention and distribution of the

1. *Ram Bharose* v. *Vishwanath Prasad*, AIR 1934 All 336.
2. *Udit Singh* v. *Kashi Ram*, (1892) ILR All 185 FD
3. *Jasti Venkateswara Rao* v. *South Central Railway, Vijayawada*, 2012 (110) 579 (AP).
4. *Nunia Mal* v. *Duni Chand*, AIR 1964 Punjab 299.

water of rivers and streams flowing in natural channels and of natural lakes and ponds, or of the water flowing, collected, retained or distributed in or by any channel or other work constructed at the public expense for irrigation;

(b) any customary or other right (not being a licence) in or over immovable property which the Government, public or any person may possess irrespective of other immovable property; or

(c) any right acquired or arising out of a relation created, before this Act comes into force.

NOTES

Section 2, clause (a) expressly saves from the operation of the Act the right of the Government to regulate, collect and distribute water in natural and artificial water-courses, lakes and ponds. This right of the Government to distribute water, and also to conserve it for public good, wherever necessary to construct works of irrigation, and maintain old ones according to the needs and circumstances of the country is, Government's obligation in an agricultural country like India. But the Government should exercise due care and caution in construction of works of public utility for irrigational purposes and to have full regard for the property rights of private owners.

Clause (b).—Customary or other rights which the Government, the public or any person may possess irrespective of other immovable property are not easements because they are unappurtenant to any tenement. They are rights in gross and Section 2, clause (b) expressly lays down that Easements Act does not apply to such rights in gross.

Customary rights.—A customary right belongs to no individual in particular, but exists for the benefit of all those persons who for the time being happen to reside in a particular locality, or who for the time happen to form a distinct class or community for whose benefit the custom or usage attached to a particular locality prevails. A custom must be ancient, reasonble and continuous and so must be a customary right.

Examples.—Right to burn Holi at a certain place on certain days of the year; right to hold musical festivals on a chabutra, right to place taziyas on a chabutra during Moharrum; or right of a certain section of public to bury their dead in another's land; a custom of the inhabitants of a village to bathe in a tank; a customary right of free pasturage over certain lands; are all examples of customary rights.

'Customary rights', 'Easement' and 'Customary Easement'—Distinction between.—A 'customary right' is not an 'easement'. An 'easement' belongs to a determinate person or persons in respect of his or their land. A fluctuating body of persons like the inhabitants of the locality cannot claim an easement. Easements are private rights belonging to particular persons, while customary rights are public rights annexed to the place in general. 'Customary right' is also different from 'customary easements' and Easements Act does not at all deal with it. On the other hand it expressly excludes it from its scope and purview. The real distinction between 'customary right' and 'customary easement' has been ably set forth in Frederick Peacock's well known treatise on the law relating to Easements in British India, at page 205 of the second edition, as follows :—

> Customary easements, as they are called in Section 18 of the Indian Easements Act, should be distinguished from the customary rights referred to in Section 2, clause (b), of the same Act. The latter are rights arising by custom, but unappurtenant to a dominant tenement. No fixed period of enjoyment is necessary to establish these rights, but the custom must be reasonable and certain."
> As a matter of fact, the distinction was clearly brought out as far back as 1895 in *Kuar Sen* v. *Mamman*,[1] when it was observed that there could be no right of easement, where there was no dominant tenement or heritage. The same distinction was pointed out in *Palaniandi Tevan* v. *Puthirangonda Nandan*.[2] Then in *Ganpat* v. *Narayan*,[3] it was observed by Pollock A.G.C. that a customary easement can exist "only for the beneficial enjoyment of the other land" and that it is "merely appurtenant to the dominant heritage and cannot exist in gross", whereas "a right over property that exists in gross and not for the beneficial enjoyment of other property is not an easement though it may be a customary right. It is thus quite clear that easement, customary easement and customary right have to be understood properly and all these three rights

1. ILR 17 All 87.
2. (1898) ILR 20 Mad 389.
3. AIR 1933 Nag 74.

are different from one another.[1]

Clause (c).—This clause lays down that all rights and obligations which were created before the Indian Easements Act came into force would be duly respected.

Before the Indian Easements Act came into force on July 1, 1882, the law as to easements was provided by certain other enactments like the Indian Limitation Act, 1871 and 1877, by certain customs and usages prevailing in the country as well as by the English Common Law. The term 'easement' was for the first time defined in the Indian Limitation Act, 1877. This definition did not include *profits a prendre* and gave the easements a much more extensive meaning than that assigned to them by the English law. The result has been the acquisition of certain rights which cannot be called easements or *profits a prendre* strictly. The rights which were thus acquired are saved by clause (c).

Profit a prendre.—A *profit a prendre* in gross—that is a right exercisable by an indeterminate body of persons to take something from the land of others, but not for the more beneficial enjoyment of a dominant tenement—is not an easement within the meaning of the Act. To the claim of such a right, the Easements Act has no application.[2]

Ryotwari proprietors.—The Government has every right to regulate water available to *ryots* in a locality. No injunction suit would lie before any civil court curtailing or restraining power of Government in irrigation matters.[3]

Aripal spring, water of natural source.—'Aripal Spring' is a natural water source so no one can claim any interest therein.[4]

3. Construction of certain references to Act XV of 1877 and Act IX of 1871.—All references in any Act or Regulation to Sections 26 and 27 of the Indian Limitation Act, 1877 or to Sections 27 and 28 of Act No. IX of 1871, shall in the territories to which this Act extends, be read as made to Sections 15 and 16 of this Act.

---

1. *Prabhawati Devi* v. *Mahendra Narain Singh*, AIR 1981 Pat 133.
2. *State of Bihar* v. *Subodh Gopal Bose*, AIR 1968 SC 281.
3. *Samayan* v. *N. Velu*, AIR 2008 (NOC) 444 (Mad).
4. *Zamindaran Lorow* v. *State*, AIR 2008 J & K 25.

NOTES

In territories to which Indian Easements Act applies, all references to Sections 26 and 27 of the Indian Limitation Act, 1877 or Sections 27 and 28 of the Limitation Act No. IX of 1871 shall be deemed to have been made to Sections 15 and 16 of the Easements Act.

CHAPTER I

OF EASEMENTS GENERALLY

4. "Easement" defined.—An easement is a right which the owner or occupier of certain land possesses, as such, for the beneficial enjoyment of that land, to do and continue to do something, or to prevent and continue to prevent something being done, in or upon, or in respect of, certain other land not his own.

Dominant and servient heritages and owners.—The land for the beneficial enjoyment of which the right exists is called the dominant heritage, and the owner or occupier thereof the dominant owner; the land on which the liability is imposed is called the servient heritage, and the owner or occupier thereof the servient owner.

Explanation.—In the first and second clauses of this section, the expression "land" includes also things permanently attached to the earth : the expression "beneficial enjoyment" includes also possible convenience, remote advantage, and even a mere amenity; and the expression "to do something" includes removal and appropriation by the dominant owner, for the beneficial enjoyment of the dominant heritage, of any part of the soil of the servient heritage or anything growing or subsisting thereon.

Illustrations

(a) *A*, as the owner of a certain house, has a right of way thither over his neighbour *B*'s land for purposes connected with the beneficial enjoyment of the house. This is an easement.

(b) *A*, as the owner of a certain house, has the right to go on his neighbour *B*'s land, and to take water for the purposes of his household out of a spring therein. This is an easement.

(c) *A*, as the owner of a certain house, has the right to conduct water from *B*'s stream to supply the fountains in the garden attached to the house. This is an easement.

(d) *A*, as the owner of a certain house and farm, has the right to graze a certain number of his own cattle on *B*'s field, or to take, for the purpose of being used in the house, by himself, his family, guests, lodgers and servants, water or fish out of *C*'s tank, or timber out of *D*'s wood, or to use, for the purpose of manuring his land, the leaves which have fallen from the trees on *E*'s land. These are easements.

(e) *A* dedicates to the public the right to occupy the surface of certain land for the purpose of passing and repassing. This right is not an easement.

(f) *A*, is bound to cleanse a watercourse running through his land and keep it free from obstruction for the benefit of *B*, a lower *riparian owner*. This is not an easement.

NOTES

What is easement.—A right that cannot be prevented from being exercised by physical interference during the period of enjoyment cannot be acquired as an easement. But before time can interfere to run under the Easements Act, there must be invasion of some legal right. Acts that are neither preventable nor actionable cannot be relied upon to claim a right of easement.[1]

"Easement", as defined in this Act, is a right, which the owner or occupier of certain land possesses as such, for the beneficial enjoyment of that land to do and continue to do something, or to prevent and continue to prevent something being done, in or upon, or in respect of, certain other land not his own.

Applicability of easement.—A relief claimed on the title is fully inconsistent with the relief claimed on the basis of other, once plaintiff having failed on question of title cannot

1. *K. Mohideen* v. *M.M. Abdullah*, AIR 1978 Mad 97.

ask for relief on the basis of easement.[1]

Right of easement.—Easement right is exercisable by a person relating to land not of his own. Ownership over a land and easementary right thereto by use cannot co-exist together. Held, that right of easement, become, extinguished the moment when two tenements become vested in one and the same person.[2]

Essentials of a right of easement.—1. There must be an owner or occupier of certain land. The person of inherence must either be the owner or occupier of certain land for the beneficial enjoyment of which the right is claimed. The word 'occupier' shows that the right can be claimed even by a person who is not the owner but who is only an occupier of land.

2. The right must be possessed by the owner or occupier of such land as such owner or occupier.

3. The right must be to do and continue to do something, or to prevent and continue to prevent something being done in or upon, or in respect of some other land. In other words, the right may either be an affirmative or assertive right which might empower an owner of a tenement to do or to continue to do, something in or upon or in respect of a certain other land not his own, or it may be a negative or restrictive right which might authorise an owner of a tenement to prevent or to continue to prevent any such thing being done in or upon or in respect of some other tenement not his own, as might be inconsistent with his right of enjoyment of his own tenement.

4. The right must be for the beneficial enjoyment of his own land.

In order to establish an easementary right, the plainitiff must prove that he is the owner or occupier of a land for the beneficial enjoyment of which he has certain rights over the defendant's land. The ownership of a deity on another's land is not necessary for the beneficial enjoyment of one's own land. Further in India it is quite common, in villages as well as in towns, for the owner of well to allow neighbours to draw water for domestic purposes, but this is a licence which has nothing to do with the beneficial enjoyment of any land.[3]

5. The other land in or upon which the right is to be exercised must not be *owned or occupied* by him (the person

1. *E. Elumalaichetty* v. *Naina Mudali*, AIR 1987 Mad 102.
2. *Swapan Sinha* v. *Smt. Usha Rani Sahana*, 2002(1) Civil LJ 328 (Cal).
3. *Hardayal* v. *Chotai*, AIR 1963 All 32.

who claims the right of easement) but it must be owned or occupied by some person. Because the owner of the dominant tenement cannot claim an easement right if he happens to be also the full owner of the servient land. With unity of ownership the lesser right of easement merges itself in the higher right of full proprietorship, and what was formerly an obligation on a separately owned tenement imposed for the benefit of the dominant heritage, becomes if, enjoyed under the new circumstances, a part of the property rights of the full owner. You cannot have the land itself and also an easement over it.[1]

A person cannot acquire an easement unless he acts with the knowledge that it is a case of dominant and servient tenement and he is exercising a right over property which does not belong to him. If he enjoys a right under the supposition that he is an owner of property he does not acquire an easement. Not only that but there can be no question of acquiring an easement of light and air over property jointly owned by him with others.[2] When both tenements are owned or held by the same person or persons, any easement by prescription cannot be acquired.[3]

It is essential for the creation of an easement that there should be two distinct heritages, that the two heritages must not belong to the same individual and that there must be some advantage derived by one tenement from or upon a neighbouring tenement greater than what would naturally and ordinarily belong to the former. No plaintiff would be allowed to take the impossible position of being the owner of and of having the simultaneous right of easement over the same land.[4]

Varieties of easement.—There may be large varieties of easement in the sense that each one of them may impose a different kind of burden on the servient heritage, but all of them are required to fall within one or another of the known categories of easement. Therefore, an easement of a novel kind cannot be devised and attached to property at the fancy or caprice of any owner.[5] In India, the principles enunciated in *Kepple* v. *Bailey* were reiterated in the case of *Hiralal* v.

1. *Ladyaman* v. *Grave* (1871) 6 Ch 763.
2. *Marghbhai* v. *Motibhai*, AIR 1932 Bombay 513.
3. *Diwan Durag Singh* v. *The State of M.P.*, AIR 1972 MP 12.
4. *Laxman Patnaik* v. *Cuttack Municipal Council, Cuttack*, AIR 1985 Orissa 90.
5. *Kepple* v. *Bailey*, (1834) 2 My and R 517.

Loknath,[1] and it was held that the courts could not be allowed to create any new species of easements which were formerly unknown to law, specially so if the novel easement claimed also constituted a nuisance.

Easements and customary and public rights.—An easement is private proprietary privilege appurtenant to a dominant tenement and, apart from statute, must be founded against common right on a grant or prescription. By contrast a public right is enjoyed by the public at large, irrespective of any interest they may have in the tenement.

An easement must appertain to a dominant tenement. An indeterminate and fluctuating body of persons, such as the public, or the community, or a section of the public, or section of the community, cannot have any right of easement. It is one thing to say that twenty years' enjoyment, as of right by some people, of a right in gross, raises a presumption of immemorial enjoyment, and another thing to say that certain persons have got a right of easement thereby assuming that there is a dominant tenement as well as a servient tenement.[2]

Easements distinguished from customary rights.—Easements are distinguished from that class of rights which exist in particular localities under special local customs whereby a wholly undefined and fluctuating body of persons is entitled to utilize the land of another person in a particular manner and for a particular purpose. Such rights founded on custom appertain to many persons as a class, and not as grantees, nor do such rights require the existence of a dominant tenement. They are analogous to easements, but are not really easements, since some necessary elements of an easement are wanting.

A customary right is a right in gross, while an easement is always appurtenant to a tenement. Customary rights are claimed for a large or fluctuating body of persons in respect of a locality and it is unnecessary to look out for their origin from grant or otherwise.[3] Private easements, on the other hand, are claimed by defined persons and arise from a grant, which is either express or implied from prescriptive user. The existence and validity of customary rights generally depends upon some local custom excluding the operation of the general

1. AIR 1961 Cal 787.
2. *Brij Bhukan Kalwar* v. *S.D.O., Siwan*, AIR 1955 Pat 1 (22); *Prabhawati Devi* v. *Mahendra Narain Singh*, AIR 1981 Pat 133 : 1981 BLJR 323 : 1981 BLJ 465 : 1980 Pat LJR 542.
3. *Maharaj Bahadur* v. *Gandhauri Singh*, 39 IC 869.

rules of law, and they are sometimes entirely independent of any express or implied agreement between the parties; they generally stand upon a different footing, and are not in all respects governed by the same principles as those which determine the boundaries of easements.

Some of the principal differences between these customary rights and easements are—

(1) Customary rights are claimed—

(a) for fluctuating body of persons,

(b) in respect of a particular locality, and

(c) it is unnecessary to look out for their origin.

Easements are claimed—

(a) by defined person,

(b) for the beneficial enjoyment of a dominant tenement, and

(c) arise from a grant which is either express or is implied from prescriptive user.

(2) Customary rights are disallowed if they are unreasonable.

Easements involve only the interests of the owners of the two tenements. An easement cannot confer the exclusive use of a servient tenement. No question of reasonableness can arise where the title to an easement is based on express grant.

Easement is a prohibitive or restrictive right of enjoyment.—An easement can be a permanent one or for a term of few years or even for an extremely limited period or subject to periodical interruptions exercisable by certain persons or at certain times. An easement may be conditional as well as limited by time. An easement is in essence a restriction of the natural rights of ownership which a true owner is otherwise entitled to enjoy as incidental to his right of ownership. Thus, easement is recognised as a burden on the owner or occupier of a servient heritage. In juxtaposition, a bare license which does not allow profits arising therefrom, to be shared, confers upon the grantee no property in the land. The grantee has a mere right of possession for achieving the object or purpose of the grant. A bare licence whether granted by deed or not and whether it is backed by consideration or not, is revocable.[1]

1. *Jasti Venkateswara Rao* v. *South Central Railway, Vijaywada,* 2012 (110) A/C 577 (AP).

Right to draw water from well standing on neighbour's land.—The mere fact that one person draws water from a well situated on another person's land does not create an easement. Under Indian social conditions a person owning a well is deemed to be under a moral or pious obligation to allow the poor or less fortunate inhabitants of the locality to draw water from his well. In almost every street in India the rich man's well is used by his poor neighbours for drawing water. The law of easement was not intended to disturb this excellent social custom by giving the drawer of water from another person's well right of easement. The presumption in view of social conditions should be that the right in all such cases is permissive and does not create an easement. The law of easement must be interpreted in the right of Indian social conditions.[1]

Dominant and servient heritages and owners.—The land for the beneficial enjoyment of which the right exists is called the dominant heritage and the owner or occupier of such land is called the dominant owner. The land on which the liability is imposed is called the servient heritage and the owner or occupier of such land is called the servient owner. It must, however, be clearly remembered that the two heritages must be owned or possessed by two different persons as no one can have a servitude on his own land. An easement right enhances the rights of the dominant owner while there is a corresponding domination in the rights of the servient owner.

An easementary right imposes no personal obligation on the owner of the servient tenement. The servient owner or occupier has merely negative duties to perform. He is prohibited from doing anything which may be found to be inconsistent with the dominant owner's right of employment.

As every easement right exists for the benefit of the owner of the dominant tenement alone, it is inherent in the nature of the right that the owner of the dominant tenement may cease to exercise it if the right ceases to be beneficial. In such cases, the owner of the servient tenement cannot insist on the continuance of the exercise of the easement right, because the exercise of the easement right does not create any reciprocal rights in the servient owner.[2]

Benefit to dominant heritage.—Another characteristic of an easement is that it must be beneficial to the dominant

1. *Chheddu Singh* v. *Kewal*, AIR 1963 All 122.
2. *Dharniwhar Sahu* v. *Bhagirathi Sahu*, AIR 1956 Orissa 89.

tenement. A right unconnected with the enjoyment or occupation of land cannot be annexed as an incident to it.[1] This is borne out by the words "beneficial enjoyment of the land" which occur in the definition. An easement is not invalid merely because in its exercise for the benefit of the dominant heritage it confers some benefit upon any other tenement.[2]

An easement exists for the benefit of the dominant heritage alone, and prima facie the servient owner acquires no right to insist on its continuance, or to ask for damages on its abandonment. [Section 50, Easements Act.] Being in its very nature a right created for the benefit of the dominant owner its exercise by him cannot operate to create a new right for the benefit of the servient owner. Like any other right its exercise may be discontinued, if it becomes onerous or ceases to be beneficial to the dominant owner. The existence of an easement does not carry with it any presumption of the creation or existence of a counter-easement, in the owner of the servient tenement, against the owner of the dominant tenement.[3]

An easement attaches itself to the land of the servient owner. In imposing itself thereon it lays a negative obligation upon the servient owner not to do anything which may interfere with the enjoyment of the dominant owner. The obligation is not, however, of general nature, but is a special obligation of well defined limits. So, an easement of way does not impose a general obligation upon the servient owner to allow the dominant owner to walk wherever he pleases, but only a passive obligation not to interfere with a special specific way.[4]

It is an essential characteristic of an easement that the dominant and servient owners must be different persons. If this characteristic is not there, there is no easement. Thus, when a right of way of carts is claimed over a village road, technically no question of easement arises for here every resident on that road can by turns be both a dominant and servient owner.[5]

An easement, as Austin describes it, "is a fractional right";

1. *Ackoryd* v. *Smith*, (1850) 10 CBNS 164 : 19 LJCP 315.
2. *Tapling* v. *Jones*, (1865) 11 HLC 290; *Simpson* v. *Godmanchester Corporation*, 1897 AC 696.
3. *Mc Evoy* v. *Great Northern Railway Co.*, (1900) 2 Ir R 325, 333, *per* Palles, CB.
4. *Doorga Churn Dhur* v. *Kally Coomar*, ILR 7 C 145.
5. *Lal Mohammad Biswas* v. *Emajuddin Biswas*, AIR 1964 Cal 548.

it is a definite right of user subtracted or broken off from the indefinite right of user which resides in him or them who bear the dominion of the subject. It is a single or particular exception, accruing to the benefit of the party in whom the right resides, from the power of user and exclusion, which resides in the owner of the thing."

Acquisition of an easement by a person claiming ownership.—The words "not his own" in Section 4 are highly significant. It is imperative that the owners of the servient tenement and dominant heritage must be different. A person cannot acquire an easementary right over his own land because all acts done by him over his own land are acts done in exercise of his rights as owner of the land and the prime requisite of 'animus' for acquisition is thereby absent. The right of easement becomes extinguished the moment the ownership in the two tenements becomes vested in one and the same person. Co-existence of an easement alongwith the ownership of the land itself is not allowed under the law. Therefore acts done by a person during a statutory period which are only referable to the purported character of owner thereto cannot validate a subsequent claim to acquisition of an easement over that property.[1]

Mere passage through land does not create easement of necessity.—Where it was claimed that there was passage through land through which villagers reached their fields, but documentary evidence suggested that there were no public streets passing through the land. Held, that mere passage through land does not create easement of necessity.[2]

Indian and English Law—Difference

(1) From the definition of easement given in Section 4 of the Indian Easement Act it is clear that in India easement can be claimed only in respect of corporeal property such as land and not in respect of incorporeal rights. But under the English law an easement can be claimed in respect of an incoporeal right also.

(2) Under the Indian law an easement also includes what in English law is called *profits a prendere*. But in English law distinction has been made between an easement and *profits a prendre*. Thus, though the English law recognizes easement as a right of light or air, it does not recognize as an easement a

1. *Sri Venkateswaraswami Varu Devasthanam* v. *Velidandala Kanakalakshmi*, AIR 1976 Andh Pradesh 250.
2. *Chahi* v. *Rajinder Singh*, AIR 2001 P & H 20.

right of pasturage over the soil of another owner or right to dig and take stones from the land of another for mending one's own road. The reason is that the latter rights which allow partaking of the soil or produce under the English law are *profits a prendre.*

(3) Under the Indian law, two tenements need not be adjacent to each other.[1] Because the words used in the section are that the servient heritage must be "certain other land" not belonging to the dominant owner. But under the English law two heritages must be adjoining ones.

Profits a prendre.—A right by which one person is entitled to remove and appropriate for his own use any part of the soil belonging to another man or anything growing in or attached to or subsisting upon his land for the sake of the profit to be gained from the property thereby acquired in the thing removed, is in English law commonly called a *profit a prendre.* Thus, a right to dig stones from the land of another for the purpose of mending one's own road or a right to cut trees from the land of the servient owner are examples of *profit a prendre. A profit a prendre,* a right to take and use something from the land of another, is not merely a privilege to do something or to prevent something being done on the land of another as is the case with easement under the English law. In *profit a prendre* there is participation in the profits of a neighbour's land. Under the Indian law, however, the term 'easement' has a much wider significance and includes even a right to enjoy profits arising out of the soil of another owner. This is made clear by the Explanation to Section 4 which lays down that the expression "to do something" includes removal and appropriation by the dominant owner, for the beneficial enjoyment of the dominant heritage of any part of the soil of servient heritage, or anything growing or subsisting thereon.

Distinction between easement under the English law and profit a prendre

Before noting the points of distinction between easement under the English law and '*profit a prendre*' it should be clearly borne in mind that there does not exist any such distinction under the Indian law. The term "easement" as defined in Section 4 of the Indian Easements Act includes what in English law is called *profit a prendre.*

1. An easement right under the English law is a privilege

1. *Misrilal* v. *Mohanlal*, AIR 1954 Ajmer 73.

without profit. It permits enjoyment of certain rights in respect of the dominant tenement without allowing the owner of the dominant tenement to share in the profits which arise out of the soil of the servient heritage, e.g., easement rights of light and air, etc. A *profit a prendre* confers a right to take from the servient tenement some part of the soil of that tenement or some part of its natural produce. A right to take stones from the servient heritage for mending one's own road or a right to cut trees from the servient heritage are examples of *profit a prendre* under the English law.

2. In *profit a prendre* there is a participation in the profits of the servient tenement but under the English law an easement can never import an interest in the land of the servient tenement. It is merely a right appurtenant to land to do something or to prevent something being done on the servient tenement.

An easement can be claimed by custom but a *profit a prendre* cannot be claimed by virtue of a custom.

Right of easement and Right in gross—Distinction between.—Rights which are not claimed by a person as appurtenant to his land as dominant tenement but by virtue of long user as a private right, or rights claimed by a community or a class of persons by virtue of customary user and not by being appurtenant to any dominant tenement, are not easements but are *rights in gross* which are incapable of being acquired under the provisions of the Indian Easements Act. To call these rights "easements in gross" is a misnomer, because no easement rights can exist unless there be both a servient as well as a dominant tenement.

Profit of prendre in gross not an easement.—A *profit-a-prendre* in gross—that is a right exercisable by an indeterminate body of persons to take something from the land of others, but not for the more beneficial enjoyment of a dominant tenement is not an easement within the meaning of the Easements Act. To the claim of such a right, the Easements Act has no application. Section 2 of the Easements Act expressly provides that nothing in the Act contained shall be deemed to affect, *inter alia*, to derogate from any customary or other right (not being a license) in or over immovable property which the Government, the public or any person may possess irrespective of other immovable property. A claim in the nature of a *profit-a-prendre* operating in favour of an indeterminate class of persons and arising out of a local custom may be held enforceable only if it satisfies the tests of a valid custom. A custom is a usage by virtue of which a class of persons belonging to a defined section in a locality are entitled to exercise specifc rights against certain other persons property in the same locality. To the extent to which it is inconsistent with the general law, undoubtedly the custom prevails. But to be valid, a custom must be ancient, certain and reasonable, and being in derogation of the general rules of law must be construed strictly. A right in the nature of a profit-a-prendre in the exercise of which the residents of locality are entitled to excavate stones for trade purposes would *ex-facie* be unreasonable, because the exercise of such a right ordinarily tends to the complete destruction of the subject matter of the profit.[1]

Rights of easement as distinguished from obligations.—An easement differs from an obligation inasmuch as it confers on the owner or occupier of the dominant tenement for the beneficial enjoyment of the dominant heritage to do something, or to prevent something being done in or upon the servient heritage; in other words, an easement confers a privilege over the land of another, while an obligation confers a right only against the owner.

It may be observed that where land is granted or demised for certain purposes, although no easement is created, an obligation may be implied on the part of the grantor or lessor which is analogous to that which arises from a restrictive covenant.

Contractural obligation and easement.—An easement right is appurtenant to a dominant tenement and is to be exercised on a servient tenement and a change in the ownership or possession of the dominant or the servient heritage does not affect the continuity of the easement right. But contractual obligations are binding only on the party making a particular contract or his heirs, assigns or successors.[2]

Easements distinguished from licence.—An easement is distinguished from a licence as to the manner in which it may be created and as to its various characteristics and qualities. The chief distinction between an easement and a licence to use land in a particular manner is that whereas an easement cannot be extinguished (except in the modes

1. *State of Bihar* v. *Subodh Gopal*, AIR 1968 SC 281.
2. *Lachhman Ram* v. *Jagbandhu Sahu*, (1962) 4 Orissa JD 349.

mentioned in the Act) merely at the will of the grantor, a licence is generally revocable at the will of the person who has given it; and whereas a licence is merely personal and does not run with the land, an easement is always appurtenant to the dominant tenement. A licence merely confers a privilege to do some act on the land without passing any estate therein, but an easement creates an estate in the land distinct from the ownership thereof. An easement possesses the qualities of inheritability and assignability, but these qualities are generally inconsistent with a licence, which is terminated by the conveyance of the land by the party giving the licence.

Whether a particular agreement creates an easement or a licence depends on the construction of its language. In cases of ambiguity or inconsistency, surrounding circumstances have to be considered. The points which generally arise from determination are—

(1) Whether the right in question is appurtenant to land or is merely personal.

(2) Whether the benefit as well as the burden are annexed to the lands or whether they are merely personal both to the grantor and the grantee.

(3) Whether the right in question creates an estate or it does not.

A licence makes an act lawful which without it would be unlawful. Instances of licences are : to hunt in a man's park; to visit a man's house but a licence to hunt in a man's park and carry away the deer killed for one's own use, or to cut down a tree and carry away its timber, is a licence as to the act of hunting and cutting the tree, but it is a grant as to the carrying away of the deer killed or the timber cut.

Claim for easementary right.—The land in dispute was open space meant for being used by persons residing in the vicinity. Opposite party who was the owner of house adjoining that land had no right or title over it to claim it as their own personal property. Persons residing in vicinity would have easementary right to use that land and maintain it as open space.[1]

Easement defined.—An easement is a right which owner has for beneficial enjoyment over the land belonging to another.[2]

1. *Nirmala Devi* v. *Ram Sahai*, AIR 2004 All 359.
2. *Bhaurao Akasar* v. *Vinod Kasar*, 2006 (2) Bom CR 201.

A right which the owner or occupier of certain land possesses, as such, for the beneficial enjoyment of that land, to do or continue to do something, or to prevent and continue to prevent something being done, in or upon, or in respect of certain other land not of his own, is said to be easement under Section 4 of the Act. Where the plaintiffs used way through property of their landlord to reach the main road and the defendant purchased some portion of that land, the claim of easement of necessity of the plaintiff would be allowed as he had no alternative way except way through defendant's property.[1]

Under the provision of S. 4 of the Act for the beneficial enjoyment of land an easementary right may be claimed. The expression 'land' has been explained in the Explanation to S. 4 according to which a house would also come under the purview of S. 4 of the Act.[2]

Servient heritage, limitation on dominant owner.—The dominant owner cannot increase the burden of the servient owner by using the immovable property of the latter for the purpose of which the dominant owner had no right to use the other person's property. The dominant owner may have easementary right for flowing rain water and water used in houses but not flowing of sewage water as it would cause nuisance to servient owner.[3]

5. Continuous and discontinuous, apparent and non-apparent easements.—Easements are either continuous or discontinuous, apparent or non-apparent.

A continuous easement is one whose enjoyment is, or may be, continual without the act of man.

A discontinuous easement is one that needs the act of man for its enjoyment.

An apparent easement is one the existence of which is shown by some permanent sign which, upon careful inspection by a competent person, would be visible to him.

A non-apparent easement is one that has no such sign.

1. *Babli Krishna Vaigankar* v. *L.S. Vaigankar*, AIR 2006 (NOC) 1349 (Bom).
2. *Ramcharan* v. *Ram Asrey*, AIR 2008 MP 105 (108).
3. *Daveshwar Prasad Tiwari* v. *Kalyan Singh*, AIR 2007 Utr. 72 (74).

Illustrations

(a) A right annexed to *B*'s house to receive light by a window without obstruction by his neighbour *A*. This is a continuous easement.

(b) A right of way annexed to *A*'s house over *B*'s land. This is a discontinuous easement.

(c) Rights annexed to *A*'s land to lead water thither across *B*'s land by an aqueduct and to draw off water thence by a drain. The drain would be discovered upon careful inspection by a person conversant with such matters. These are apparent easements.

(d) A right annexed to *A*'s house to prevent *B* from building on his own land. This is a non-apparent easement.

NOTES

Section 5 divides easements into continuous or discontinuous easements and apparent or non-apparent easements. *Continuous easements* are those whose enjoyment is, or may be, continued without the act of man. A right to receive light or air are examples of continuous easements, because for their enjoyment no act of man is needed.

A *discontinuous easement* is one that needs the act of man for its enjoyment. But the 'act of man' necessary to secure the enjoyment of a discontinuous easement should be brought into play upon the soil of the servient tenement during the course of the enjoyment of the right. A right of way is an example of discontinuous easements, because for its enjoyment an act of man is needed and the act is done on the soil of the servient owner. A right to drain sullage water on the servient tenement has been held to be a continuous easement.[1]

The performance or non-performance of an 'act of man' is the sole criterion to distinguish a continuous from a discontinuous easement. The act of man, so far as it affects the easement being continuous or discontinuous is something done upon the land belonging to the servient owner.

Discharge through drain of foul water for domestic purposes whether continuous or discontinuous easement.—So long as the domestic water remains on the land belonging to the dominant owner and it is there that the

1. See *Brij Mohan Lal* v. *Hazari Lal*, AIR 1966 All 90 (FB).

act of a man comes in—the exercise of the easement does not begin. It begins when it leaves the land belonging to the dominant owner and begins to flow on to the servient tenement. So far as its flow in the latter is concerned, no act of man intervenes, and unless it is a case in which the flow of water is not possible without the dominant owner doing something on the land of the servient owner, for instance, opening a passage which is closed except where he desires to lead the water, the right is a continuous easement.[1]

The weight of authority, therefore, may be taken to be for the proposition that no distinction can be drawn between a drain or watercourse which carries rain-water and one which conveys water that has been used for domestic purposes because in both cases a continuous easement is enjoyed without an act of man.[2]

Right of way which can be used only intermittently and which requires an act of man to be beneficially enjoyed is a discontinuous easement.[3] The right of access for repairs, as for instance, a party wall, is a discontinuous easement, as it can be exercised periodically during limited period and for the specific purposes of repairs.[4]

Apparent easement.—An "apparent easement" is one the existnce of which is shown by some *permanent sign*. The permanent sign may either be visible by every observer or by competent person on careful inspection. Doors, windows, skylights, drains, etc. are such works which are visible to every observer but underground drains and sewers can be discovered only by a man conversant with such matters and that too after careful inspection.

Non-apparent easement.—Non-apparent easements have no permanent sign on the servient heritage which may be visible to an observer. A right annexed to A's house to prevent B from building on his own land or to build above a certain height, are non-apparent easements. A right of way on

1. *Brij Mohan Lal* v. *Hazari Lal*, 1935 ALJ 1330 (FB).
2. *Brij Mohan Lal* v. *Hazari Lal*, 58 A 662 : AIR 1936 A 90 : 160 IC 879 : 1936 ALJ 1330 (FB), *per* Niamatullah, J.; *Bamber Nath* v. *Jagannath Prasad*, AIR 1915 A 249 : 29 IC 695; *Morgan* v. *Kirby*, 2 M 47 at p. 51; *Pearson* v. *Spencer*, (1861) 1 B & S 571 : 4 LT 769; *Pyer* v. *Carter*, (1857) 1 H & N 916 : 26 LJ Ex 258.
3. *Naryana Gajapatiraju* v. *Sree Rani Janaki*, 53 M 449 : 124 IC 593 : AIR 1930 M 609; *Krishnamarazu* v. *Marraju*, 28 M 495; *Esa Abbas Sait* v. *Jacob Haroon Sait*, 33 M 327 : 4 IC 425.
4. *Varadarajulu Chettiar* v. *Muthukannu Ammal*, AIR 1966 Mad 158.

the servient tenement may be an apparent easement or a non-apparent easement according to the circumstances of each case. Where a right of way is shown by a permanent doorway and a formed path, it is an apparent easement. But where there is neither permanent doorway nor a formed path, the right of way cannot be said to be an apparent easement.

Apparent and non-apparent easements.—Distinction.—An apparent easement, here defined, is one, the existence whereof is shown by some permanent sign, which, upon careful inspection by a competent person, would be visible to him. The phraseology here used is borrowed from the famous English case of *Pyer* v. *Carter*,[1] which has been the subject of much adverse criticism in subsequent cases.[2] By a competent person is meant a person who is ordinarily conversant with the subject.[3] By a permanent sign is meant not only such a sign as must necessarily be seen or be apparent to every man but also such a sign as would be discernible by a person ordinarily conversant with the subject or expert in the matter on his careful inspection. For instance, an easement of drainage is an apparent easement,[4] existence of vents through which adjoining lands were irrigated is evidence of an apparent and continuous easement and the fact that an act of man, for instance, the opening and closing of the vents, is necessary in the course of enjoyment of the right, does not render it non-continuous,[5] although it may not be visible to the naked eye of every man but may be known only on excavation or on a careful comparison of the level of the ground of the dominant and servient heritages. *See* also Synopsis heading "General" under Section 5.

There are two criteria for judging whether or not an external sign is permanent. The objective criterion is the nature of the construction and the material employed. The subjective criterion is the intention of the party constructing it.[6] Where, however, a person intending to put up a permanent

1. 26 LJ Exch. 258.
2. *Per* Martin, B. in *Dodd* v. *Burcheel,* 31 LJ Exch. 364; *Ewart* v. *Cochrane,* 5 LT 1; *see* also Goddard, pp. 173, 181.
3. Goddard, p. 174; *see* also *Pyer* v. *Carter* (1857), 1 H & N 916 (per Watson, B.); *Suffield* v. *Brown,* 9 LT 627.
4. *Sultani* v. *Ram Saran Das,* 1900 PR 49 : 1900 PLR 173.
5. *Morala* v. *Thota,* 45 MLJ 724. But *see* per contra; *Sajidunnissa* v. *Hidayat Hussain,* AIR 1924 A 748.
6. *Faqirullah* v. *Wali Khan,* 97 IC 537 : AIR 1926 A 714; *Anand Nath* v. *Jokhu,* 113 IC 757.

structure owing to financial stringency employs poor and easily perishable material and thereby fails to make it a permanent structure according to the notions of well-to-do people, the structure will be regarded permanent in the eye of law. Thus it has been held that a mud hut is as good a permanent construction as the proudest of edifices may claim to be.[1]

6. Easement for limited time or on condition.—An easement may be permanent, or for a term of years or other limited period, or subject to periodical interruption, or exercisable only at a certain place, or at certain times or between certain hours, or for a particular purpose, or on condition that it shall commence or become voidable on the happening of a specified event or the performance or non-performance of a specified act.

NOTES

Easements may be either permanent or temporary. Both the types of easements may be capable of continuous enjoyment or they may be subject to interruption, or they may be capable of being enjoyed at fixed intervals only.

A temporary easement may even be a contingent one. In other words, it may be of such a nature as may become void or voidable on the happening of a specified event or the performance or non-performance of specified act. A temporary easement might be extinguished on the death of a Hindu widow.

Temporary easements are those which can be enjoyed only for a limited period, while permanent easements are enjoyable for all times to come.

Rights acquired by prescription also can be limited.—Rights acquired by prescription are not excluded from the clear terms of the section. Therefore, the limitations as to time, place, purpose or condition are applicable to such rights. The language of the section is permissive and not mandatory and can, therefore, neither control nor extend the language or the effect of any other section of the Act.

1. *Nasirulzaman Khan* v. *Azimullah*, 28 A 741 : 3 ALJ 765; *Anand Nath* v. *Jokhu*, 113 IC 757; *Vithaldas* v. *Goma*, AIR 1924 N 254; *Mathuri* v. *Bhola Nath*, 149 IC 389 : AIR 1934 A 517; *Gauri Shanker* v. *Mithai*, 84 IC 264 : AIR 1924 A 750; *Bhaddar* v. *Khairuddin*, 29 A 133; *Shyam Lal* v. *Munne*, AIR 1935 O. 69 : 140 IC 880; *Daya Ram* v. *Deora*, 94 IC 923 : AIR 1926 Nag. 376; *Amjad Khan* v. *Shafiuddin*, AIR 1923 A 203.

Generally, most of the cases of limited easements acquired by prescription are limited to a purpose, occasion or season; thus a right of way for scavengers or for agricultural purposes is an easement limited to a purpose and capable of being acquired by prescription, while a right to take water for a second crop from a source of water during a particular season is an easement limited to a season and capable of being acquired by prescription. A right to perform religious ceremonies, e.g., on the day of the *Holi* festival, is a right limited to a particular occasion.

The Act does not contemplate any acquisition on an easement against an occupier and not against an owner. An easement is acquired in the land and not against one or more of the persons interested in the land. By Section 15 of the Act, the acquisition of the easements by prescription, such as the right to access and use of light or air to and for any building, support from one person's land or things affixed thereto, or the right of way or any other easement, is made absolute against all persons connected with the land whether as owner or as occupiers.[1] So also a right of access to a neighbour's land for effecting periodical repairs to a dividing party-wall is an easement for a specific purpose and for particular periods.[2]

There is nothing in Section 16 itself to impose any restriction on a prescriptive easement, which is perpetual.[3]

An easement can be permanent, or for a limited period under Section 6. But an easement for a limited period cannot be acquired by prescription. In the absence of clear legislative language, courts should not be justified in recognising a prescriptive right to light and air by way of a limited period, such as during the occupation of the servient heritage by a lessee, when it is clear that no such right has been ever recognised by English law.[4]

Temporary or contingent easements.—Easements which terminate with the efflux of a certain specified period or on the happening of certain ascertained events are temporary easements. They are distinguishable from contingent easements. Contingent easements become void or voidable only

1. *B.N.W. Ry Co.* v. *Muneshwar Ram*, ILR 1937 A 511 : 1937 ALJ 259 : 169 IC 666 : AIR 1937 A 423 (429).
2. *Varadarajulu Chettiar* v. *Muthukannu Ammal,* AIR 1966 Mad 158.
3. *Koyyammu* v. *Kuttiammoo,* 42 M 567 : 50 IC 291 : 37 MLJ 28.
4. *Parkum* v. *Kuttiammoo,* AIR 1919 Mad 338, 340, 341, 343 (*per* Abdul Rahim, J., with Philips, J. contra); *Koyammu* v. *Kuttiammoo,* ILR 42 Mad 567 (DB) : 50 IC 291 : 37 MLJ 28.

on the happening of a particular uncertain event, or on the performance or non-performance of some act which may or may not be performed. But a temporary easement necessarily terminates due to a cause inherent in it, after a certain time. For instance, a temporary easement may terminate on the death of a widow who was a limited owner before the Hindu Succession Act, 1956, came into operation.

Easements subject to periodical interruption.—By periodical interruption is here meant such interruption as may have been agreed to by the grant, or agreement, or may be necessary and unavoidable under the circumstances in which the easement is enjoyed, or may be due to some other unavoidable cause, and does not mean actual interruption by the servient owner himself without right or in derogation to the claim of the right of easement itself as under Section 15, *infra.*[1] An interruption of the latter kind destroys the easement, or prevents its growth, as we will see when we come to discuss Section 15, *infra.*

Conditional easements.—Easements acquired on transfer or bequest mentioned in Section 13, *infra,* are examples of easements which are to commence on the performance of a certain specified act.[2] The easements acquired from or against a life-tenant are examples of the easements which becomes void on the happening of a certain specified event, *viz.,* death of the life-tenant.[3] Similarly, easements acquired from or against a lessee for a term of years exceeding three years are an example of easements, which are voidable at the termination of the period, if the lessor exercises his option to avoid them within three years of such termination by laying resistance to their enjoyment.[4] Conditions attached to an agreement by which an easement is imposed are valid and binding provided they refer to a certain specified act, or event, and are not vague for uncertainty and therefore, incapable of having a binding effect for want of certainty.[5]

Future easements.—Where easements are created *in praesentia* so as to become vested as a right in some persons

1. *Ram Sunder* v. *Woomakant,* 1 WR 217; *Omar* v. *Ramzan,* 10 WR 363; *Mookoondonath* v. *Shiv Chunder,* 22 WR 332; *Sheikh Mohammad Ansari* v. *Sheikh Seffatollah,* 22 WR 340; *Koylash Chunder* v. *Sonatun,* 7 C 132; *Budhu Mandal* v. *Maliat Mandal,* 30 C 1077.
2. *See* Section 13, infra.
3. *See* Illustration (b) to Section 8 *Infra.*
4. *See* Section 16, *Infra.*
5. *See* the Indian Contract Act, 1872, Chapter III., Section 29.

immediately, they cannot be said to offend against the rule of perpetuities even if the benefit in respect of them is to accrue in future and the easements so created are valid in law.[1] In the above cited case an easement right to discharge water on the servient tenement from the second storey of the house which was in contemplation at the time of the imposition of the right was held to have been lawfully acquired by the dominant owner. But the case is different from those easements which are to be created in future as they actually offend against the rule of perpetuities. Thus, where a mere agreement to grant some future right of easement alone exists, without any present right, over any particular tenement being conveyed to the dominant owner, the rule against perpetuities is operative.[2]

7. Easements restrictive of certain rights.—Easements are restrictions of one or other of the following rights (namely)—

(a) *Exclusive right to enjoy.* The exclusive right of every owner of immovable property (subject to any law for the time being in force) to enjoy and dispose of the same and all products thereof and accessions thereto.

(b) *Rights to advantages arising from situation.* The right of every owner of immovable property (subject to any law for the time being in force) to enjoy without disturbance by another the natural advantages arising from its situation.

Illustrations of the rights above referred to :

(a) The exclusive right of every owner of land in a town to build on such land, subject to any municipal law for the time being in force.

(b) The right of every owner of land that the air passing thereto shall not be unreasonably polluted by other persons.

(c) The right of every owner of a house that his physical comfort shall not be interfered with materially and unreasonably by noise or vibration

1. *Bhagwan Sahai* v. *Narsingh Sahai*, 31 A 612.
2. Gray on Perpetuities, 3rd Ed., 316; *Smith* v. *Colbourne*, (1914) 2 Ch 533 : 84 LJ Ch 112.

caused by any other person.

(d) The right of every owner of land to so much light and air as pass vertically thereto.

(e) The right of every owner of land, that such land in its natural condition, shall have the support naturally rendered by the subjacent and adjacent soil of another person.

Explanation.—Land is in its natural condition when it is not excavated and not subjected to artificial pressure : and the "subjacent and adjacent soil" mentioned in this illustration means such soil only as in natural condition would support the dominant heritage in its natural condition.

(f) The right of every owner of land that, within his own limits, the water which naturally passes or percolates by, over or through his land shall not, before so passing or percolating, be unreasonably polluted by other persons.

(g) The right of every owner of land to collect and dispose within his own limits of all water under the land which does not pass in a defined channel, and all water on its surface, which does not pass in a defined channel.

(h) The right of every owner of land that the water of every natural stream which passes by, through or over his land in a defined natural channel shall be allowed by other persons to flow within such owner's limits, without interruption and without material alteration in quantity, direction, force or temperature, the right of every owner of land abutting on a natural lake or pond into or out of which a natural stream flows, that the water of such lake or pond allowed by other persons to remain within such owner's limits without alteration in quantity or temperature.

(i) The right of every owner of upper land that water naturally rising in, or falling on, such land, and not passing in defined channels, shall be allowed by the owner of adjacent lower land to run naturally thereto.

(j) The right of every owner of land abutting on a natural stream, lake or pond to use and consume its water for drinking, household purposes and watering his cattle and sheep; and the right of every such owner to use and consume the water for irrigating such land, and for the purposes of any manufactory situate thereon: provided that he does not thereby cause material injury to other like owners.

Explanation.—A natural stream is a stream, whether permanent or intermittent, tidal or tideless, on the surface of land or underground, which flows by the operation of nature only and in a natural and known course.

NOTES

Section 7 lays down that easement rights are restrictions of ownership rights. It classifies ownership rights into two categories : (1) an exclusive right of the owner to enjoy and dispose of within the boundaries of his land, the soil, the products of the soil, and all the accessions thereto, (2) a right to enjoy without disturbance all those natural advantages which arise out of the situation of the land.[1]. In other words, according to Section 7 an easement right either restricts an exclusive right of the owner to enjoy and dispose of within the boundaries of his land, the soil, the products of the soil, and all the accessions thereto or it restricts the right of an owner to enjoy without disturbance all those natural advantages which arise of the situation of his land. "Easements are acquired rights abstracted from the ownership of one land and added to the ownership of another."

Natural rights.—Natural rights are those incidents and advantages which are provided by nature for the use and enjoyment of man's property. Right to receive light which falls vertically on a tenement is a natural right. Similarly, the right of every owner of land to receive from the adjoining tenement air free from obnoxious fume or gases is a natural right. Every piece of land receives support from adjoining lands. This natural right of support is a right of property attached to the soil itself which, though it does not prevent an adjoining owner from doing anything on his own land, yet prevents him from

1. *Husain Sahib* v. *Subayya*, AIR 1926 Mad 449

doing anything so as to withdraw support of his land to a neighbouring land. Every owner may dig in his own land as deep as near to his boundary or to the surface as he chooses, yet he may do so subject to one limitation, *viz.*, that he cannot dig so deep and so near as to cause the neighbour's land to sink, unless he substitutes some efficient support. These natural rights form part of ownership rights and are available against the whole world (i.e., natural rights *in rem*).

Characteristic features of natural rights.—Natural rights are those incidents and advantages which are provided by nature for the use and enjoyment of a certain property. These rights are, in law, the ordinary incidents of the ownership of property and annexed to land wherever land exists. Natural rights secure to the owner of a piece of land the full enjoyment thereof undiminished by any wrongful act of his neighbour. They are regarded by law as incident to the ownership of land and as inherent in land by the law of nature, and are rights *in rem* enforceable against all the world, subject only to curtailment by an easement. Whereas easements are acquired by restrictions of the complete rights of property, natural rights are themselves part of the complete rights of property, and exist wherever land, the subject of ownership, exists. Just as easements cannot exist apart from a dominant tenement, even so natural rights cannot exist apart from the land in which they are inherent.[1]

On the creation of an easement adverse to the natural right, the latter is not extinguished, but merely remains suspended during the continuance of the easement and revives upon the extinction of the easement.[2]

The characteristic features of natural rights were elaborately considered in *Moidin* v. *K. Gopalakrishna*.[3] It was recognized that natural rights are by law annexed to, and are inherent in, land *ex jure nature* (natural right), and exist, prima facie, in all cases as between a landowner and his neighbour, otherwise no man would be assured that his land would not, at any moment, be rendered useless by a

1. *Rowbotham* v. *Wilson*, (1860) HLC 348; *Stockport Waterworks Co.* v. *Potter*, (1864) 3 H & C 300.
2. *Tenant* v. *Goldwin*, (1705) 2 Ld. Raymd, 1089, 1092; *Rylands* v. *Fletcher*, (1868) LR 3 HL 330; *Madras Railway Co.* v. *Zamindar of Carcetnagaram*, (1874) 1 IA 364.
3. AIR 1953 M 849 : (1953) 1 MLJ 816.

neighbour's act otherwise lawful, or a neighbour might deprive a landowner of the benefit of certain things, which, in the course of nature, have been provided for the common good of mankind. Natural rights are rights *in rem*, that is enforceable against all who may violate them, and they are either affirmative rights to do something, or negative, as rights which every owner of immovable property has, that his neighbour shall not disturb the natural conditions under which he enjoys his property.

It was pointed out that natural rights, though resembling easements in some respects, are clearly distinguishable from them. The essential distinction between easements and natural rights appears to lie in this that easements are acquired by restrictions of the complete rights of property, or to put it in another way, "acquired rights", abstracted from the ownership of one man and added to the ownership of another, whereas natural rights are themselves part of the complete incidents of property and are *ipso facto* enforceable in law. Natural rights are themselves subject to restriction at the instance of easements. "The natural corollary of these natural rights is that they are subject to the rights of adjoining owners, who for the benefit of the community, have and must have rights in relation to the use and enjoyment of their property that qualify and interfere with those of their neighbour's rights to use their property in the various ways in which property is commonly and lawfully used."[1]

Natural right to the flow of light and air.—Every owner or occupier of land has a natural right to receive and enjoy so much light and air as come vertically thereto and to open doors and windows in his own wall which adjoins another's land, unless he is under a legal obligation not to do so.[2] Light and air are *publici juris*.[3] Every man is free, in the lawful enjoyment of his own property, to take and use so much light and air as come thereto. And his neighbour's right is the same as his own, but these rights of enjoyment are mutually qualified, for neither can prevent the other from making such lawful use of his land as he pleases. A man who is deprived of light and air by an act of his neighbours, as by the erection

1. *Per* Bramwel, LJ in *Bryant* v. *Lefever,* (1879) 4 C.P.D. 172 (176).
2. *Paramatma Prasad* v. *Sampatti*, AIR 1968 All 184.
3. *Bagram* v. *Khettranath Karformah,* (1869) 3 Beng LR OC 18 at p. 43; see *Baban Mayacha* v. *Nagu Shravucha,* ILR (1876) 2 B 52.

of a building, has still the right to so much of light and air as come to him and he cannot complain of the obstruction however serious unless he can establish his title to an easement of light and air. The natural rights of property, as defined by the maxim "*cujus est solum, ejus est usque ad coelum*" enable a man to build as he pleases on his own land.[1] It is well recognised principle that unless easementry rights to light and air are obstructed, the adjacent owner has a right to put up his own wall at the boundary of his property and the owner of the other adjacent property can have no grievance against the same.[2]

Natural right to the purity of air.—Every owner of land has the right that the air passing thereto shall not be unreasonably polluted by other persons. Since private health is considered of greater importance than public benefit, it is essential to the health of the community that this should be so. But it is not every pollution that gives a cause of action, and in some cases, even discomfort of itself is not a sufficient ground for relief. Unpolluted air means, not necessarily air as fresh, free and pure as at the time of building the plaintiff's house, the atmosphere then was, but air not rendered to an important degree incompatible with the physical comfort of human existence, having regard to the climate and habits of the locality.

Natural rights in water of streams or rivers.—All riparian proprietors who have the occupation or ownership of lands abutting on running streams or rivers have certain natural rights to the usufruct of the water.[3] These rights do not depend upon a grant, or upon the ownership of the bed of the stream, but are natural rights incident to the ownerhip of the soil of the land abutting the stream.[4]

The word "stream" means water running in a defined channel, and the term "natural stream" denotes a stream that

1. See *Ranchod Shamji* v. *Abdullabhai,* ILR 28 B 428.
2. *(Dr.) K. Panduranga Nayak* v. *Jayshree,* AIR 1990 Kant. 236.
3. *Wood* v. *Waud,* (1849) 3 Ex 748 at p. 775; *Dinkar* v. *Narayan,* ILR 29 B 357.
4. *Rawstron* v. *Taylor,* (1855) 11 Exch. 369 at p. 382; *Chasemore* v. *Richards,* (1859) 7 HLC 349, 379, 382; *Court of Wards* v. *Raja Leelanund Singh,* (1870)13 WR 48; *Ramessur Pershad Narain Singh* v. *Koonj Bihari Pattuk,* ILR 4 C 633 : 76 IA 33; *North Shore Railway Co.* v. *Pion,* (1889) 14 App Cas 612 (PC).

flows at its source by the operation of nature, and in a defined channel, whether on the surface of the land or underground.[1]

Natural rights exist in intermittent as well as permanent natural streams.[2] But there are no natural rights in artificial streams, that is, streams which flow at their source by the operation of man.

Riparian proprietors in natural private streams have subject to similar natural rights of upper and lower proprietors, the right to have water come to them in its ordinary and accustomed course, undiminished in flow, quantity and quality and unaffected in temperature, and to go from them without obstruction.[3] And riparian owners on a public river have all the rights of riparian owners on a private stream or river, subject to the right of the public, and *inter se* are under the same obligation.

Rules regarding the ownerships of the soil of the bed of non-tidal streams.—The rules may be shortly formulated thus—

(1) The ownership of the soil of the alveus, or bed, of a non-tidal stream, whether it be navigable or not, prima facie belongs to the riparian proprietors on both sides, not in common but in severalty, the *medium filum aquae*, or the middle thread of the streams, being the dividing line between the shares of the two proprietors respectively.

The test of tidality is not strictly applicable in India, where the bed of a navigable river is regarded as public domain or public territory. But there is no doubt that the rule that the beds of small and shallow rivers, or streams, or of those portions of rivers, which are above the point where navigability ceases, prima facie belong to the riparian proprietors *ad medium aquae*, has been accepted and applied in India.[4]

1. Section 7, Explanations, Easements Act; *Chasemored* v. *Richards,* (1859) 7 HLC 349, 379.
2. *Narayan* v. *Keshav*, ILR 23 B 506.
3. Section 7, Illustration (h), Easements Act; *Ramessur Pershad Narain Singh* v. *Koonj Bihari Pattuk,* ILR 4 Cal 633; *Debi Pershad Singh* v. *Joynath Singh,* ILR 24 C 865 (PC); *Dinkar* v. *Narayan,* ILR 29 B 357; *Baldeo Singh* v. *Jugal Kishore,* ILR 33 A 619.
4. See *Kali Kissen Tagore* v. *Jadoo Lal,* 5 CLR 97 (PC); *Khagendra Narain* v. *Matangini Debi,* ILR 17 C 814 (PC).

(2) As a corollary of this rule, if the course of such a stream be permanently diverted and the old alveus or bed be left dry, each riparian proprietor becomes entitled to it up to the line which coincides with what was the middle thread of the stream.

(3) When the lands on both banks of such a stream belong to the same person, the presumption of law (though rebuttable) is that the ownership of the whole alveus or bed belongs to such person.

(4) The ownership of the alveus or bed of such a stream may be claimed by a person who does not own land on either bank of it, though this is generally not the case.[1]

Easement and natural right distinguished.—Easement is a specific right subtracted from the general rights constituting ownership of one property and attached to the ownership of another property. In the language of the Act an easement is a restriction of a natural right. One of such natural right is the right of every owner of upper land to allow water to drain off to the adjacent lower land.[2]

Right to lateral support.—The right to lateral support is a right recognised in law as between owners of adjacent lands. No owner of a land can treat his land in such a manner as to remove the lateral support from the adjoining land or to impair it substantially so as to cause subsidence of land of the adjoining owner. Such subsidence would be caused by an owner of land removing the soil from his land on the boundary of his property to an appreciable degree unless it be that his property is in a higher level and the soil is removed therefrom so as to bring it down to a level of the land of the adjoining owner. Otherwise the removal of the soil would result in the caving in of the portions of the land of the adjoining owner and would infringe the right of lateral support of such owner. Any person who is threatened with injury to his right of lateral support could seek an injunction from a civil court to restrain such an act, in appropriate cases where the injury had already been caused a mandatory injunction may issue to restore the lateral support by any means the court finds feasible.[3]

1. *Jagdish Chandra Deo* v. *Indian Copper Corporation Ltd.*, AIR 1953 P 283.
2. *Chanti Chaina Venkatareddy* v. *Kulasani Koti Reddy*, AIR 1967 Andh Pra 81 : (1966) 2 Andh WR 80 : (1966) 2 Andh LT 177.
3. *Dr. I.K.J. Jacob* v. *K. Nandgopalan and others*, AIR 1983 Kerala 177.

Right of support to building.—The owner of a land has a right to the support of his land in its natural state from the adjacent and subjacent land of the neighbouring owners. This right is not an easement but a natural incident of his ownership. The natural right of support from neighbour's land is available only in respect of land in unburdened and natural or of his land burdened with the additional weight of his buildings unless such a right has been acquired as an easement. If there is no easement to have such lateral support, the neighbour is within his right to make excavation provided that he does not act negligently. If there is no negligence, the plaintiff is not entitled to any damages caused to his building.[1] There is no natural right of support for buildings, but such a right may be acquired as an easement. A right to receive lateral support from adjacent land acquired by building by 20 years' user openly, continuously and without interruption.[2] An acquired right is similar in character to a natural right. If the adjacent or subjacent support is withdrawn so as to cause land to subside, and the subsidence has not been caused by the additional weight of the buildings or other erections upon the land, the landowner is entitled to recover, in addition to damages for the subsidence of his land, damages for injury to his buildings or other erections although he has not acquired right of support in respect of them.

There is no natural right of support for buildings, and therefore a landowner may make an excavation on his own land notwithstanding that by so doing he may cause his neighbour's building to fall provided, of course, there is no negligence in the excavation operations. Also, if in pulling down his own home he removes the support of his neighbour's house, he is not bound to shore up his neighbour's house or take any other active steps for protection. But if his neighbour has an easement of support for his buildings from the adjoining buildings, he must not pull down his own building so as to remove the support from his neighbour's building.[3]

Section 7 gives an exclusive right to every owner of immovable property to enjoy and dispose of the same. It also gives a right to every owner of immovable property to enjoy,

1. *Bengal Provincial Railway Co.* v. *Rajani Kant*, AIR 1936 Cal 564. See also *Rasiklal* v. *Savailal*, AIR 1955 Bombay 285.
2. *Dalton* v. *Angus*, (1881) 6 AC 740.
3. *Ramgopal* v. *Gopi Krishna*, 1957 MPC 442.

without disturbance by another, natural advantages arising from its situation. Where the defendant's land is 10 feet lower than that of the plaintiff, the plaintiff's land in its natural condition will have the support naturally rendered by the defendant's land. The explanation to Section 7 makes it also clear that land to have this right should not have been subjected to artificial pressure. The land subject to artificial pressure from another person's land can have this benefit of support if an easement is acquired under Section 15, satisfying its conditions. When the plaintiff is unable to satisfy that the abovementioned conditions of Section 7 and Section 15 are satisfied, his suit for damages on the ground that the compound wall was damaged due to quarrying on the defendant's land would fail.[1]

Questions as to support have arisen where the title to land *A* has been severed from the title to land *B* which is subjacent to land *A* vertically; or from the title to land *C* which is adjacent to land *A* laterally. The prima facie rule in these cases is that (independently of the result of any facts or instruments connected with the severance) the owner of land *A* is of common right entitled to have it supported vertically by land *B*[2] and laterally by land *C*.[3] But the obligation to support land *A* laterally only binds that portion of the adjacent land *C*, the existence of which in its natural state is necessary for the support of land *A*.[4]

Where for instance, the lessees of the surface soil and a mine underneath are different persons, the mine-holder is entitled to work the mine without causing any injury to the surface owner in his right of support from the sub-soil. The surface owner's right of support from the subjacent soil is a natural right independent of any easement. It is a right to have the surface kept at its ancient and natural level and comes into being on the severance of the interest in the surface and the mine.[5] And, if at the time of the severance, the surface soil is burdened with any structure such as a building, the mine-owner will have to bear the weight of the additional

1. *Gopalakrishna Panickar* v. *Thirunakkara Devaswom*, AIR 1959 Ker 202.
2. *Humphries* v. *Brogden*, (1850) 12 QB 739; *Caledonian Ry.* v. *Sprot*, (1856) 2 Macq 449 (HL); *Backhouse* v. *Bonomi*, (1861) 9 HLC 503; *N.E. Ry.* v. *Elliot*, (1860) 1 John & M 145.
3. *Hunt* v. *Peake*, (1860) John 705; *Dalton* v. *Angus*, (1881) 6 App Cas 740.
4. *Birmingham Corporation* v. *Allen*, (1877) LR 6 Ch D 284.
5. *Nimcha Coal Co.* v. *Sriniwas Goenka*, (1965) 70 Cal WN 1108.

burden also into consideration in working his mine. The liability in such cases arises in tort and the surface owner is entitled to damages measured by the full value of the land depillarised.[1]

Surface water.—In each case, the question whether or not particular water is surface water is one of fact to be determined by the circumstances attending its origin and continued existence. If the water is spread out and flows sluggishly over the surface, losing itself by percolation and evaporation, it is surface water, although it has its source in springs. But the mere fact that the water spreads out of some place, and flows sluggishly without sufficient force to form a channel for itself, does not make it surface water if the flow has sufficient force to maintain itself, and it is subsequently gathered together into a channel so as to form a water course.[2]

Merely because water spread itself over the upper field before it gets into the lower field, it does not fulfil the definition of surface water. If it flows in a well defined course into an upper land, spreads itself over the whole field which is irrigated by it, and then flows over the field ridge to another or into an intermediate channel through which it comes into another field, it could not be regarded as surface water. So long as the identity and the existence of the water that flows through the channel is maintained as a water body, it could not be described as surface water.[3]

The owner of a lower heritage cannot escape the burden of receiving the water which falls from a piece of higher ground merely because the water flows across an intervening tenement belonging to another person.[4]

The contention that the right of discharge of rain water of every owner of upper land, given Legislative recognition in Section 7, illustration (i) of Easements Act, is limited to the adjacent land and the moment somebody else's property intervened, the said right could not be extended to the property beyond that intervening property, cannot be accepted. The reason is that what has been observed in the illustration is only illustrative in character and not definitive in import. If the intervening owner readily accepts the burden, which then

1. *Khas Joyrampur Colliery Co. Ltd.* v. *Net Ram Marwari,* AIR 1966 Pat 405.
2. *Adinarayana* v. *Ramudu,* AIR 1914 Mad 507.
3. *Venkataramaniah* v. *Subbaramayya,* AIR 1962 Andhra Pradesh 245.
4. *Natabar Sasmal* v. *Krishna Chandra Bera,* AIR 1942 Cal 261.

passes on further, the intervening owner is not a necessary party to any such litigation. The first claimant can very well have a cause of action against the property standing third in order, if that person tries to arrest the flow of his water via that intervening property.[1]

Drainage of surface water.—The natural right of drainage to discharge water possessed by the upper heritor, cannot be limited merely to the natural regulation of the water, according to the law of gravitation. It includes a right to collect in a body all the natural surface water which may be found on a tenement, and to discharge it down, without causing more injury than it would have caused by its natural unregulated flow. The lower owner has no cause for complaint if he receives without additional injury the upper water in a body instead of receiving it in its diffused natural state.[2]

Where a right is based upon illustration (i) the owner of higher land can pass even flood water received by him on to the lower land, at any rate where the flood is a usual or a periodic occurrence in the locality. Where the owner of the lower ground by creating an embankment impedes the natural flow of water he would be obstructing the natural outlet for that water. It makes little difference that the water happens to be not merely rain water but flood water, provided the flood is of the kind to which the higher land is subjected periodically. The only right which a riparian owner may have is to protect himself against extraordinary floods. But even then he would not be entitled to impede the flow of the stream along its natural course.[3]

The principle of law that a reparian owner is entitled to a protective step on his own land with a view to prevent the flood water causing damages to his land will not apply in a case where something is sought to be done in the nature of raising an artificial dam on a piece of land which belongs to others and specially when it is found that raising of dam was not in the nature of a protective step but a malicious one calculated to injure certain other persons and not a step meant to protect their own interest.

A complete reversal of the direction of a flow of the rain

---

1. *Uka Amra* v. *Dhuda Vira*, AIR 1979 Guj. 42.
2. *K.P.V. Pillai* v. *R.N.A. Nadar*, AIR 1955 Trav-Cochin 112.
3. *P. Dudrayya* v. *Venkayya*, AIR 1961 SC 1821 : (1961) 2 SCJ 662.

water due to the construction of a dam cannot be said to be a natural use and anyone who seeks to do something of this kind cannot claim that he is merely taking protective steps against flood water.[1]

The right of a person to draw up water or divert the course of naturally flowing water or provide a particular channel for the flow of accumulated water is not an unrestricted right. It is subject to the obligation of seeing that no injury was caused to the property of another.[2]

An owner of land has a natural right not only to collect and retain within the limits of his own land surface water not flowing in a defined channel, but also a right to draw it off on to his neighbour's lower land,[3] or put it to whatever use he pleases.[4]

This principle applies to rain or flood waters naturally accumulating on land of higher level which must find its level by draining into the lower land.

This is a natural right independent of an easement, grant or custom.[5]

No natural right to discharge foul refuse water.— The natural right of an owner of the upper land in regard to water naturally rising or falling in his land is only a limited right mentioned in illustration (i). He cannot claim a right to flow water in a defined channel like a drain as a natural right nor can he claim a right to discharge that water on the lower land which does not naturally arise on his land or fall upon it. No natural right to discharge through drain, foul refuse water of a factory situated on the upper land can therefore be claimed on the ground that the land on which the water is being discharged is situated on the lower level.[6]

A perusal of the illustrations (f), (g), (h), (i) & (j) of Section 7 shows that there is right by way of easement to discharge

1. *Hari Ram* v. *Siya Ram*, AIR 1977 All 244.
2. *Maung Bya* v. *Maung Kyi Nyo*, AIR 1925 PC 236.
3. *Chasemore* v. *Richards*, (1859) 7 HLC 349, 379, 382; *Kopil Pooree* v. *Manick Sahoo*, 20 WR 287; *Subbramaniya* v. *Ramchandra*, ILR 1 M 335; *Imam Ali* v. *Poresh Mundul*, ILR 8 C 468; *Ramaswamy* v. *Rasi*, ILR 38 M 149; *see* Sec 7, Illustration (i), Easements Act; *Sampuran Singh* v. *Arjan Singh*, AIR 1961 Punj 414 at 415.
4. *Chasemore* v. *Richards*, (1857) 7 HLC 349.
5. *Sumanlal Bhagwandas* v. *Naginlal Bhagwandas*, ILR 1966 Pat 166.
6. *Chandami Lal* v. *General Manager, Western Railway*, AIR 1962 All 159 : 1961 ALJ 768.

the dirty water of the drain of one's house or property on another person's land. That would be allowing a right to create or cause nuisance on another person's land. An easement of that kind is not contemplated by the Easements Act.[1]

Right to open door or windows in wall.—Every owner has a right to open windows, apertures or doors in his own wall and unless by doing so he violates the right of privacy or any other pre-existing and well established right vested in his neighbour, the latter cannot compel him to close the doors or windows or apertures.[2]

Right to consume water of natural stream.—A riparian owner has right to consume water of a natural stream for his household or domestic purposes and to meet the wants of his cattle or sheep. In the *bona fide* exercise of this right for such purposes he is free to satisfy his wants without any regard to the effect which such diminution of water caused by his user, might have on the other proprietors lower below. In this primary use of water he may even exhaust it altogether without being liable to other riparian owners. The case, however, would be different when water is utilized for agricultural or manufacturing purpose. For such purposes he cannot utilize the water at all if as a result of such user the water of the stream is materially diminished to the prejudice of the lower riparian owners. Where a stream does not contain sufficient water to enable every riparian owner to utilize it freely for secondary needs, e.g., agricultural or manufacturing purposes, each owner must get only his proportionate share of the water as determined by the number of owners and the area for which the water is to be applied by each to an equally beneficial use. It is thus clear that the upper riparian owner with respect to the natural stream is not entitled to exclusive use of the water in the natural stream. He cannot complain of the use of the water by the lower riparian owner, and in law he has *locus standi* during a suit against a lower riparian owner putting up a bund across the natural stream and diverting the water for purpose of irrigating his land.[3]

Nuisance—Locality, in what cases relevant?—Gale on Easements[4] dealing with nuisance states as follows :

The result of an inquiry whether there is a nuisance

1. *Prabhu Narain Singh* v. *Ram Niranjan and others*, AIR 1983 All 223.
2. *Jodha* v. *Jhiguria*, MBLJ 1953 HC 703.
3. *Dr. K. Anantha Bhatt* v. *K.M. Ganpathy Bhatta*, AIR 1981 Ker 102.
4. Gale on Easements, (1959), 13th Ed. by Bowles, p. 228.

may differ according to the locality of the building affected; but in cases of nuisance by obstruction to ancient lights locality is of very much less importance in determining whether such obstruction amounts to an actionable nuisance than in cases relating to other nuisance;[1] but it is probable that no variation in locality can justify the diminution of light below a minimum standard;[2] or afford grounds for reducing the light, passing to a room in a manufacturing town, to the standard of other inadequately lighted rooms in the neighbourhood. In the case of nuisance other than obstruction to light, the question varies with the locality.[3]

According to Knight Bruce, V.C. in the case *Walter* v. *Salfe*,[4] (affirmed on appeal), the question in each case is this :

> Ought this inconvenience to be considered in fact as more than fanciful, more than one of mere delicacy or fastidiousness, or as an inconvenience materially interfering with the ordinary comfort physically of human existence, not merely according to elegant or dainty modes and habits of living, but according to plain, sober and simple notions among the English people.

For the purpose of answering this question, said Warrington, J. :[5]

> I am not to look at the defendants' operation in the abstract and by themselves, but in connection with all the circumstances of the locality, and in particular, in reference to the nature of the trades usually carried on there, and the noises and disturbances existing prior to the commencement of the defendants' operations.[6] But if after taking these circumstances into consideration, I find a serious and not merely a slight additional interference with the plaintiff's comfort as above defined, I think it is

1. *Fishendon* v. *Higes & Hill Ltd.*, 79 S.J. 434 : (1935) 53 LT 128 at 140 (*per* Romer, LJ and at pages 142, 143, *per* Maugham, J.); *see* also (1904) AC at pp. 183-185 (*per* Lord Halsbury and p. 210 *per* Lord Lindley); *Kiney* v. *Jolly*, (1905) 2 Ch at p. 297 (*per* Romer, L.J.).
2. *Horton's Estate Ltd.* v. *James Beattie Ltd.*, (1927) 1 Ch 75 (*per* Russell, J.).
3. *Rushmer* v. *Polsue*, (1906) 1 Ch 234, 250 : 1907 AC 121.
4. (1851) 4 De. G & S 315 : 20 LJ Ch 433 : 17 LT 103.
5. *Rushmer* v. *Polsue*, (1906) 1 Ch 234; approved in *Polsue* v. *Rushmer*, (1907) AC 121.
6. *Sturges* v. *Bridgman*, (1879) 11 Ch D 852; *St. Helen's Smelting Co.* v. *Tipping*, (1865) 11 HLC 642.

the duty of the court to interfere.[1] This seems to me to be the true result of the authorities.

Distant tenements and their supposed state is not relevant in determining the question. Nor are the personal idiosyncracies to be taken into account for this purpose.[2]

A nuisance from noise and vibration is more difficult to prove than in the case of injury arising from a visible or tangible cause.[3] But proceedings have been taken successfully in respect of bell-ringing;[4] noise from confectioner's mortar;[5] noisy machinery;[6] electric station;[7] rifle practice;[8] loud music;[9] a circus or organs;[10] noisy crowds;[11] building operations;[12] and hotel activities.[13] As regards the establishment of a school, it is stated in Comyn's Digest[14] : "If a man sets up a school so near my study who am of the profession of the law that the noise interrupts my studies, no action lies."

Natural stream.—A natural stream as defined in the Explanation in connection with riparian rights, is a stream, whether permanent, intermittent, tidal or non-tidal, on the surface of land or underground, which flow by the operation of nature only and in a natural course. If the body of the water

1. *Crump* v. *Lambert*, (1867) LR 3 Eq. 409.
2. *Phiraya Mol* v. *Emperor*, 9 P.H. 1904 (Cr).
3. *Gaunt* v. *Fynney*, (1872) LR 8 Ch App 81.
4. *Soltan* v. *De Held*, (1851) 2 Sim (NS) 133.
5. *Sturges* v. *Bridgman*, (1879) 11 Ch D 852.
6. *White* v. *Cohen*, (1852) 1 Drew 312; *Eaden* v. *Firth*, (1863) 1 H & M 573; *Fenwick* v. *London Ry.*, (1875) LR 20 Eq. 544; *Heather* v. *Pardon*, (1877) 37 LT 393; *Rushmer* v. *Polsue*, (1906) 1 Ch 234.
7. *Shelter* v. *City of London Co.*, (1895) 1 Ch 287; *Colwell* v. *St. Pancras*, (1904) 1 Ch 707; see *Knight* v. *Isle of Wright*, (1904) 90 LT 410.
8. *Hawley* v. *Steele*, (1877) 6 Ch D 521.
9. *Christie* v. *Davey*, (1893) 1 Ch 316.
10. *Inchbald* v. *Robinson*, 1869 LR 4 Ch 388; *Lambton* v. *Mellish*, (1894) 3 Ch 163.
11. *Bellamy* v. *Wells*, (1891) 60 LJ Ch 156; *Germaine* v. *London Exhibitions*, (1896) 75 LT 101; *Dewar* v. *City Racecourse*, (1899) 1 Ir R 345 (*see* also to the obstruction of a highway by crowds); *Lyons* v. *Gulliver*, (1914) 1 Ch 631; *Barber* v. *Penley*, (1893) 2 Ch 447. (The defendants must have done something to create the crowd); *Dwyer* v. *Mansfield*, (1946) 1 KB 437, 440 (queue outside defendant's shop caused by shortage of potatoes. *Held*, no action would lie). Distinguished in *Fabbri* v. *Morris*, (1947) 176 LT 172 (where evidence held by the Divisional Court to justify finding of fact by Justices that the defendant had done something to create the crowd).
12. *Lipman* v. *Pulman*, (1904) 91 LT 132.
13. *Vanderpant* v. *Mayfair*, (1930) 1 Ch 138; *see* Gale on Easements, 13th Ed.,

is found to flow in a well-defined channel it is enough, and it is not essential that its banks should be unchangeable or its flow constant or the size uniform and its waters be entirely unmixed with mud or clay. As it is not possible for law to fix any limits for variations in these particulars, they may be found to differ considerably in each particular case.[1] As stated above, the definition of stream as given in the Explanation to Illustration (i) [(formerly) (j)] includes a subterranean stream flowing in a defined and known channel. But the illustration contemplates neither an underground water which does not flow in a defined channel but merely percolates through the strata of the earth, nor a stream the existence whereof cannot be ascertained except by excavation.[2] In the above-cited case the owner of the soil was held not liable for draining a pond, the water whereof escaped and squandered itself when it rose above a particular point, into a natural stream, but not in a defined course. The reason of this rule has been lucidly stated by Tindal, C.J., in the following words : "But in the case of a well sunk by a proprietor on his own land, the water which feeds it from neighbouring soil does not flow openly, in the sight of neighbouring proprietors but through the hidden veins of earth beneath the surface. No man can tell what changes these underground surfaces have undergone in progress of time. It may well be, that it is only yesterday's date that they took the course and direction which enabled them to supply the well. Again, no proprietor knows what portion of water is taken from beneath his own soil, how much he gives originally, how much he transmits only, or how much he receives. On the contrary, until the well is sunk, and the water collected by draining into it, there cannot properly be said, with reference to the well, to be any flow of water at all."[3]

Ownership of land, what includes.—The ownership of land includes the right to draw underground water from the land, fixers to land like trees etc. The right of every owner of upper land that water naturally rising in, and passing in defined channels is recognised by law as restricted easement. The right of every owner of the land to the natural flow of water by natural stream without interruption and without

1. *Gopala Krishna* v. *Secretary of State*, 26 IC 800 (Mad); *Rassett* v. *Salisbury Manufacturing Co.*, 43 N.H. 369; *see* also *Narasimhalu* v. *Bhadrayya*, AIR 1933 M 10; *Basavana* v. *Narayana*, AIR 1931 M 284.
2. *Broadbent* v. *Ramsbotham*, (1856) 11 Exch 602 : 25 LJ Ex 115 : 24 WR 1011.
3. *Acton* v. *Bhundell*, (1843) 12 M & W 324 : 7 RR 361 : 13 LJ Ex 299.

material alterations is also recognised. The right, however, of an owner to claim a share in the water in a well constructed in a separate and distinct land is not recognised in law.[1]

Restrictive right to privacy.—Where a party opens window, invading privacy of neighbour, he is at liberty to raise a wall in his site to prevent that party from overlooking into his site.[2]

Right of support—Damage.—Where excavation work on part of adjacent owner resulted in collapsing of wall which was constructed by the plaintiff along hillock for beneficial use of his land, the suit for easementary right of lateral support from adjacent wall would be maintainable.[3]

---

1. *Nadupari Narayana* v. *Ijjada Narayana*, AIR 2002 AP 387.
2. *Perumalla R. Maharishi* v. *Musumuri Balat Sundaramma*, (AP) 2007 (2) LS 359.
3. *Ningappa Eranakegowda* v. *R. Shankarappa*, AIR 2007 (NOC) 314 (Kar).

CHAPTER II

THE IMPOSITION, ACQUISITION AND TRANSFER OF EASEMENTS

8. Who may impose easements.—An easement may be imposed by any one in the circumstances, and to the extent, in and to which he may transfer his interest in the heritage on which the liability is to be imposed.

Illustrations

(a) *A* is a tenant of *B*'s land under a lease for an unexpired term of twenty years, and has power to transfer his interest under the lease. *A* may impose an easement on the land to continue during the time that the lease exists or for any shorter period.

(b) *A* is a tenant for life of certain land with remainder to *B* absolutely. *A* cannot, unless with *B*'s consent, impose an easement thereon which will continue after the determination of his life interest.

(c) *A*, *B* and *C* are co-owners of certain land. *A* cannot, without the consent of *B* and *C*, impose an easement on the land or on any part thereof.

(d) *A* and *B* are lessees of the same lessor. *A* of a field *X* for a term of five years, and *B* of a field *Y* for a term of ten years. *A*'s interest under his lease is transferable; *B*'s is not. *A* may impose on *X*, in favour of *B*, a right of way terminable with *A*'s lease.

NOTES

GENERAL.—Easements, being right which are superadded to the ordinary natural incidents of the ownership of a dominant tenement, and which connote a corresponding burden on a servient tenement against common right, may be created or passed only by deed, that is by grant, reservation or covenant, or by prescription, which presupposes a grant. This rule, however, is subject to some exceptions, as under some circumstances an easement may be created by operation of law, such as by estoppel; by agreement, express or implied, by part performance of an oral agreement, or by special statutory proceedings providing for the acquisition of a private road or right of way over the lands of another; or by statute; or an easement may be created or recognized by a judgment or decree; or may be acquired by necessity. An easement may also exist by custom, but as custom has the force of customary law within the locality where it obtains, a right existing by custom is not strictly an easement.

An easement may rest—

(i) upon an express grant actually subsisting, or

(ii) upon a presumed grant, or

(iii) upon a grant arising by mere implication.

An easement existing by presumed grant is an easement claimed under the doctrine of prescription; or on the doctrine of a lost modern grant, all of which rest upon the fact of long undisturbed enjoyment of the right constituting the easement.[1]

An easement existing upon a grant arising by mere applicability is virtually created by express grant, since the creation of the easement is effected by the legal construction of the instrument, although it contains no express mention whatever of the easement.

Whether or not the right created by a particular agreement or instrument constitutes an easement depends on the intention of the parties, as ascertained from the language of the agreement or instrument in question, or in case of doubt, from the surrounding facts and circumstances.

Whatever be the origin of an easement, the quality of the right, where validly subsisting is the same, irrespective of whether the right has been created by long enjoyment or by grant, express or implied. But there is a difference in respect of quantum of right between an easement created by express grant or arising by implication of law and an easement claimed under a presumed grant. In the former case, the easement may be created for interests analogous in their duration to all manner of interests and estates, in the latter case, the

1. *Phillips* v. *Halliday,* 1891 AC 228 (HL) at p. 231, *per* Lord Herschell; *Clippens Oil Co.* v. *Edinburgh & District Water Trustees,* 1904 AC 64 (HL) at p. 69, *Per* Lord Halsbury, L.C.

easement exists in perpetuity.

Under Section 8, every owner or occupier of land having a transferable interest in it can impose over it an easement to the extent of his own right. Such owner or occupier cannot, however, create an easement which exceeds in any case his own transferable interest over the heritage. The reason is that an easement diminishes the rights of the servient owner and no one can be allowed to diminish another's rights without his consent. Absolute and indefeasible easement rights might, therefore, be imposed over the servient heritage by the full owner of the land himself or by his duly authorized agent in this behalf. So an owner who has previously contracted to sell his property, cannot impose easement over it. Limited owners can impose easement to the extent of their own interests. Thus, a Hindu widow having only a life-interest in a property cannot impose an indefeasible easement which might be detrimental to the interests of the reversioners.

Difference between imposition and transfer of easements.—The imposition of an easement should be distinguished from the transfer of an easement. Imposition of an easement means the creation of an easement by the owner or occupier of the land on which it is to be exercised, while transfer of an easement means the transfer of an existing right by the dominant owner.[1] The former is the voluntary creation of a right which did not exist before, while the latter is only a voluntary conveyance of the existing right.

No writing necessary for creating an easement.—A grant of an easement may be made orally without any writing, because the creation of easement by the servient owner over the land in his ownership or occupation does not amount to a transfer of ownership.

Grant as basis of easements.—Theoretically all easements have their origin in some sort of grant by the servient owner. The grant may be express, or it may be implied from the circumstances and conduct of the parties to the easement or it may be presumed from long user or it may be inferred from some usage prevailing in the locality.[2]

In the case of an express grant of the easement, the limit

1. *Sultan Nawaz Jung* v. *Rustomji* 20 B 704; *see* also *Gopichetti Narayanaswami Naidu* v. *Madala Venkanna,* AIR 1915 M 571; *Parkum* v. *Kuttiammoo,* AIR 1919 Mad 339 : ILR 42 Mad 567 (DB).
2. *See* Peacock on Easements, p. 311 (3rd Ed.).

depends on the words used.[1] The easement granted may be such as altogether to exclude the owner of the servient tenement and others from participation in the enjoyment of the easement,[2] or it may be one which is to be shared in common with others. In the latter case, the principle that a lessor impliedly contracts to give to the lessee possession of the property demised at the beginning of the term, can have no application to an easement to be enjoyed in common with other people.

In the case of *Shri Swayam Prakash Ashram* v *Anandveli Amma*,[3] the plaintiff and the defendant found that some land was being used by the owner for the Ashram. According to the will of the owner, some land was granted by the defendant to the plaintiff. The disputed route was the only way to enter the land granted to the plaintiff. The plaintiff was using this route for a longtime. The other way was also not told by the respondent. The Supreme Court held it to be an implied easement by grant. It was not necessary to mention it in the grant letter.

Form of grant and registration.—No particular form or language is necessary to constitute a grant. It is enough, if the words used convey the idea of an unequivocal grant, of easement by the servient owner for the beneficial enjoyment of the dominant heritage by the dominant owner. Any words which clearly show the intention to give an easement which is by law grantable are sufficient to effect that purpose.[4] It need not be in writing[5] or registered.[6]

Constructive grant by acquiescence.—There are numerous cases in which an agreement to grant an easement

1. See *Taylor* v. *St. Helena*, (1877) 6 Ch D 264.
2. See *Lee* v. *Stevenson*, (1858) EB & E 512; *Southport* v. *Ormskirk*, (1894) 1 QB 196; *Biyan* v. *Whistler*, (1828) 3 B & C 288.
3. AIR 2010 SC 622.
4. *Rowbotham* v. *Wilson*, 8 E & B 123; *see* also *Gum Som* v. *Cassim Dalla*, 34 IC 95.
5. *Krishna* v. *Ravappa*, 4 MHC 98; *Meer Helaloodeen* v. *Chowdhry Abdul Sattar*, 9 WR 351; *see* also *Musunoori Satyanarayan Murtin Chekka Lakshmayya*, AIR 1929 M 79 : 31 A 612.
6. *Sewanath* v. *Faqir Chand*, AIR 1965 J. & K. 62 (FB); *Bhagwan Sahai* v. *Narsingh Sahai*, 31 A 612; *Suraj Prasad* v. *Maheshwari Prasad*, 96 IC 276; *Sewa Nath* v. *Faqir Chand*, AIR 1965 J. and K. 62 (FB) in which it was explicitly ruled that for relinquishment of right of easement, writing is not required to be registered and the case of *Subramanya Chettiar* v. *Meyyammal Achi*, AIR 1943 Mad 522 was distinguished; *see* also *Sital Chandra* v. *(Mrs.) Allen Delanney*, 34 IC 450 : AIR 1917 C 681 contra.

or some other right has been inferred—or more correctly has been imputed to the person who is in a position to make the grant, on account of some action or inaction on his part. These cases rest on the equitable doctrine of acquiescence, but they may be referred to, for the purpose of classification, as imputed or constructive grants.

The party acquiescing is subsequently estopped from denying the existence of easement. It is as if such person had made an actual grant of the easement.

Applicability of illustration (c).—Illustration (c) to Section 8 applies where a co-owner seeks to impose an easementary right on the land or any part thereof. But where the plaintiffs claim easementary right only as an alternative ground but the main ground on which they based their claim is on the right of co-ownership, illustration (c) to Section 8 has no application.[1]

Co-owners.—An easement by way of passage stipulated in the sale deed cannot be imposed by some of the co-owners in view of Section 8 read with illustration (c).[2]

Section 8, illustration (c) does not apply where a co-owner seeks to exercise a right of co-ownership.[3]

Easement by grant, by implication.—An easement by grant can be by implication. The fact that the pathway mentioned in the plaint was left in the settlement would be no ground to hold that there was not implied easement by grant. Where the trial court and High Court had reached the conclusion that the plaintiff had acquired the right of easement in respect of impugned pathway, by way of implied grant, the finding of fact arrived at by the courts below would not be upset.[4]

Grant as basis of easements.—In *Hero Vinoth (Minor)* v. *Seshammal*,[5] the principle is elucidated thus :

> 26. The question whether an easement is one acquired by grant (as contrasted from an easement of necessity) does not depend upon absolute necessity of it.

1. *Ayyaswami Gounder and others* v. *Munnuswamy Gounder and others*, AIR 1984 SC 1789.
2. *(Mst.) Naffisan Nisa* v. *Mohd. Ishaque*, AIR 1975 All 431.
3. *Ayyaswami Gounder* v. *Munnuswami Gounder*, AIR 1984 SC 1789, 1790 : (1984) 4 SCC 376 : (1985) 1 MLJ 36, 38, 39 (SC).
4. *Sree Swayam Prakash Ashramam* v. *Anandavally Amma*, AIR 2010 SC 622 (628).
5. 2007 2 LW 945 (SC).

It is the nature of the acquisition that is relevant. Many easements acquired by grant may be absolutely necessary for the enjoyment of the dominant tenement in the sense that it cannot be enjoyed at all without it. That may be the reason for the grant also. But easement of grant is a matter of contract between the parties. In the matter of grant the parties are governed by the terms of the grant and not anything else. Easement of necessity and quasi easement are dealt with in Section 13 of the Act. The grant may be express or even by necessary implication. In either case it will not amount to an easement of necessity under Section 13 of the Act even though it may also be an absolute necessity for the person in whose favour the grant is made. Limit of the easement acquired by grant is controlled only by the terms of the contract. If the terms of the grant restrict its user subject to any condition, the parties will be governed by those conditions. Anyhow the scope of the grant could be determined by the terms of the grant between the parties alone. When there is nothing in the term of the grant in this case that it was to continue only until such time as necessary, was absolute. In fact even at the time it was granted, it was not one of necessity. If it is a permanent arrangement uncontrolled by any condition, that permanency in user must be recognised and the servient tenement will be recognized and the servient tenement will be permanently burdened with that disability. Such a right does not arise under the legal implication of Section 13 nor is it extinguished by the statutory provision under Section 41 of the Act which is applicable only to easement of necessity arising under Section 13.

27. An easement by grant does not get extinguished under Section 41 of the Act which relates to an easement of necessity. An easement of necessity is one which is not merely necessary for the reasonable enjoyment of the dominant tenement, but one where dominant tenement cannot be used at all without the easement. The burden of the servient owner in such a case is not on the basis of any concession or grant made by him for consideration or otherwise, but it is by way of a legal obligation enabling the dominant owner to use his land. It is limited to the barest necessity, however inconvenient it is irrespective of the question whether a better access could be given by the servient owner or not. When an alternate

access becomes available, the legal necessity of burdening the servient owner ceases and the easement of necessity by implication of law is legally withdrawn or extinguished as statutorily recognized in Section 41. Such an easement will last only as long as the absolute necessity exists. Such a legal extinction cannot apply to an acquisition by grant and Section 41 is not applicable in such case.

9. Servient owners.—Subject to the provisions of Section 8, a servient owner may impose on the servient heritage, any easement that does not lessen the utility of the existing easement. But he cannot, without the consent of the dominant owner, impose an easement on the servient heritage which would lessen such utility.

Illustrations

(a) *A* has, in respect of his mill, a right to the uninterrupted flow thereto, from sunrise to noon, of the water of *B*'s stream. *B* may grant to *C* the right to divert the water of the stream from noon to sunset : Provided that *A*'s supply is not thereby diminished.

(b) *A* has, in respect of his house, a right of way over *B*'s land. *B* may grant to *C*, as the owner of a neighbouring farm, the right to feed his cattle on the grass growing on the way : Provided that *A*'s right of way is not thereby obstructed.

NOTES

Section 9 lays down that a servient owner may burden his servient tenement with as many easements as he may choose to impose on his heritage provided he does not thereby infringe the right of enjoyment of the dominant owner. For example, if A has, in respect of his mill, a right to the uninterrupted flow thereto, from sunrise to noon, of the water of B's stream, then B may grant to C the right to divert the water of the stream from noon to sunset, provided that A's supply is not thereby diminished.

As every new easement which is inconsistent with a dominant owner's right of lawful enjoyment is bound to affect the interest of the dominant owner, it has been expressly provided in Section 9 that no easement which is in derogation of the rights of the dominant owner can be imposed over the servient heritage without the consent (express or implied) of the dominant owner. But if the dominant owner gives his consent to the imposition of a new easement in derogation of his own rights, a servient owner is free to do so.

Right of servient owner to impose additional easements on the servient heritage.—The right of servient owner to use and enjoy the servient heritage is limited by the existence of an easement over it. He can only deal with it subject to such restrictions as are imposed on it by the easement concerned.[1] His power of transfer is also restricted to the extent that he cannot transfer any interest which would interfere with the full enjoyment of the easement by the dominant owner. If a servient heritage or any interest therein is transferred it goes burdened with the liabilities imposed by the existing easement on it.

Power of imposing an easement is subject to the same limitations as the power of transfer. So no servient owner can impose an additional easement which would interfere with the full enjoyment of the existing easement in the way, to the extent and under the circumstances as it was enjoyed before such imposition. So practically Section 9 is only a corollary to Section 8. The propositions laid down by Section 9 and Sections 10 and 11 are covered by the general proposition laid down by Section 8 and do not need much explanation. In fact Sections 9 to 11 are only an amplification of the principle laid down in Section 8 and are intended by the Legislature only to exemplify that principle. But the sections do no appear to be very happily worded and the clause "subject to the provisions of Section 8" added to Sections 9 and 10 appears, at first sight, to suggest that these sections are otherwise an exception to the rule laid down in Section 8, which is not, in fact, the meaning which the Legislature intends to convey thereby. In fact Sections 9 to 11 are superfluous and cases intended thereby to be covered are already covered by the sufficiently broad principle laid down by Section 8.

Consent of the dominant owner.—In order to validate an easement imposed by the servient owner which affects the utility of the easement already existing, the consent of the dominant owner is, of course, indispensable as it is in every case where a third party's interest is being adversely affected by a grant. But such consent may be express or implied from the circumstances and conduct of the dominant owner. An

1. *See* Section 7, *ante*.

acquiescence in the enjoyment of an easement adversely affecting his own interest as dominant owner, for a sufficiently long time raises a strong presumption that he consented to its imposition by the servient owner and if there has been such a change of position as converts an acquiescence into an estoppel, the dominant owner cannot question it.

10. Lessor and mortgagor.—Subject to the provisions of Section 8, a lessor may impose, on the property leased, any easement that does not derogate from the rights of the lessee as such, and a mortgagor may impose, on the property mortgaged, any easement that does not render the security insufficient. But a lessor or mortgagor cannot, without the consent of the lessee or mortgagee, impose any other easement on such property, unless it be to take effect on the termination of the lease or the redemption of the mortgage.

Explanation.—A security is insufficient within the meaning of this section unless the value of the mortagaged property exceeds by one third or if consisting of buildings, exceeds by one-half, the amount for the time being due on the mortagage.

NOTES

Section 10 deals with the rights of a lessor or a mortgagor to impose easements on his land which has been leased or mortgaged during the continuance of the lease or mortgage, and lays down that a mortgagor or a lessor can impose such easement on his tenement which does not prejudicially affect the rights of the mortgagee or the lessee. But a lessor or a mortgagor is quite free to impose any easement on his land which is to take effect on the termination of the lease or on the redemption, of the mortgage.

In the case of a mortgage, the mortgagor can impose an easement which does not render the security insufficient, i.e., the value of the property is not reduced to such an extent that from the amount due on the mortgage it would not exceed by one-third and in the case of buildings by one-half of such amount. This criterion of the security being sufficient is the same as given in Section 66 of the Transfer of Property Act, 1882, and bears the same meaning. A mortgagor is free to impose any easement of whatsoever character, if its enjoyment is to begin after the redemption of the mortgage. The principle, laid down in this section had been acted upon in Punjab, where the Indian Easements Act and Transfer of Property Act do not apply, as a principle in consonance with justice, equity and good conscience.[1]

Mortgagor cannot create an easement over mortgaged land, to the detriment of the mortgagees in possession, without the consent of the latter.[2]

11. Lessee.—No lessee or other person having derivative interest may impose on the property held by him as such an easement to take effect after the expiration of his own interest, or in derogation of the right of the lessor or the superior proprietor.

NOTES

The words "derivative interest" mean interest short of full proprietorship. The person holding a derivative interest can impose only those easements which do not affect the interest of full owner, because no person can be allowed to do an act which injures the rights of others.

The easements which such persons can impose are only those which do not affect the interest of the full owner for no person can be allowed by law to do an act which injures the right of others.

12. Who may acquire easements.—An easement may be acquired by the owner of the immovable property for the beneficial enjoyment of which the right is created or, on his behalf by any person in possession of the same.

One of two or more co-owners of immovable property may, as such, with or without the consent of the other or others, acquire an easement for the beneficial enjoyment of such property.

No lessee of immovable property can acquire, for the beneficial enjoyment of other immovable property of his own, an easement in or over the property comprised in his lease.

1. *(Mst.) Bhagwan Devi* v. *Bunyadi*, 85 PR 1902; *Jhandu Lal* v. *Munshi Lal*, AIR 1934 Lah. 199, 200 : 149 IC 949.
2. *Jhandu Lal* v. *Munshi Ram*, AIR 1934 Lah. 199, 200 : 149 IC 949 (2).

NOTES

Who may acquire easements.—An easement may be acquired by the *owner* of the immovable property or by some one, on behalf of the owner, who is in possession of the immovable property. If there are several owners of an immovable property, one of them with or without the consent of others can acquire an easement for the beneficial enjoyment of their joint tenement. The easementary right thus acquired becomes annexed to the heritage itself and is to be enjoyed by all the joint owners equally.

No lessee can acquire an easement over the immovable property leased to him for the beneficial enjoyment of another property of which he happens to be the owner. This restriction is based on the recognition of the rule that during unity of possession of two or more tenements no fresh easement rights can be acquired by prescription for the advantage of the one tenement over the other tenements under the same occupier.

An easement by presumption under Sections 12 and 15 of the Act is in fact an assertion of a hostile claim of certain rights over another man's property and in order to acquire the easement the person who asserts the hostile claim must prove that he had the consciousness to exercise that hostile claim on a property which is not his own and where no such consciousness is proved, he cannot establish a prescription of the right. Therefore, if the owner of a dominant tenement has, during the period of prescription, exercised rights on the footing that he is the owner but which he later on claims as an easement over a servient tenement, then, his exercise of those rights is not exercised as an easement and he must fail in a claim for an easement.[1]

Acquisition of easement by tenant.—A tenant cannot by prescription acquire a right of way over land belonging to the landlord. Because for the existence of an easement two tenements owned by two different persons are necessary.[2] A tenant of one of the several joint owners of a village cannot acquire a right of easement against the others so long as there has been no partition as he is a tenant of the whole proprietary body and cannot acquire a right of easement against his own landlords.[3]

1. *Chapsibhai Dhanjibhai Dand* v. *Purushottam*, AIR 1971 SC 1878.
2. *Imdad Ali* v. *Feral Mia*, ILR (1954) 6 Assam 237.
3. *Bahadur* v. *Khashi Ram*, 11 ALJ 990.

Though one tenant can claim right of easement against another tenant on the basis of implied grant, he cannot claim right of easement against another tenant on the basis of prescription.[1]

An easement implies an absolute outright grant to some person of an incorporeal right as appurtenant to his corporeal property. Such a grant cannot be conceived as made to a mere tenant in respect of a tenement in which his interest is precarious. A grant of this kind, therefore, cannot in such a case be implied, or in other words, there can be no easement claimed by a tenant as against his landlord.[2]

Easement on servient tenement.—Easement over passage of land was created by 'express grant' by owner in favour of transferee. Transferee became dominent owner over plot of land to him and passage of land over which easement was imposed became servient tenement. Though as per terms of sale deed, creator of easement continued to be owner of passage of land, transferee would not have *'nistari'* right of way on land. Transferee had acquired right of passage on land in dispute for beneficial enjoyment of plot purchased by him as per Section 12 of the Act. Held, that as plaintiffs were subsequent transferees of that plot servient tenement also stood transferred to plaintiff by virtue, as per Section 19 of the Act.[3]

Exclusive right of easement, who can claim.—Where in original sanction plan, provision is made for two gates to the suit building, the fact that the northern gate has not been used for six years, cannot translate it into a right in favour of the respondents/plaintiffs so as to contend that the said gate cannot be opened at all in posterity. Also there is no provision in the documents executed between the parties preventing the appellant to do so, who is the lessee in respect of the demised land and is also owner of ground floor premises and basement. The argument of the respondents that northern gate cannot

1. *Bhadu Bala Devi* v. *Gobardhan Chattaraj*, AIR 1978 Cal 425.
2. *Krishna* v. *Venkatachalla*, 7 MHCR 60 (64); *Wheaton* v. *Maple & Co.*, 3 Ch 48 : *Kilgour* v. *Gaddes*, (1904) 1 KB 457; *Gayford* v. *Moffat*, LR 4 Ch App 133 (135); *Outram* v. *Maude*, 17 Ch D 391; *Bayley* v. *G.W. Ry. Co.*, 26 Ch D 441; *Derry* v. *Saunders*, (1919) 1 KB 223; *Bahadur* v. *Khushi Ram*, 11 ALJR 990; *Abdul Rashid* v. *Braham Saran*, AIR 1938 A 293 : ILR (1938) A 538 : 1938 ALJ 436; *Abdul Haq* v. *Tarabannessa*, AIR 1937 Cal 572; *Abdulla* v. *Municipal Corporation, Karachi*, AIR 1939 Sindh 39, confirmed in, AIR 1941 Sindh 211.
3. *Dhananjay Bisen* v. *Devi Bai*, AIR 2002 M.P. 79.

be opened or operated at all, cannot be countermanded. Both the appellant and the respondent had common right to jointly enjoy the common passage. Appellant only cannot claim exclusive right.[1]

13. Easements of necessity and quasi-easements.—Where one person transfers or bequeaths immovable property to another—

(a) if an easement in other immovable property of the transferor or testator is necessary for enjoying the subject of the transfer or bequest, the transferee or legatee shall be entitled to such easement; or

(b) if such an easement is apparent and continuous and necessary for enjoying the said subject as it was enjoyed when the transfer or bequest took effect, the transferee or legatee shall, unless a different intention is expressed or necessarily implied, be entitled to such easement;

(c) if an easement in the subject of the transfer of bequest is necessary for enjoying other immovable property of the transferor or testator, the transferor or the legal representative of the testator shall be entitled to such easement;

(d) if such an easement is apparent and continuous and necessary for enjoying the said property as it was enjoyed when the transfer or bequest took effect, the transferor or the legal representative of the testator, shall, unless a different intention is expressed or necessarily implied, be entitled to such easement.

Where a partition is made of the joint property of several persons—

(e) if an easement over the share of one of them is necessary for enjoying the share of another of them, the latter shall be entitled to such easement; or

(f) if such an easement is apparent and continuous and necessary for enjoying the share

1. *Shatrughan Sinha* v. *Gurudev Singh*, 2006 (6) Mah. LJ 213.

of the latter as it was enjoyed when the partition took effect, he shall, unless a different intention is expressed or necessarily implied, be entitled to such easement.

The easements mentioned in this section, clauses (a), (c) and (e) are called easements of necessity.

Whether immovable property passes by operation of law, the sons from and to whom it so passes are for the purpose of this section, to be deemed, respectively, the transferor and transferee.

Illustrations

(a) *A* sells *B* a field then used for agricultural purposes only. It is inaccessible except by passing over *A*'s adjoining land or by trespassing on the land of a stranger. *B* is entitled to a right of way, for agricultural purposes only, over *A*'s adjoining land to the field sold.

(b) *A*, the owner of two fields, sells one to *B*, and retains the other. The field retained was at the date of the sale used for agricultural purposes only and is inaccessible except by passing over the field sold to *B*. *A* is entitled to a right of way, for agricultural purposes only, over *B*'s field to the field retained.

(c) *A* sells *B* a house with windows overlooking *A*'s land which *A* retains. The light which passes over *A*'s land to the windows is necessary for enjoying the house as it was enjoyed when the sale took effect, *B* is entitled to the light, and *A* cannot afterwards obstruct it by building on his land.

(d) *A* sells *B* a house with windows overlooking *A*'s land. The light passing over *A*'s land to the windows is necessary for enjoying the house as it was enjoyed when the sale took effect. Afterwards *A* sells the land to *C*. Here *C* cannot obstruct the light by building on the land, for he takes it subject to the burdens to which it was subject in *A*'s hands.

(e) *A* is the owner of a house and adjoining land. The house has windows overlooking the land. *A* simultaneously sells the house to *B* and the land to *C*. The light passing over the land is necessary for enjoying the house as it was enjoyed when the sale took effect. Here *A* impliedly grants *B* a right to the light, and *C* takes the land subject to the restriction that he may not build so as to obstruct such light.

(f) *A* is the owner of a house and adjoining land. The house has windows overlooking the land. *A*, retaining the house sells the land to *B* without expressly reserving any easement. The light passing over the land is necessary for enjoying the house as it was enjoyed when the sale took effect. *A* is entitled to the light, and *B* cannot build on the land so as to obstruct such light.

(g) *A*, the owner of a house, sells *B* a factory built on adjoining land. *B* is entitled, as against *A*, to pollute the air, when necessary, with smoke and vapours from the factory.

(h) *A*, the owner of two adjoining houses, *Y* and *Z*, sells *Y* to *B*, and retains *Z*. *B* is entitled to the benefits of all the gutters and drains common to the two houses and necessary for enjoying *Y* as it was enjoyed when the sale took effect, and *A* is entitled to the benefit of all the gutters and drains common to the two houses and necessary for enjoying *Z* as it was enjoyed when the sale took effect.

(i) *A*, the owner of two adjoining buildings, sells one to *B* retaining the other. *B* is entitled to a right to lateral support from *A*'s building and *A* is entitled to a right to lateral support from *B*'s building.

(j) *A*, the owner of two adjoining buildings, sells one to *B* and the other to *C*. *C* is entitled to lateral support from *B*'s building and *B* is entitled to lateral support from *C*'s building.

(k) *A* grants lands to *B* for the purpose of building a house thereon, *B* is entitled to such amount of lateral and subjacent support from *A*'s land as is necessary for the safety of the house.

(l) Under the Land Acquisition Act, 1870, a

Railway Company compulsorily acquires a portion of *B*'s land for the purpose of making a siding. The Company is entitled to such amount of lateral support from *B*'s adjoining land as is essential for the safety of the siding.

(m) Owing to the partition of joint property, *A* becomes the owner of an upper room in a building, and *B* becomes the owner of the portion of the building immediately beneath it. *A* is entitled to such amount of vertical support from *B*'s portion as is essential for the safety of the upper room.

(n) *A* lets a house and grounds to *B* for a particular business. *B* has no access to them other than by crossing *A*'s land. *B* is entitled to a right of way over that land suitable to the business to be carried on by *B* in the house and grounds.

NOTES

Section 13 deals with easement rights after the severance of a tenement into several independent units has taken place by transfer, bequest, partition or by operation of law. Two kinds of easement rights which arise on severance of a tenement are : (1) Easements of necessity, and (2) *Quasi* easements.

Easements of Necessity.—An easement of necessity is that which is *absolutely necessary* for the enjoyment of a tenement into several independent units. Mere convenience is not the test for an easement of necessity. Where in a suit for injunction restraining the defendants from using a particular passage in front of the plaintiff's house, the defendants rely on the right of way as an easement of necessity and not as an easement acquired by prescription, it must be shown that without the use of this passage the enjoyment of the property becomes impossible, i.e., it must be established that there is no other means of access into the southern lane and it cannot be pleaded that disputed passage is a more convenient means of access to the southern lane.[1] Clauses (a), (c) and (e) of Section 13 deal with easement of necessity.

Example.—A sells B a field then used for agricultural purposes only. It is inaccessible except by passing over A's adjoining land. B is entitled to a right of way, for agricultural purposes only, over A's adjoining land to the field. Thus B's

1. *M. Ammal* v. *Pandaram*, AIR 1956 Mad 584.

right to have a right of way over A's adjoining land is an easement of necessity because without such a right of way B cannot approach and hence enjoy his land at all.

An easement of necessity is an easement without which a property cannot be used at all and not one merely necessary to the reasonable enjoyment of the property.

An easement of necessity has also to answer the general definition of an easement as generally defined in Section 4. Unless, therefore, it falls within the definition and answers the description of an easement as defined therein, one cannot take the second step of considering as to whether it amounts to an easement of necessity, because it has to fall within the general category of an easement first and only thereafter the question may arise as to what particular category of easement it belongs and whether it amounts to an easement of necessity.[1] Where one property is severed from another property either in possession, or in ownership, or in both, by a transfer, bequest, or partition, or by operation of law, and these two are so relatively situated that the one cannot be enjoyed without the exercise of a particular privilege, in or upon, or in respect of the other, such privilege is called an easement of necessity.[2] The first condition under Section 13 which is required to be fulfilled is that the immovable property as such has to be transferred or bequeathed and creation of sub-lease, would not amount to such transfer as is contemplated in Section 13. May be the transfer is in the form of only an interest in the property and may, therefore, include letting out of the property. But it must be by the owner of the property because it has to be connected with another property belonging to the transferor and unless the transferor is the owner of that other property, the question of creating an easement of necessity cannot arise in respect of such property.[3]

An easement of necessity is an easement needed absolutely for the enjoyment of property. It is not merely for convenience or reasonable enjoyment. If a person can have access to his property by making alteration in his own building he cannot claim easement of necessity in the property of another.[4]

Where a property is severed by the grant of a portion of

1. *State* v. *Hiralal*, AIR 1980 Guj. 146 at pp. 147, 148.
2. See *Morgan* v. *Kirby*, 2 M 46.
3. *State* v. *Hiralal*, AIR 1980 Guj. 146 at p. 148.
4. *K. S. Vaidyanathan* v. *(Messrs.) Bubari & Sons (P) Ltd.*, (1969) 1 MLJ 435.

it, there can be no implied reservation in favour of the property retained of an easement of convenience but only of an easement of necessity. If a passage is not the subject matter of a lease, the lessee cannot have better right than the lessor. If an alternative passage has been provided to the lessee it would obviate the necessity which forms the foundation of easement.[1]

Easement of necessity arises only where by a transfer, bequest or partition, a single tenement is divided into two or more tenements and any of those is to be situated that it cannot be enjoyed at all without certain privilege on another such tenement. In such a case, implied grant or reservation will be presumed in favour of the person holding the former tenement.[2]

The creation of an easement of necessity is an outcome of the prior relationship between the tenements. The disposition which terminates the common ownership and gives rise to an easement by implication of law, may be of either tenement, or may be a simultaneous disposition of both tenements. Where a man transfers or bequeaths part of his land which affords accommodation to the part retained, that accommodation, upon severance, ripens into an easement, if it is absolutely necessary for the enjoyment of the part retained and the accommodation is such that it is capable of constituting the subject matter of an easement.[3]

The mere fact that the two tenements belong to a common owner, does not give rise to an easement of necessity. There must be proof that both the tenements constituted one tenement (the single unit). It must further be established that after the severance, the situation was such that the dominant tenement cannot be used at all without the easement claimed in the suit over servient tenement. Further, the necessity must be absolute necessity and not merely for reasonable and convenient enjoyment of the property.[4]

An easement of necessity can be granted only when the

1. *Bank of India* v. *Sarathy Brothers.*, AIR 1970 Mad 37 : 82 MLW 191.
2. *Earsad Ali* v. *Mohammad Yakub Khan.*, AIR 1969 Orissa 201 : (1968) 84 Cut. LT 835.
3. *Dwijesh Ch Dutta* v. *Kalyani Das*, (1985) 2 Gauhati Law Rep. 426, 432, para 10.
4. *Usharani Das* v. *Bhaktahari Monahty*, AIR 1984 Orissa 97, 102, 104.

necessity is what may be termed "absolute".[1] Sweepers passing through residential houses would give rise to such a state of inconvenience as to make the houses for all practical purposes uninhabitable for the people of ordinary decency and clean habits. Where plaintiff's houses were solely dwelling-houses and the locality was in which respectable people dwelt and the part over which the right of sweepers to carry buckets after clearing plaintiff's latrine was claimed, was already being used by the sweepers who carried buckets from the defendant's latrine, it was held that to compel the plaintiff to have his nightsoil buckets carried out through the houses would destroy as residential dwellings the houses which were the properties sold by the original owner of the whole plot of land as dwelling-houses and, as such, it was an easement of necessity.[2] Inconvenient an alternate access is, if it is available, there is no place for an easement of necessity.[3] Plaintiff is not to establish absolute necessity in the sense that there should be no other manner of such enjoyment available in any circumstance whatever. Section 13 contemplates that an easement of necessity exists having regard to the normal way of life of the person who claims and of persons belonging to his category. Hindus are averse to the entry of sweepers through the courtyard inside the house itself.[4]

An easement of necessity runs with the property like any other right appurtenant thereto, by virtue of an implied grant, or reservation, and no express words are necessary for the conveyance, or reservation thereof.[5]

Certain property was partitioned between two co-owners. The house allotted to the defendant was surrounded by land allotted to the plaintiff. It was found that it was necessary for the defendant for the reasonable enjoyment of his house to pass over the plaintiff's land but that a door could be opened

1. *Daw Gyan* v. *U. Maung Maung* 1935 R 127 : 156 IC 775; *Daw Tint* v. *Maung Kywe*, 154 IC 468 : AIR 1935 P 56; *Anant Ram* v. *Kashiva Lunia Kumbi*, 1942 NLJ 441; *Rajalu* v. *Malak*, AIR 1939 N 197 : ILR 1939 N 580 : 1939 NLJ 297 : 186 IC 155; *Ramanandan* v. *Ramjiban*, AIR 1939 Pat 164 : 178 IC 803; *Mahboob Khan* v. *Govindarajulu*, AIR 1936 M 142 : 160 IC 955.
2. *Daw Gyan* v. *U Maung Maung*, AIR 1935 R 127 : 156 IC 775; *Lodha Singh* v. *Kanhaya Lal*, 1969 Cut LJ 868 (Punj).
3. *R.R. Mohan* v. *N. Namboodiripad*, 1990 (1) KLJ 89 at 92.
4. *Narayani Devi (Smt.)* v. *Phool Chand*, AIR 1981 All 99 at p. 101; *See* also *Annapurna Datta* v. *Santosh Kumar*, AIR 1937 Cal 661 and *Chintamani Hargovan* v. *Ratanji Bhun*, 20 (Bom) ILR 1131.
5. See *Morgan* v. *Kirby*, 2 M 46.

on defendant's land which, however, would diminish the utility of the house, *held*, that the defendant was not entitled to right of way claimed, inasmuch as the user of that right was not absolutely necessary for the benefit of his share of the house.[1]

Where in a partition proceedings a *pucca* well was allotted to the plaintiff without reserving any right for the defendant; *held*, that the defendant had no easement of necessity inasmuch as he could dig another well for the enjoyment of his land.[2]

Easement of necessity would no longer be available when alternative way is available to the claimant of that right.[3]

An easement of necessity is an easement without which the property cannot be enjoyed at all, it is not merely a reasonable enjoyment and in determining the necessity it is not a convenience alone but it must be absolute necessity. In a suit for injunction if the defendant claims it is an easement and not one acquired by presumption, it must be shown that without using it the enjoyment of the property becomes impossible. It is not sufficient to plead that it would be more convenient to enjoy the property.[4]

In the suit for permanent injunction prohibitory or mandatory, plaintiff has to establish his title to the property in respect of which he is claiming the injunction and right which he wants to enforce. Thus, where the injunction was sought by plaintiff on ground that their precedessor-in-title from whom plaintiff had acquired property by way of sale deed, have been enjoying the easementary right of light and air and thereafter under the sale deed they have been enjoying easement of necessity and hence acquired the same.[5]

If there is a formed pathway, though the easement may be apparent, it is discontinuous. Rights of way, therefore, unless they are easements of absolutely necessity, do not pass by implied grant. Where the plaintiff was using *puramboke* land by side of road for ingress and egress to road, he can sue for the relief of injunction without alleging possession over

1. *Sukhdei* v. *Kedarnath*, 8 ALJ 280.
2. *Gaddar* v. *Kalla*, ALJ 672.
3. *Ramesh Chandra Bhikabhai Patel* v. *Maneklal Maganlal Patel*, AIR 1978 Guj 62.
4. *Mariya Ammal* v. *Aruchala*, AIR 1966 Mad 88.
5. *Moulasab Rajasab Mullanavar and another* v. *Naganagouda Parvatagouda Harlapur and another*, 1998 AIHC 1927.

the property.[1]

The ownership rights were acquired by the appellants-plaintiffs in a house in their possession by operation of law, i.e., by way of adverse possession and it was proved that the house in possession of both the parties are contiguous to each other. The defendants had been using house courtyard for reaching cattle-shed since last 40 years and so they had acquired easement of necessity regarding the courtyard in the form of right of passage through it.[2]

In *Prem Lal Yadav* v. *Rajendra Prasad Chandrawansi*,[3] where decree for permanent injunction after removing obstruction made by defendant was not granted in favour of plaintiff but the plaintiff had established his easementary rights over suit land. By Chhatishgarh High Court he was held entitled for consequential relief of permanent injunction restraining defendant from interfering with use of said land.

Easement of Necessity—Principle on which based.— "When on severance of the ownership of the tenement it is found that some act for the enjoyment of the severed properties is necessary to be performed either by the grantee or by the grantor and further that without its performance the property either of the grantor or of the grantee becomes incapable of enjoyment, a presumption arises that the right to perform such an act, and to utilize all those lawful means by which the desired enjoyment is to be attained, was granted, or reserved (as the case might be) for the beneficial enjoyment of the granted or reserved tenement by the very same instrument or deed which operated to cause the severance." As an easement of necessity cannot arise in any other way than on severance of tenements no claim to it (Easement of Necessity) can be advanced unless unity in ownership of the dominant and servient tenement at some period is established.

The right of easement of necessity does not arise in a case in which the property becomes useless without an easement being raised in favour of the party claiming it. The right is implied only in cases of severance of tenments and unity of ownership of the dominant and servient tenement at sometime or other is essential.[4]

1. *Varrakkaru Muslim Thaikkarupally* v. *Narayana Purshan*, 1991 (2) KLT 477 : 1991(2) KLJ 526 : ILR 1992(1) Ker 221.
2. *Hari Singh* v. *Jaswant Singh*, 2011 AIR CC 2717 (P & H).
3. AIR 2022 Chhat. 73.
4. *Santosh Kumar Banerjee* v. *Krishna Kant Gupta and another*, AIR 1985 Patna 12.

Easement of necessity according to Section 13 arises only where by a transfer, bequest or partition, a single tenement is divided into distinct and separate tenements and any of the separate tenements is so situated that it cannot be used at all without enjoying an easement over the other such tenement or tenements.

It is an established proposition of law that the mere fact that the servient and dominant tenements belong to a common owner does not give rise to an easement of necessity. It must be established that both the tenements had constituted a single unit and after the severance, the situation of a dominant tenement became such that it cannot be used at all without the easement claimed in the suit over the servient tenement.

In order to find an easement of necessity, the necessity must be absolute necessity and not merely a convenient mode of enjoyment of the property. In other words, an easement of necessity is an easement without which the property cannot be used at all and not merely for reasonable and convenient enjoyment of the property.[1]

In *Smt. Narayani Devi* v. *Phool Chand and another*,[2] it has been laid down that this is not the requirement of law that before being entitled to claim an easement by way of necessity it must be established by the plaintiff that the claim is one of absolute necessity in the sense that there should be no other manner of such enjoyment available in any circumstances whatsoever. Section 13 contemplates that the easement, which is claimed as an easement of necessity, can be claimed as the only possible mode of enjoyment of the right claimed having regard to the normal way of life of the person belonging to his category.

Under Section 13, where a person transfers or bequeaths, immovable property to another and an easement in other immovable property of the transferor is necessary for enjoying the subject of the transfer, the transferee shall be entitled to such easement and where an easement in the subject of the transfer is necessary for enjoying other immovable property of the transferor, the transferor, shall be entitled to such easement.

Where before the transfer of a house, the service latrine in the house used to be cleaned by the sweeper by approaching it through an adjacent open strip of land owned by the

1. *Smt. Usarani Das* v. *Bhaktahari Mohanty and others*, AIR 1984 Orissa 97.
2. AIR 1981 Allahabad 99.

transferor and the strip was thus open to enjoyment to the transferor as an easement of necessity, the transferee, a Hindu lady, also would be deemed to have established easement of necessity in respect of the strip notwithstanding the fact that the sweeper could clean the latrine by approaching it from within the house. The reason is that the transferee being a Hindu lady, it is well known that Hindus are generally averse to permitting entry to sweepers inside the house for the purpose of cleaning a service latrine.

Easement of necessity arises as the severance of tenements. The rationale or the legal basis of this kind of easement can be traced to the creation of an implied grant. Really, easement of necessity is an easement, which under particular circumstances the law creates by virtue of the doctrine of implied grant to meet the necessity of a particular case. As far as the Indian law is concerned, the contour of this doctrine of implied grant to create an easement of necessity are well delineated in the section itself. It has to be remembered that it is an easement which is not merely necessary for the reasonable enjoyment of the dominant tenement, but one without which that tenement cannot be used at all.[1] It has to be remembered that an easement of necessity arises where normally both the dominant and servient tenements have been in common ownership so that the creation of an easement by implication of law may be said to be the outcome of the former jointness of the two tenements. The disposition which causes a cessation of the common ownership that gives rise to the creation of an easement may be of either tenement, or a simultaneous disposition of both tenements.[2]

Easement of necessity must be an absolute necessity and not a merely convenient mode of enjoyment of property. Existence of alternative pathway, however inconvenient, is sufficient to reject a claim of easement of necessity.[3]

Quasi-Easement.—The term quasi-easement has been applied to those easements which are not easements of absolute necessity but which come into existence for the first time by presumed grant on severance of two or more

1. *Aldridge* v. *Wright* (1929) 2 KB 117 CA and *Union Lighterage Co.* v. *London Graving Dock Co.* (1902) 2 Ch 557.
2. *Maniyan Krishnan and another* v. *Maniyan Nanukuttan*, AIR 1986 Kerala 75.
3. *Mathu Injodikkaran Anthony* v. *Varied*, AIR 1989 NOC 53 (Ker); *Zachariah* v. *Kaliyani Amma*, (1961) Ker LT 829 relied on; *Kali Pada Bose* v. *Fani Bhusan Roy*, AIR 1924 Cal 363 Disting.

tenements formerly united in the sole ownership of one person.[1] Easements of necessity are absolutely essential and without them severed tenements to the extent to which they were enjoyed before the unity of the tenements under single ownership broke up. Quasi-easements must be : (1) apparent, (2) continuous, and (3) necessary for enjoying the dominant heritage as it was enjoyed before severance. Therefore, non-apparent or discontinuous easements cannot be claimed as quasi-easements. A right of way is a discontinuous easement, because it needs the act of man for its enjoyment. Therefore, a right of way cannot be claimed as quasi-easement even though an apparent track proves its former user and existence. Clauses (b), (d) and (f) of Section 13 deal with quasi-easements. Quasi-easements can come into existence where they are found to have been expressly or by implication excluded from the terms of the grants which caused the severance of the tenements. The quasi-easements claimed must be in existence at the time when the severance takes place, so that there may be possibility of an implied grant, or an implied reservation. If they were not present at the time of severance but came into existence afterwards, such rights cannot be claimed as quasi-easements under Section 13.

Example.—A sells B a house with windows overlooking A's land which A retains for himself. The light which passes over A's land to the windows is necessary for enjoying the house as it was enjoyed when the sale took effect. B is entitled to the right, and A cannot afterwards obstruct it by building on his land. A quasi-easement exists in favour of B.

Easements of necessity and quasi-easement—How arise.—On severance of common ownership there are two ways in which quasi-easement pass to the grantee. One such is where accommodation is required to be continued even after severance, provided its continuance is found essential for the beneficial and reasonable enjoyment of the severed tenement, to the extent to which accommodation was enjoyed before the unity of the tenements under single ownership broke up. In such a case the continuance or reservation may be inferred or implied. Another case is where such accommodation is expressly reserved by the owner. The quasi-easement of way, as of necessity, may be inferred to have been reserved by the

1. *Bhola Nath*, 51 Cal 789.

owner.[1] It is not necessary to mention creation or transfer of easement with dominant heritage in the sale deed executed in favour of purchaser.[2]

The quasi-easements claimed must be in existence at the time of the severance of the tenements.—The quasi-easements claimed must be in existence at the time when the severance takes place, so that there may be a possibility of an implied grant, or an implied reservation. If they were not in existence at the time when the severence took place but came into existence afterwards, such rights cannot be claimed as quasi-easements under this section.[3] So, where an artificial channel was cut after the severance of the tenement by the sale thereof by the owner to two different persons it was held that the right to flow water through such channel could not be claimed as quasi-easement under this section, though it was an apparent and continuous easement.[4]

Quasi-easement under the Indian law and the English law distinguished.—Under the Indian Easements Act quasi-easement can be acquired both by a transferee as well as a transferor. But under the English law only a transferee can acquire a quasi-easement by express words in the instrument of transfer. Therefore, if in England a person owns a house and land and transfers the land keeping the house himself, the transferee would be free to build on the land so as to block the windows of the house of the transferor unless the transferor expressly lays down that the transferee would not be allowed to build on the land so as to block the windows. There is no distinction between the English law and the Indian Easements Act so far as easements of necessity are concerned.

Way of necessity.—A plaintiff who claims a right of passage through the field of another under Section 13(a) of the Act has to prove that he has no alternative means of access, however inconvenient, to his field. He cannot be said to have

1. *Harilal Bandopadhya* v. *Gora Chand Malik*, AIR 1960 C 592 at 596 : (1879) 12 Ch D 31; *Chidambara Rao* v. *Secretary of State*, (1934) 1 KB 435, relied on.
2. *Gundali Basavanyappa* v. *G.S. Basavaraja*, (1996) 1 Civil Court Cases 303 at 306 (Karn).
3. *Kuttah Krishan* v. *Chathu Menon*, 5 IC 740 : 33 M 207 : 1910 MWN 319 : 7 MLT 72; *Sultani* v. *Ram Saran*, 49 PR 1900 (Cr); *Faiz Mohd.* v. *Latif*, AIR 1924 Lah. 724 (2); *see* also *Chidambra Rao* v. *Secretary of State*, 26 M 66; *Leela* v. *Ambujakshy*, 1989 (2) KLT 142.
4. *Kuttath Krishnan* v. *Chathu Menon*, 5 IC 740 : 33 M 207 : 1910 MWN 319.

an alternative way unless he had lawful right to use that way. The grant which arises by implication of law in the case of such easement is a grant of a right of way until such time as the grantee may acquire the power from some other source of reaching his tenement without using the tenement of the grantor.[1]

The claimant for an easement of necessity has to prove that though in order to enjoy the tenement granted or reserved by him he did actually employ all those means which people situated as he was, were generally in the habit of employing in the circumstances, yet he found himself incapable enjoying his share without the claimed additional aid of right. Unless such proof is forthcoming, no court can be justified in compelling an adjacent proprietor to submit against his will to such a detrimental right as an easement of necessity over his land. A court may with perfect justice ask a claimant whether all usual means were employed by him before he pressed his claim and in cases of doubt may refuse to grant him any relief.[2]

Under Section 13(b) read with Section 5 of the Easements Act, a right of way, though apparent, if it is a formal way, is a discontinuous easement, as it requires an act of man to enjoy it, and, therefore, it does not fall under Section 13(b) and hence cannot be regarded as quasi-easement, it can only be claimed as an easement of necessity.[3]

"Transferror" and Transferee.—A plain reading of the provisions of Section 13 shows that where immovable property passes by operation of law, the persons from and to whom it so passes are, for the purposes of this Section, to be deemed respectively, the transferor and transferee.[4]

Joint Property—Right of way

So long as partition does not take place, even co-owner of a joint property is entitled to use any and every part thereof consistently with the right of user of the other co-owners and such user by a co-owner should be reasonable in the sense that it should not amount to ouster of the other co-owners. Subject to that limitation the reasonable user by a co-owner of co-ownership property consistent with the right of other

1. 1942 NLJ 451.
2. *Zakariah* v. *Kaliyat Amma*, 1961 Ker LJ 67.
3. AIR 1942 Bom 305.
4. *Hari Singh* v. *Jaswant Singh*, 2012 (116) AIC 642 (P & H).

co-owners is perfectly justified. In fact, such user would be a necessary concomitant of the co-ownership right.[1]

Where the two termini are known, the right to the way does not fall merely for want of a defined track between them, and if the owner of the servient tenement does not point out the line of such way, the dominant owner must take the nearest way he can. If the owner of the servient tenement wishes to confine him to a particular track, he must set out a reasonable way, and then the person is not entitled to go out of the way merely because the way is rough, and there are ruts in it and so forth."[2]

If the plaintiff in a suit for a declaration of a right of way establishes the terminal from which and to which the way runs, he is entitled to have his right of way declared and right would be enjoyed in the way that the owners of the servient tenement point out as being the track over which the way should be enjoyed and if no track is pointed out, the plaintiff would be entitled to enjoy the right by nearest route.[3]

Drain.—A drain is an apparent and continuous easement and Section 13(f) of Easements Act applies to the same. If the easement is necessary, not in the sense of absolute necessity, but necessary for enjoying the share of the dominant tenement as it was enjoyed when the partition of joint property took effect, it would pass to the owner of the dominant tenement.[4]

Easementary right of way.—In the present matter the plaintiff had purchased part of property. Right to approach that property was through portion of land occupied by tenant of defendant. Defendant *in lieu* of that land had gifted big piece of land to tenant. Held, that the denial of right to plaintiff and mandatory injunction on ground that there was no privity of contract between him and tenant was improper.[5]

Division of tenement.—When by a transfer, bequeath or partition a single tenement is divided into two or more separate and distinct tenements, and any of these tenements (whether transferred or reserved) is so situated that it cannot be used at all without the enjoyment of a certain privilege on any other of such tenements, the law presumes the implication

1. *Girdharbhai Becharbhai Patel* v. *Gordhanbhai Parshottamdass*, AIR 1981 Guj 93.
2. *Ramhary Pal* v. *Nidhi Mohanty*, AIR 1934 Pat 420.
3. *Lakhi Kanta Roy* v. *Raj Chandra Saha*, AIR 1919 Cal 476; *See* also *Achhelal Mahto* v. *Harichand Mahto*, AIR 1976 Pat 5.
4. AIR 1944 Mad 441.
5. *Prithvi Singh* v. *Banshi Lal*, AIR 2004 Raj 100.

of a grant or reservation of such privilege in favour of the person holding such tenements. The right thus implied is known as easement of necessity.[1]

Using pathway through another's land as easement of necessity.—When a person wants to use a pathway through another's land as an easement of necessity then he should restrict his right only to the shortest possible area. It appears from the judgment of Courts below that the pathway of 43 feet in length and 4 feet in width running straight from defendant No. 1/appellant's house to the public pathway lying to the south of the suit property of plaintiff/respondent No. 1 and adjacent east to the land of proforma respondent No. 2 was declared to be defendant No. 1/appellant's pathway. Defendant No. 1/appellant was granted the use of said pathway through the suit property of plaintiff- respondent No. 1 as an easement of necessity. As per plaint the plaintiff/respondent No. 1 was in possession of 2 decimals of land though as per his purchase deeds he purchased 2-1/4 decimals of land. If that be the factual position then the plaintiff/respondent No. 1 was not entitled to a decree of declaring his right over 2-1/4 decimals of land. His right, title and possession can only be restricted to the suit property measuring 2 decimals of land with a rider that the defendant No. 1/appellant was entitled to use the pathway measuring 43 feet in length and 4 feet in breadth running through the western border of the suit property as an easement of necessity.[2]

Common passage included in purchased property—Easement of necessity may still prevail.—Even if the common passage was found to be included in the purchased property of the plaintiffs still the plaintiff was not entitled to get a decree as prayed for. It came out from the report of the Advocate Commissioner as well as from the other evidence on record that the suit passage was the only pathway through which one can come out from the property of the defendants to the main public road. It also came out that the suit passage was used even after sale of the property to the plaintiff by plaintiff's vendor and thereafter defendant No. 1 and lastly the present defendants as purchasers of the property lying to the adjacent south of plaintiff's property. The Indian Easements Act, 1882 has no application in the State of West Bengal, but the principles of said Act are squarely applicable.

---

1. *Smt. Bina Ghorai* v. *Hatton Show*, (2013) 129 AIC 604 (Cal).
2. *Sakina Bewah* v. *Akkal Ali*, 2013 (127) AIC 482 (Cal).

In view of the above, the High Court held that the lower Appellate Court did not commit any wrong by declaring that the suit passage was a common passage and that it was not included in the purchase deed of the plaintiff appellant.[1]

Suit for declaration of right of way.—This suit was filed for a decree of declaration of plaintiff's right of easement over a certain plot. The trial court decreed the suit in favour of the plaintiff. The defendant appellant had challenged the said decree. Appeal was dismissed by the ADJ Midnapur. The defendant again challenged the decree.

The High Court held that the material issues have not been considered by the courts below and as such remanded the case back for fresh enquiry.[2]

In the case of *Sakina Bewah* v. *Akkil Ali*,[3] the right of pathway was involved.

At the appellate stage defendant appellant submitted that the courts below admitted that defendant No. 1 had no way other than the pathway running through the suit property. The plaintiff submitted that the courts below allowed said land of 43 feet in length and 4 feet in width.

After going through the submissions of both the parties the High Court held that the appellant was entitled to use the pathway running 43 feet in length and 4 feet in width.[4]

Easement of necessity.—The plaintiff had claimed right of prior purchase of adjoining property on ground of easement of necessity of light and air. There was no specific pleading that said necessity was absolute necessity. As no evidence could be produced in support of the said plea, hence, plaintiff was not entitled for relief sought for.[5]

Where alternative remedy pathway is admittedly available to the plaintiffs, the claim for easement may not be made on the grounds that alternative pathway is inconvenient.[6]

Effect of availability of alternative passage in claim of easement of necessity.—Easementary right of necessity could not be claimed even if alternative passage was inconvenient or bit longer. As there was nothing on record to clarify the factual position whether alternative passage was

1. *Smt. Bina Ghorai* v. *Hattan Show*, (2013) 129 AIC 604 (Cal).
2. *Bhutnath Bhuria* v. *Sri Manta Kumar Maity*, 2012 (117) AIC 443 (Cal).
3. *Sakina Bewah* v. *Akkil Ali*, 2013 (127) AIC 482 (Cal).
4. *Sakina Bewah* v. *Akkil Ali*, 2013 (127) AIC 482 (Cal).
5. *Avinash Chandra* v. *Satya Devi*, AIR 2003 NOC 487 (J & K).
6. *Ponnaiyan* v. *Karuppakkal*, AIR 2002 Mad 443.

usable and remained so throughout the year. Hence, matter was remanded for reconsideration afresh.[1]

Necessity of easement.—In the case of *Alo Rami Banerjee* v. *Smt. Malati Roy*,[2] it was argued that the grant implicit in the representation came into existence when the purchasers of the plots acted on the representation by purchasing such land and as such the defendant is estopped from challenging the plaintiff's claim. In support of his contention he has relied on a single bench decision of this Court in *Nirmal Kumar Moulik* v. *Smt. Champabala Roy*.[3] In that case the plaintiff was the owner of land of the colony. The plaintiff by showing the suit land as a park in the plan at the time of sale or settlement of the plots of the colony induced her prospective purchasers or lessees that the suit land would remain as such park and there would be grant of user of the land as such park. This is a representation made by the plaintiff to the defendant to purchase or to take a lease of the plot. It has been held that it is necessary that there must be recital about user of the park in the *kobalas* or in the various settlement-deeds of the defendants. Mere absence of recitals in the *kobalas* about user of the park does not indicate that it was never meant to be a part though it was shown as such by the plaintiff in the plan. Estoppel is a rule of evidence which prevents one party from denying the existence of a fact which he represented as existing and upon which representation another person has been induced to act to his detriment. It has been held that the plaintiff is barred by estoppel from having a declaration from the Court that the instant land was her private land and she could do whatever she likes in respect of the suit land and prevent other people from entering into the said land. It has further been held that no document in writing is required for grant of user of any land. The plan was the basis of representation and in that plan, the suit land was shown as park. There were also roads which are also shown in the said plan. It would be obvious to represent the grant of user of roads as also user of suit land as a park. Even though there was no express grant or dedication, as soon as the defendant acted on the said representation by purchasing or taking lease of the plots for consideration the grant implicit in the representation came in existence. In the instant case, Court have already seen that

1. *Rama* v. *Megha*, AIR 2002 Raj 309.
2. AIR 1992 Cal 302.
3. 76 CWN 556.

the disputed strip of land has been described as a new road in the document and the evidence shows that there was specific representation by the vendor that the said strip of land was set apart as the common passage of the prospective buyers including the plaintiff and as matters of fact the said passage was shown in a sketch map which the defendant is withholding. It must, therefore, be held that there was representation of grant on use of the disputed road even though there was no express grant of dedication. As soon as the plaintiffs acted on the said representation by purchasing the suit plots for consideration the grant implicit in the representation came into existence and the defendant claiming through the original vendor is, therefore, estopped from challenging the implied grant of user of the disputed strip of land. It is quite obvious that had not the plaintiffs been induced to believe that they would have right of use of the disputed strip of land, they would not have purchased portions of the plot as in that case they would have no means of access to or exit from their plots of land where they would construct residential buildings.

In *Achutan Nair* v. *Vasudevan*,[1] it was held that—whether a claim of easement of necessity is mutually incongruous or destructive with that of a claim of prescriptive right of mutually destructive and hence a claim based on easement of necessity and prescriptive rights of easement can not be maintained in a suit.

Acquisition of land due to easement of necessity.—There was acquisition of land due to easement of necessity, possession of acquired land was taken. Held, that right of passage by way of necessity enjoyed by respondents over acquired land, would not be extinguished by reason of acquisition.[2]

Claim for easement of necessity not allowed as necessity must be absolute and not convenient mode of enjoyment.—Easement of necessity arises on severance of tenements. Plaintiff had no case that both servient and dominant tenements were in common ownership. Alternative inconvenient pathway was no ground to claim easement of necessity as necessity must be absolute and not convenient mode of enjoyment. There was no allegation of prior joint ownership and it was shown by evidence that two tenements

1. 2021 (1) Civil Court cases Ker 296.
2. *H.P. State Electricity Board* v. *Shiv K. Sharma*, AIR 2005 SC 954.

had been owned by different persons. As such, there could not be any question of easement of necessity.[1]

Easement of necessity must be absolutely necessary.—The plaintiff was claiming right of passage to reach her house as an easement of necessity. But it was proved that plaintiff was using alternative passage since past 20-22 years which was more accessible and shorter passage. It could not be said that suit passage was matter of necessity. Suit passage could not be claimed as matter of right. Moreover, after a lapse of ten years from the date of alleged obstruction, plaintiff had also failed to establish right over suit passage by way of prescription. Relief by way of mandatory injunction to leave the suit passage to plaintiff was illegal.[2]

Easement right by prescription, who can claim.—An easement of necessity is one which the law creates according to doctrine of implied grant in a particular case and is one without which the dominant tenement cannot be used at all. Where the right of access is claimed not as owner of property but as an easement of necessity and was proved that it was being used since over last 58 years, the contention that plaintiff's right to use was only permissive and not perspective right would not stand.[3]

Right to use hall and stairways.—The plaintiffs cannot be denied their right of passage from residential premises to the PWD road, where evidences do not disclose existence of any alternate path.[4]

Easements of necessity and quasi-easement—How arise.—On severance of common ownership there are two ways in which quasi-easement pass to the grantee. One such is where accommodation is required to be continued even after severance provided its continuance is found essential for the beneficial and reasonable enjoyment of the severed tenement, to the extent to which accommodation was enjoyed before the unity of the tenements under single ownership broke up. In such a case, the continuance or reservation may be inferred or implied. Another case is where such accommodation is expressly reserved by the owner. The quasi-easement of way, as of necessity, may be inferred to have been reserved by the

1. *Gouri Amma Krishnamma* v. *Seethalakshmi Amma*, AIR 2004 Ker 75.
2. *R. Paramasivan* v. *T. Anasuya*, AIR 2005 Kant 240.
3. *Babli Krishna Vaigankar* v. *Laxman S. Vaigankar*, 2006 (5) Bom CR 277.
4. *Monwar Ali* v. *Rayachan Bewa*, AIR 2006 Gau. 146 (148).

owner.[1]

It cannot be denied that access to any property which is severed from the road, on account of partition, is an acute necessity for the use of it. If the respondents were able to prove that there existed an alternative and convenient road or path, the necessity for recognition of the easement can certainly be doubted.[2]

If the right of way is given for passing of men and cattle, the same can be used for taking tractors provided there is sufficient width.[3]

In *Manisha Mahendra Gala & Ors.* v. *Shalini Bhagwan Avatramani & Ors.*,[4] Supreme Court held that an easement of necessity cannot be claimed if there is any alternative way to access the property, even if that alternative is longer or inconvenient. The Court emphasized that necessity ends the moment an alternative route becomes available. This effectively raises the bar for claimants to prove they are completely landlocked with absolutely no other option.

In *Baby* v. *Lakshmi*,[5] Kerala High Court upheld a claim for easement by necessity following a partition. The deciding factor was the concurrent finding of fact by lower courts that no other viable route existed for the dominant heritage (the beneficiary land) other than the path through the northern portion of the partitioned land.

In *Jayrambhai Jasrajbhai Patel* v. *Ranchhodbhai Shivabhai Patel*,[6] Gujarat High Court reaffirmed that one cannot claim an easement of necessity through the middle of another's property to "destroy or divide it" if an alternative route (even if less convenient) is available.

Easement, extinguishment of.—An easement by grant does not get extinguished under Section 41 of the Act which relates to easement of necessity. The right of way provided under partition deed to particular sharer would not extinguish only because such sharer has an alternative way.[7]

1. *Harilal Bandopadhya* v. *Gora Chand Malik*, AIR 1960 C 592 at 596 : (1879) 12 Ch D 31; *Chidambara Rao* v. *Secretary of State*, (1934) 1 KB 435, relied on. See also *Monwar Ali* v. *Mustt. Rayachan Bewa*, AIR 2006 Gau. 146.
2. *Pakeer Pitchi Reddy* v. *Pakeer Papi Reddy*, 2006 (1) ALT 626.
3. *Undavilli Mangayamma (Died) by L.R.* v. *Undavilli Veerayamma*, 2007 (1) ALT 671.
4. 2024 INSC 293.
5. 2025 Supreme(Online)(Ker) 58333.
6. 2025 Supreme(Online)(Guj) 12487.
7. *Hero Vinoth* v. *Seshammal*, AIR 2006 SC 2234 (241).

The right of passage by way of necessity which was enjoyed by respondents over the land would not be extinguished if that land is acquired and possession thereof is taken.[1]

14. Direction of way of necessity.—When a right to a way of necessity is created under Section 13, the transferor, the legal representative of the testator, or the owner of the share over which the right is exercised, as the case may be, is entitled to set out the way, but it must be reasonably convenient for the dominant owner.

When the person so entitled to set out the way refuses or neglects to do so, the dominant owner may set it out.

NOTES

The right to set out the direction of a way of necessity is vested in the transferor, the legal representative of the testator or the owner of the tenement over which the right is exercised. These persons while setting out the directions of a way of necessity must keep in mind the reasonable convenience of the dominant owner. When once a way has been set out, it cannot be changed without the concurrence of both the parties. When the servient owner refuses or neglects to set out of right of way, the dominant owner can do so himself, but while doing so the dominant owner should be careful to see that no injury is inflicted on the servient owner which can be avoided. The dominant owner cannot be said to have acted in a *bona fide* manner in cutting out a new track through the servient tenement if a well-formed road suitable for this purposes is available to him thereon. A defence in such circumstances, that the available road was not the shortest route to his premises cannot prevail.

Non-availability of easementary right

It is only in the absence of effective opposition on the part of the servient tenant that the right of an easement matures. Unless the servient owner has got a right to obstruct the passage of air and light there is no question of acquiring easement right. When the lane in between the tenements is 6 feet wide, there is no question of servient tenement raising any objection and there is no question of acquiring any

1. *H.P. State Electricity Board* v. *Shiv K. Sharma*, AIR 2005 SC 954.

easement.[1]

Landlord can change the passage.—In *Balbir Singh* v. *Sawan Singh*,[2] it was held by the court that in terms of Section 14 of the Basement Act, the tenant is given an option to set out a reasonably convenient passage for the landlord through site on rent with him to the vacant plot of the landlord. It he fails to do so, it shall be open to the landlord to set out such passage for himself.

Doctrine of lost grant

A right of easement is also created by grant and a grant of such right is presumed from long use or possession although the actual transaction of making such a grant cannot be discovered. If a party has been using a particular land for a particular purpose from time immemorial, it can be said that he has earned that right on the basis of doctrine of lost grant. There is no period fixed for the time immemorial. It depends on facts of each case.[3]

15. Acquisition by prescription.—Where the access and use of light or air to and for any building have been peaceably enjoyed therewith, as an easement, without interruption and for twenty years,

and where support from one person's land or things affixed thereto, has been peaceably received by another person's land subjected to artificial pressure or by things affixed thereto, as an easement, without interruption and for twenty years,

and where a right of way or any other easement has been peaceably and openly enjoyed by any person claiming title thereto, as an easement, and as of right, without interruption, and for twenty years,

the right to such access and use of light or air, support or other easement shall be absolute.

Each of the said periods of twenty years shall be taken to be period ending within two years next before the institution of the suit where the claim to such period relates is contested.

1. *Misrilal* v. *Mohanlal*, AIR 1954 Ajmer 73.
2. AIR 1987 P & H 174.
3. *Nathu Lal* v. *Ram Swaroop*, AIR 1987 Raj 169 at 173, 174 : 1986 Raj LR 812 : 1987 Raj LW 98.

Explanation I.—Nothing is an enjoyment within the meaning of this section when it has been had in pursuance of an agreement with the owner or occupier of the property over which the right is claimed, and it is apparent from the agreement that such right has not been granted as an easement, or if granted as an easement that it has been granted for a limited period, or subject to a condition on the fulfillment of which it is to cease.

Explanation II.—Nothing is an interruption within the meaning of this section, unless there is an actual cessation of the enjoyment by reason of an obstruction by the act of some person other than the claimant, and unless such obstruction is submitted to or acquiesced in for one year after the claimant has notice thereof and of the person making or authorising the same to be made.

Explanation III.—Suspension of enjoyment in pursuance of a contract between the dominant and servient owners is not an interruption within the meaning of this section.

Explanation IV.—In the case of an easement to pollute water the said period of twenty years begins when the pollution first prejudices perceptibly the servient heritage.

When the property over which a right is claimed under this section belongs to Government, this Section shall be read as if for the words "twenty years" the words "thirty years" were substituted.

Illustrations

(a) A suit is brought in 1883 for obstructing a right of way. The defendant admits the obstruction, but denies the right of way. The plantiff proves that the right was peaceably and openly enjoyed by him claiming title thereto as an easement and as of right, without interruption, from 1st January, 1862 to 1st January, 1882. The plaintiff is entitled to easement.

(b) In a like suit the plaintiff shows that the right was peaceably and openly enjoyed by him for twenty years. The defendant proves that for a year of that time, the plaintiff was entitled to possession of the servient heritage as lessee thereof and enjoyed the right as such lessee. The suit shall be dismissed, for the right of way has not been enjoyed "as an easement" for twenty years.

(c) In a like suit the plaintiff shows that the right was peaceably and openly enjoyed by him for twenty years. The defendant proves that the plaintiff on one occasion during the twenty years had admitted that the user was not of right and asked his leave to enjoy the right. The suit shall be dismissed, for the right of way has not been enjoyed "as of right" for twenty years.

NOTES

Application.—Section 15 has no application where the right claimed does not rest on a prescriptive easement.

Prescription.—Prescription means acquisition of a right or title the user of possession had during the period and in the manner prescribed by law. A man who cannot show any other title may acquire property or certain rights by showing that he has been in possession of the property or enjoying rights for a very long time.

The reason, why the law encouraged this mode of acquiring rights is that if a man after long, continued and uninterrupted use, was required in every case to prove the origin of his title, especially in the olden times when writing was not in vogue, it would result in great hardship and injustice to him. So the law, in order to safeguard the interests of persons claiming title by long and immemorial user, invested them with a title on the natural presumption that such user had a legal origin, which the person questioning could not legally dispute at an earlier date when the evidence of such right might be forthcoming for no man could be presumed to allow his own property to be used by any other man for such a long time without title.

Fiction of lost grant.—The doctrine of prescription is based on the fiction of a lost grant, for law in such cases of long uninterrupted enjoyment presupposes that there was once a grant validly made and simply due to the efflux of time has been lost or destroyed (English notion). In India, however, the right depends upon positive enactments and it is not necessary that any presumption of supposed grant and its subsequent loss need be made.[1]

Conditions for acquisition of easement rights by prescription

1. Easement rights of way and other varieties of easement rights can be acquired if—(1) they have been enjoyed, (2) as an easement, (3) for twenty years, (4) without interruption by a person claiming title to them, (5) openly, (6) peaceably, and (7) as of right.

2. Easement rights of light, air and support can be acquired if they have been peaceably enjoyed, without interruption, as an easement, for twenty years. The rights of light, air and support need not be enjoyed either 'openly', or 'as of right' or 'by a person claiming title thereto'. Such easements can be acquired by peaceable enjoyment without its enjoyment being as of right. It is only in case of other easements that it is necessary to enjoy them as of right in order to acquire an absolute right in respect of them.

All the above 7 ingredients of an easement right must be proved to have been present during the whole of the prescriptive period of 20 years. The statutory period of 20 years must be proved to have been completed within two years next before the institution of the suit wherein the claim to such easement right is contested.

A scrutiny of Section 15 reveals that the following conditions should exist before an easement can become absolute by prescription : (1) There must be a pre-existing easement which must have been enjoyed by the dominant owner, (2) the enjoyment must have been peaceable, (3) the enjoyment must have been as an easement, (4) the enjoyment must have been as of right, (5) the right must have been enjoyed openly, (6) the enjoyment must have been for a period of 20 years, and (7) the enjoyment for 20 years must have been without interruption.

This section is the statutory recognition of the principle of English Common Law relating to acquisition of easement by prescription with some modifications. Prescription as a source of right in English law is generally described as being applicable only in situations where the servient owner could be regarded as having acquiesced in the user. The authoritative statement on this matter is made by Fry, J. in his advice to

1. AIR 1931 Lah 395.

House of Lords in *Dalton* v. *Angus*.[1] The learned Judge observed :—

> In many cases—first, the doing of some act by one man upon the land of another; secondly, the absence of right to do that act in the person doing it; thirdly, the knowledge of the person affected by it that the act is done; fourthly, the power of the person affected by the act to prevent such act either by act on his part or by action of the courts; and lastly, the abstinence by him from any such interference for such a length of time as renders it reasonable for the courts to say that he shall not afterwards interfere to stop the act being done.

In *Krishna Narain Agarwal* v. *Carlton Hotel (P) Ltd.*,[2] the Supreme Court has laid down that to establish the clause under Section 15, continuous user of 20 years as of right to do the act complained of in assertion of a title, peaceably and openly must be made out. The enjoyment must not he permissive. What is permissive is that which depends not on right, but on the will of another person. The Indian condition in regard to user of other's land for convenient access to main roads is a common and prevalent practice and that such user is not a user as of right. Such use of neighbour's land never depends on right but on the consent and the good sense of the neigbour. The meaning of the word 'user' as of right can be understood clearly from Halsbury's Laws of England. The user as of right having been enjoyed *nee vi, nec clom, nec precario* (neither as the result of force, secrecy or evasion) nor as dependent upon the consent of the owner of the servient tenements. Consent or acquiescence on the part of the servient owner lies at the root of prescription, and a grant cannot be presumed from long use without his having had knowledge or at least the means of knowledge. He cannot be said to acquiesce in an act enforced by mere violence, or in an act which fear on his part hinders him from preventing, or in an act which he has no knowledge actual or constructive, or which he contests and endeavors to interrupt, or which he sanctions only for temporary purposes, or in return for recurrent consideration. In substance it means that the enjoyment should be without violence, without stealth and without permission. The importance is that the user must be peaceable, open and non-permissive.

1. (1881) 6 AC 740.
2. 1969 SCD 1105.

The Courts are bound to take note of the habits of the people in considering whether a portion of land was used by the neighbour for an easy cross-cut to the main road. The Calcutta High Court in *Khoda Buksh* v. *Shaik Tajuddin*,[1] said, "Having regard to the habits of the people in India, it would not be right to draw the same inference from mere user that would be proper and legitimate in a case arising in England. The question is a question of fact, and the propriety of the rule that the presumption from user should be that it is as of right must depend upon the circumstances not only of each particular case but also of such particular country, regard being had to the habits of the people of that country."

In England, the presumption of long user being as of right is readily drawn because the social conditions and the nature of the landed property there are such that landowners are particularly jealous of their exclusive right over the land. In India, such rigid and jealous views of the exclusives of the landed property do not prevail and very often an owner of a piece of waste land never raises any objection to the passage of strangers over such land.

Where there has been a long enjoyment of property in a particular manner it is the habit, and the duty of the Court, so far as it lawfully can, to clothe the fact with right.

Where a claim to a right of way is supported by evidence of user only, the Court must satisfy itself whether or not the user was founded on actual right, the guiding principle being that open user of another's land for the purposes of a road or pathway, if continued without interruption for a long time and not attributable to permission or sufferance, induces the presumption that the user was as of right.

A user which is long, open and peaceable would be presumed to be as of right. But it is open to the servient owner to rebut this presumption by alleging and proving circumstances that point to permission or by alleging some other facts.[2]

Using a land as *rasta* land openly, peacefully and without interruption as of right for 20 years can be acquired by way of prescription but under the garb of such pleadings laying sewer line in the land of another cannot be allowed. No easementary right accrues to the plaintiff to lay sewer line on the land of another person and discharge sewer water through

1. (1903-04) 8 Cal WN 359.
2. *Maniyan Krishnan* v. *Maniyan Nanukuttan*, AIR 1986 Kerala 75.

it.[1]

The provision under Section 15 of the Act, so far as right of way is concerned, lays down that right of way can be acquired by prescription, if such right of way has been peaceably and openly enjoyed by any person claiming title thereto, as an easement and as of right, without interruption and for 20 years. The plaintiff shall not be entitled to right of easement by prescription where he had occupied some property as tenant of municipality for some years and claimed right of way thereon.[2]

Where plea of plaintiffs that they have no other passage for their land was not substantial in the absence of any '*Akshajra*' depicting that there was no other passage for the land of plaintiffs. On the contrary, defendants had produced copy of '*Akshajra*' which clearly demonstrated that there was no passage through the land of defendant. The rejection of plaintiff's claim was held to be proper.[3]

To prescribe a right under Section 15 of the Act, the user must be 'open'. If the user is secret or surreptitious, the fiction of supposed grant or acquiescence is untenable. Actual knowledge on the part of servient owner is not necessary for an enjoyment to be open under Section 15 of the Act. It is sufficient that the user is open, not intentionally secret or surreptitious.[4]

Acquisition of easement by prescription.—In *Dhaniya Bai* v. *Jiwan*,[5] it was held that since appellant constructed house adjacent to that of respondent and respondent being brother of appellant actively participated in construction and allowed her to take support of his wall and never objected but two years later respondent turned around and claimed either demolition or removal of construction. In such circumstances order of appellate Court for demolition by placing reliance on Section 15 of the Easement Act which provides for acquisition of easement by prescription, would not be proper because easement was never claimed by appellant.

1. *Mansha Ram Payal* v. *Ved Prakash*, AIR 2010 Uttr. 14 (16) : 2010 AIHC (NOC) 308 (Utr). See also *Bimla Devi* v. *Sohan Lal*, AIR 2009 (NOC) 1545 (HP).
2. *Alimoddin Faizuddin* v. *Siddi Mumtaz Ahmad Sakadar*, AIR 2010 Bom 59.
3. *Mangat Ram* v. *Central State Form, D.B., Hisar*, 2011 AIR CC 1273 (P & H).
4. *Pankajakshi Amma* v. *Gourikutty Amma*, AIR 2010 Ker 55.
5. AIR 2003 MP 71.

It has been held that even if the plaintiff has enjoyed easementary right for more than 20 years, he can maintain a suit by filing the same within 2 years of the challenge made by the servient owner to the right of the dominant owner.[1]

Enjoyment of right

The first condition to acquire an easement by prescription is that the claimant of the right must have *actually enjoyed* the right over the servient tenement. Actual user does not mean continuous enjoyment for the whole period of 20 years. There may be breaks in enjoyment but the break must be such as may be found consistent with a presumption of continued enjoyment of the right. For example, a person may be said to be in enjoyment of a right of way during a period of time, though he does not actually use the way every moment. Mere non-user for a time of an easement, which the owner might if he pleased to enjoy during every hour of that time, but which for some good reason he does not care to enjoy is not necessarily discontinuance of the enjoyment of the right.

Peaceably.—In order that an easement may be termed as peaceful, it is necessary that the claimant's enjoyment of his right during the prescriptive period must be free from all kinds of violence or physical force on his own part or on the part of the servient owner.

Openly.—Except in the case of easement rights of air, light or support, the enjoyment must be open and manifest and clandestine. But it is not necessary that the servient owner should have knowledge of the enjoyment of the right.

As of right.—A user 'as of right' simply means a user in the assertion of a right. The true meaning of the expression 'as of right' is that the enjoyment or the right should not be secret or by stealth or by sufferance or by leave and licence of another person. The words 'as of right' denote that it is not enough that the right is merely exercised but it should be exercised consciously in assertion of the right claimed. A mere user of the right of way by passing and repassing may not as such be conclusive evidence on the question whether the user has been as of right or not. But persons who exercise the right of way need not openly proclaim that they are doing so because they have a right to do so. Long continued user gives rise to a presumption, which, however, is rebuttable by proof to the contrary, that it must have been as of right and not with the leave or licence of another. A claimant cannot be said to have

1. *Smt. Asha Devi* v. *Govinda Singh*, 2013 (127) AIC 842 (Uttar).

enjoyed his right 'as of right' during the whole of the statutory period of 20 years if, at any time, within such period, leave or permission of the servient owner is found to have been taken or if there happens to be a unity of ownership or possession.

'As an easement'.—The claimant must have enjoyed the right as an easement. Where there is unity of possession or ownership in the same person of both the tenements, there cannot be any enjoyment as an easement during the period of unity.

Once the easement is acquired by prescription, there is no scope for issuing a mandatory injunction to put an end to the mode of enjoyment which has given rise to the easement.[1]

'Without interruption'.—Interruptions are those stops in the continuity of a claimant's user which are caused by physical obstructions placed on the servient tenement by persons acting adversely to the claimant and with a view to preventing his enjoyment of the right. Mere verbal protests, however long continued, or however vigorously expressed, if unaccompanied by any physical obstruction cannot amount to interruptions. The fact that the mode of enjoyment was changed from time to time during the period of 20 years does not cause an interruption within Section 15 where the change in the mode of enjoyment is due to an act on the part of the dominant owner himself.[2]

For twenty years.—In order to acquire an easement right by prescription, the right must have been enjoyed as an easement and as of right for twenty years. Till the period of twenty years has elapsed, the right remains an inchoate one, and no court will protect an inchoate right. The claimant of an easement right cannot succeed merely by showing that he did enjoy the right for the full period of 30 years, he must further prove that he continued to enjoy the right down to a date which was within two years before the institution of the suit wherein the claim relating to the alleged easement right was contested. In other words, no length of enjoyment by itself gives under Section 15 an absolute right. The right becomes absolute only when questioned and decreed in litigation. If somehow the enjoyment, whatever its duration, ceases and no suit is initiated within two years of the cessation thereof, the

1. *Tulasamma* v. *Nandula Buchairamiah*, AIR 1949 Mad 826 : (1949) 1 MLJ 314.
2. *Ram Sahai* v. *Man Singh*, AIR 1952 All 398.

enjoyment has lost all efficacy for the purpose of acquiring an easement.[1]

Example.—A is the owner of a house and has enjoyed a right of way over B's land from January, 1924 to January, 1946. In January, 1946 B prevents A from exercising his right. A brings a suit to establish his prescriptive right in 1949. A must fail, although his enjoyment of right has been for 22 years but as he brought the suit more than two years after the interruption by B, his enjoyment does not end within two years next before the institution of the suit.

When does the period of twenty years commence?—The period of twenty years prescribed by this section commences when the right first begins to be enjoyed in accordance with the terms of the section. It continues only so long as the right continues to be so enjoyed and ceases as soon as the enjoyment becomes otherwise than in accordance with the terms of this section.

In the case of easement to pollute water, the period of twenty years begins when the pollution begins to perceptibly prejudice the servient heritage.[2] So the period does not begin to run if the pollution is so slight that it does not injuriously affect the servient heritage. It commences when the servient owner first becomes conscious of the injury and has an opportunity of resisting the user by suit for action.[3] But the enjoyment of light and air need not be brought to the notice of the servient owner. The reason is that in case of light and air, actual enjoyment of the building by user or occupation of it is not ordinarily necessary to start the prescriptive period which begins to run as soon as the apertures capable of admitting light and air are put in the dominant house.[4]

For acquiring easement by prescription one has to plead and prove that the right claimed must have been enjoyed independently of any agreement with the owner or occupier of the land over which the right is claimed. The right must have been enjoyed peaceably, openly, as of right, as an easement, without interruption for twenty years or more. In the case of *Chapsibhai* v. *Purushottam*,[5] it was held that an easement by prescription is in fact an ascertain of a hostile claim of certain

1. *T.M. Jadavji* v. *S.S. Randidas*, 7 Saurashtra LR 183.
2. *See* Explanation IV *ante*; *see* also *Goldsmid* v. *Turnbridge Well Improvement Commissioners*, (1866) LR Ch App 394.
3. Goddard, p. 331.
4. *Gajadhar* v. *Ramavatar*, AIR 1952 N 103 : 1952 NLJ 210.
5. AIR 1971 SC 1878.

rights over another man's property and in order to acquire the easement the person who asserts the hostile claim must prove that he had the consciousness to exercise that hostile claim on a property which is not his own and where no such consciousness is proved, he cannot establish a prescriptive acquisition of the right. In the said case it was further held that if the owner of a dominant tenement has, during the period of prescription, exercised rights on the footing that he is the owner but which he later on claims as an easement over a servient tenement, then, his exercise of those rights is not exercised as an easement and he must fail in a claim for an easement. It was further held that where a person has pleaded ownership and has failed, he cannot subsequently turn around and claim that right as an easement by prescription.[1]

Statutory prescriptive title is possible only after a suit.—The fifth paragraph of Section 15, which applies to both continuous and discontinuous easements, seems to render it impossible to acquire a statutory prescriptive title to an easement unless and until the claim thereto has been contested in a suit.[2]

In *Siti Kantapal* v. *Radha Gobinda Sen*,[3] a Division Bench of the Calcutta High Court has further made the position lucid.

> It has been authoritatively held that title to easement is not complete merely upon the effluxion of the period mentioned in the Statute, *viz.*, 20 years and that however long the period of actual enjoyment may be, no absolute or indefeasible right can be acquired until the right is brought in question in some suit, and until it is so brought in question, the right is inchoate only and in order to establish it when brought in question, the enjoyment relied on, must be an enjoyment for 20 years up to within 2 years of the institution of the suit.

It is, therefore, necessary that in a suit for injunction based on a prescriptive easement right, the plaintiff should seek for a declaration from the Court that he has so acquired the prescriptive right of easement.[4]

Acquisition of prescriptive rights—Distinction between Government and other persons if violates

1. See *Santosh Kumar Banerjee* v. *Krishna Kumar Gupta and another*, AIR 1985 Patna 124.
2. *Sultan Ahmad* v. *Waliullah*, 10 ALJ 227.
3. AIR 1929 Cal 542.
4. *D. Ramanatha Gupta* v. *S. Razaack*, AIR 1982 Karnataka 314.

Article 15 of the Constitution.—The question is whether the distinction made by the Legislature in respect of prescriptive rights held by Government and other persons violates Article 15 of the Constitution. Private ownership of land is limited as compared to Government ownership. A private owner is in a better position than Government to safeguard his rights and to prevent the acquisition of prescriptive rights by others. It cannot be said that there is no reasonable nexus between the distinction made and the purpose of the legislation. Hence, the distinction does not violate Article 15 of the Constitution.[1]

Conclusion.—It follows from the above discussion that to establish a claim by prescription under this section, the claimant must establish—

(a) an enjoyment as of right; this would seem to involve some knowledge, or means of knowledge, on the part of the servient owner against whom the right is claimed, that the dominant owner is setting up a right of easement; but in India it is not necessary that the enjoyment of the easement should be known to the servient owner;

(b) the enjoyment has been open, and not by stealth, that is, of such a character that an ordinary owner of the land, diligent in the protection of his interest, will have, or must be taken to have, a reasonable opportunity of becoming aware of that enjoyment;

(c) the enjoyment has been without interruption, that is continuous;

(d) an enjoyment for the full period of twenty years ending within two years next before the institution of the suit wherein the claim to which the period relates is contested;

(e) the enjoyment has not been had in pursuance of an agreement;

(f) there had not been an actual cessation of enjoyment by reason of an obstruction by the act of some person other than the claimant; in any case the obstruction, if any, was not submitted to or acquiesced in for one year after the claimant had notice thereof and of the person making or authorising the same to be made; non-acquiescence or non-submission to obstruction may be shown also by any act other than the institution of a suit;

1. *Chandami Lal* v. *General Manager, Western Railway,* ILR 1962 All 58 : 1961 ALJ 768 : 1961 AWR (HC) 581 : AIR 1962 A 159.

thus, there is no acquiescence if there is correspondence between the attorneys of the parties; the obstruction is not effectual, unless the claimant has allowed it to continue for one year without any act on his part to show that he resists it.

It may be noted that an inchoate right of easement cannot be perfected after the commencement of the action. It is essential that the servient owner must have had knowledge, or a reasonable opportunity of knowing, that an easement was being enjoyed as an easement, and having had that knowledge and also the power to prevent its enjoyment, must have failed to prevent its use.

The subject may well be illustrated by the undermentioned cases.

The user cannot be said to be as of right, if it is not established that the servient owner was aware of the claimant's user of the land.

Extent of right of easement.—If the plaintiff has been receiving light and air through the two openings for over the statutory period and has thus acquired an easementary right to receive light and air through those two ventilators, then he can insist that he is entitled to continue to receive the same amount of light and air as before through the two ventilators though he might be getting insufficient light and air by other means.[1]

Sections 15, 28, 33 and 35 of the Easements Act should be read together in the matter of prescriptive right with regard to the flow of the light and air. Mere diminution of air and light would not give the plaintiff a cause of action to use for injunction. It should be substantial interference with the normal enjoyment of light and air so as to disturb the usual mode of life of the inhabitants of the building. In other words, it should amount to an actionable nuisance.[2]

Statutory prescriptive title is possible only after a suit.—An easement by statutory prescription cannot be acquired under Section 15, paragraph 5 of the Indian Easements Act, unless and until the claim thereto has been

---

1. *Santhannagori Ramayya* v. *N.N. Chetty*, AIR 1968 Andhra Pradesh 151.
2. *Ligory Minezes* v. *J.C. Lobo*, AIR 1970 Mysore 76. See *D. Ramanatha Gupta* v. *S. Razaack*, AIR 1982 Kanataka 314.

contested in a suit,[1] and received judicial sanction.

The suit might be filed after the expiry of prescriptive period either by the claimant himself or by the owner of the servient heritage with a view to contesting or destroying the claim.[2]

It is true that a lessee of land cannot acquire a right of way or any other easement over land owned by his lessor as having been peaceably and openly enjoyed by a person claiming a title thereto and as of right within the meaning of these words in clause 3 of Section 15, Easements Act, for in such a case the tenant's occupation is in the sight of the law that of his landlord. But where a lessee of land owns a building built upon land, leased to him, he may, so far as the use of light or air or support for his building are concerned acquire rights of easement in respect of such light, air or support under clauses 1 and 2 of Section 15, and these rights cannot be objected to as being incapable or being acquired by him on behalf of his landlord as well as against his landlord for these rights are acquired by him for himself and for none other than himself, as the owner of the building.

Right of way.—If the right of way has been acquired from one point to another in a particular direction or according to a particular route, the servient owner cannot at his choice substitute another way between the same points by a different route which might be less convenient to the dominant owner. The right of way acquired whether it is by custom or by way of a lost grant or by way of prescription should be limited to the part of the area of the servient tenement over which it has been actually exercised.[3]

India is predominantly an agrarian country where, generally speaking the relation between cultivators is cordial and rests on mutual regard for the convenience of others. It is, therefore, too common for one cultivator to pass over the

1. *Muthu* v. *Anantha*, 31 IC 528 (Mad); *see* also *Goddard*, p. 208 commenting on Section 4 of the English Prescription Act; *Sultan Ahmed* v. *Walliullah*, 10 ALJR 227, on appeal *Basdeo Singh* v. *Bhagwat Prasad*, AIR 1923 Oudh 29, *Siti Kanta Pal* v. *Radha Gobinda Sen*, AIR 1929 Cal 542 : 56 Cal 927 : 33 CWN 517; *Mahantha Saya Ram Dass* v. *Lahore Electric Supply Co.*, AIR 1942 Lah. 134; 200 IC 438; *Saghar Singh* v. *Patta Singh*, 1957 All WR (HC) 186.
2. *Abdullah Harron* v. *Karachi Corporation*, AIR 1941 Sind 211 at p. 214 : 207 IC 85; *Abdul Rashid* v. *Brahman Saran*, AIR 1938 All 293 : ILR 1938 All 538 : 1938 ALJ 436 (FB).
3. 1962 Andhra Weekly Reporter, 607.

mend of another cultivator as a means of access to his own field and such user of the *mend* of one's field by another for purposes of agricultural operations and allied activities is, generally speaking, never objected to and is, therefore, nothing but permissive. No easementary right, therefore, can be acquired in this country by use of a *mend* as a way unless there is clear evidnce of such user as a matter of right.[1]

Presumption and burden of proof.—The law is jealous of a claim to an easement, and the burden is on the party asserting such a claim to prove it clearly. This he must do by showing a grant conferring an easement in express terms, or by necessary implication, or, where an easement is claimed by prescription, he must prove the facts essential to the acquisition of a prescriptive title. Thus he must show that the user was open and notorious, that it was with the knowledge and acquiescence of the owner of the servient tenement, that the use was continuous and uninterrupted, hostile and under a claim of right, exclusive, and continued for the period requisite for the acquisition of an easement by prescription, without change or material variation. The existence of any other elements made necessary by statute to the acquisition of an easement by prescription must also be proved. Where an easement is claimed as appurtenant to certain land, the burden is on the party claiming it to show that the original grantee of the easement was the owner of the land in question at the time of the grant. When the party claiming the easement has made a prima facie showing of a prescriptive title, it is then incumbent on the owner of the servient tenement to show by sufficient affirmative proof that the use has been by virtue of a licence or permission, or any other defence, which would destroy the prima facie showing. On the other hand, where the servient owner sets up the defence of bona fide purchaser and proves the purchase, payment for, and ownership of, the land, the burden then shifts to claimant to show that such owner had actual or constructive notice of the easement before the purchase. The law in America presumes that land belongs to the owner of the paper title. Continuous user of 20 years openly as of right and peaceably must be proved. The evidence from which a lost grant may be inferred is not very different from the evidence on which a claim for prescriptive easement may be established.[2]

1. *Vidya Sagar* v. *Ram Das*, AIR 1976 All 415 and *Smt. Bailey* v. *Rama Shankar Lal*, AIR 1975 All 461.
2. *Krishna Narain Agrawal* v. *Carlton Hotel (P) Ltd.*, (1970) 1 SCWR 110.

Adverse possession.—Where defendant himself admitted that he was a license in the disputed room and the evidence had shown that plaintiff allowed the defendant to continue his such possession till the defendant had expressed his sole right of ownership, *held* that the defendant did not acquire title to the disputed property by adverse possession.[1]

Acquisition of easement against Government : Different period not violative of Article 14 of the Constitution.—An easement by prescription may be acquired against Government by sixty years' enjoyment.

In providing for the limitations and conditions the legislature made a distinction under the Act between land belonging to the Government and land belonging to other persons. In respect of the former, it prescribed a longer period during which the right to be acquired had to be exercised. Private ownership of land as compared to Government ownership being limited in extent, a private individual is in a better position to safeguard his rights and to prevent the acquisition of prescriptive rights by others. It cannot, therefore, be said that there is no reasonable nexus between the distinction made and the purpose of the legislation.[2]

Claim of acquisition of easement against transferee from Government.—A person claiming an easement against a transferee from the Government would have an option of either basing his claim upon user for a period of sixty years against Government and the transferee combined or if he so prefers, he can ignore the period of prescription against the Government and have his claim entirely upon user for a period of 20 years while the property was in possession of the transferee.[3]

But in *N. Nagappa Shetty* v. *Babu Achari*,[4] the Mysore High Court has held the observations in AIR 1943 All 362 to be obiter and laid down that the words 'belongs to Government' appearing in the last paragraph of Section 15 mean that at the time when the right is claimed in a suit the servient tenement must belong to Government. If it does not, then the rule of sixty years' user cannot be applied and the person claiming the prescriptive right against a private individual can succeed if he establishes the user over the servient tenement

1. *Sushila Hati & others* v. *Subhas & others*, AIR 1985 Cal 197.
2. *Chandami Lal* v. *General Manager, Western Railway*, 1961 ALJ 768 : AIR 1962 All 159.
3. AIR 1943 All 362.
4. AIR 1962 Mys. 179.

for a period of 20 years ending within two years next before the filing of the suit.

Where the property over which the prescriptive right of easement is claimed, previously belonged to the Government and the Government had assigned it to private persons, the claimant can tack on the previous user against the Government in proving his acquisition of easement right for 20 years ending within two years next before the institution of his suit.

Acquisition of easementary right on basis of immemorial user

A tenant who has been irrigating his field from the well of his landlord for the last more than 45-50 years uninterruptedly can acquire an easementary right. It is true that a tenant cannot acquire a prescriptive right of easement in land or well belonging to his lessor but he may claim a right of easement based on immemorial user, for, in such a case there is strong presumption that the enjoyment of the right had its origin under an agreement of grant.[1]

Right to use common property.—In the case of joint wall each co-owner is entitled to a reasonable user of the wall owned in common and so long as each co-owner used it reasonably without interfering with the enjoyment of that wall by the other co-owner or without doing anything which would weaken, damage, increase or diminish the wall enjoyed in common, he is entitled to do what he likes. The other co-owner will have no cause for complaint unless the acts alleged amount to his ouster or to the destruction of the party wall.[2]

Easements relating to water.—Both under the provisions of the Easements Act and Limitation Act for the acquisition of all easements relating to water, the following conditions must be fulfilled :

(1) the enjoyment of the easement must have been peaceable;

(2) the enjoyment of the easement must have been open;

(3) the enjoyment of the right must have been as a right of easement;

1. *Girdhari Singh* v. *Gokul*, AIR 1976 Raj 10.
2. *M. Nageswara Rao* v. *S. Ramachandra Rao,* AIR 1973 AP 86 at 91 : (1972) 2 An Pra LJ 397 : (1973) 1 An LT 128 : (1973) 2 An WR 36; *Rajubhai Mohanbhai* v. *Lalbhai Mulchand,* AIR 1926 Bom 545 (1); *Marghabhai Vallabhai* v. *Motibhai Meetabhai,* AIR 1932 Bom 513; *Chapsibhai* v. *Purushottam,* AIR 1971 SC 1878 : 1971 SCD 601 : (1971) 2 SCA 61.

(4) the enjoyment of the easement must have been as of right;

(5) the enjoyment of the easement must have been without interruption;

(6) the enjoyment must have continued for twenty years; and

(7) the said period of twenty years must end within two years next before the institution of the suit wherein the claim is contested.

Right of pasturage.—Where a right of pasturage is claimed by villagers, there is no dominant tenement to which the right can attach and therefore a prescriptive right of easement is wholly untenable where villagers claimed a right of pasturage.[1]

Right to burial.—The residents of a village cannot in law acquire the right of burial either as easement or by prescription.[2]

Enjoyment must have been adverse.—The user of enjoyment to raise the 'presumption of a grant of an easement in water', must have been adverse, that is, interfered with the enjoyment of the servient owner.

A user, which is neither physical, capable of prevention of by the owner of the servient tenement, nor actionable, cannot support an easement.

Easements relating to the flow of water.—A right may be acquired by an upper riparian owner to divert, obstruct or consume the water in a natural stream and thus prevent it from flowing in its accustomed course to the lower riparian estate though an owner of land through which a river runs, cannot by enlarging a channel through which the water has been accustomed to flow before any appropriation of it by another, divert more of it to the prejudice of any other riparian owner, who had, at any time before such enlargement, appropriated to himself the surplus water which did not escape by the former channel. Such a right may be acquired by statute or grant, or prescription.

Right to commit nuisance cannot be acquired by prescription.—Throwing night soil on another's land is a wrongful act called nuisance, and no one can acquire a prescriptive right to commit nuisance on another's land. There

---

1. *N.G. Dutta* v. *K.C. Banerjee*, AIR 1952 Cal 108.
2. *N.G. Dutta* v. *K.C. Banerjee*, AIR 1952 Cal 108.

is distinction between walking across another's land and throwing filth on it. The former is an act of trespass if committed without the consent of the other side, while the later is a nuisance. A right of way may be acquired by prescription if it is exercised openly and with the knowledge of the owner of the servient tenement, but a right to commit a nuisance cannot be acquired by prescription no matter how often the act of nuisance is repeated.[1]

Acquisition of easementary right to light and air through windows in common wall by prescription

A person cannot acquire an easement unless he acts with the knowledge that it is a case of dominant and servient tenement and he is exercising a right over property which does not belong to him. If he enjoys a right under the supposition that he is the owner of the property he does not acquire an easement. He cannot acquire an easement of light and air over property jointly owned by him with others. It is not possible for a person to acquire an easement of light and air through window in a joint wall belonging to himself as well as to the owner of the other premises.

The rationale behind the above views is that when one of the owners of a common wall opens windows in that common wall, he does so in exercise of his rights as a co-owner and, therefore, he cannot acquire a right of easement in respect of the windows against the co-owner. A right which cannot be prevented from being exercised by physical interference during the period of enjoyment cannot be acquired as an easement. Before time can commence to run under the Easements Act, there must be an invasion of some legal right. Acts which are neither preventable nor actionable, cannot be relied upon to found an easement. In the case of a common wall, each co-owner is entitled to a reasonable user of the wall owner in common and so long as each co-owner uses it reasonably without interfering with the enjoyment of that wall by the other co-owner or without doing anything which would weaken, damage, increase or diminish the wall enjoyed in common, he is entitled to do what he likes and the other co-owners will have no cause for complaint unless the acts alleged amount to his ouster or to destruction of the party wall. The opening of the apertures in the common wall by the plaintiff should, therefore, be treated as incidental to the enjoyment of the common property and it does not amount to trespass upon the

1. *Bankey Lal* v. *Kishan Lal*, AIR 1967 Allahabad 43.

right of the other co-owner which would entitle him to prevent such trespass by physical obstruction or by an action in a court of law. When there is no scope for such an action, the plaintiff cannot be deemed to have acquired a right of easement by prescription to ancient light, and air through those apertures.[1]

In *Nageswara Rao* v. *Ram Chandra Rao*,[2] a Bench of the Andhra Pradesh Court has held that the co-owner of a joint wall could not acquire an easement in respect of light and air through the windows in the joint wall whatever may be the period of his enjoyment prior to the date of the suit, as the normal method of enjoyment of joint wall also includes the enjoyment by opening windows or ventilators which could not give rise to any trespass so as to give a cause of action for an obstruction or a suit in a Civil Court to prevent it at the instance of the other owner.

Peculiarities of easement of way acquired by prescription.—Easements of way are governed by different principles applicable to easement of light and air inasmuch as, while the former arise from the uninterrupted user of the servient tenement, the latter arise by implied covenant on the part of the servient owner derived from the mere occupation of the dominant tenement,[3] and while the former are unlawful in their origin, the acts being a trespass, in the case of the latter, the acts are in themselves lawful acts done in the lawful occupation and user of a man's own land.[4]

Acquisition by prescription.—A right of way may be acquired by prescription where the same has been peaceably and properly enjoyed by any person claiming title thereto, as an easement, and as of right, without interruption, and for twenty years. A right of way may be acquired by prescription, and is so acquired where a user for the prescriptive period is accompanied by the elements necessary to create an easement by prescription. When by prescription, the right of easement of way becomes absolute and indefeasible, the owner of the servient tenement cannot close or wrongfully obstruct it.

Where a right of way is acquired by prescription for over 20 years, the right passes to the transferee with the transfer

1. *K. Mohideen Ibrahim* v. *M. Muhammad Abdullah*, AIR 1978 Mad 97; *Narayan Balwant* v. *Shankar Waman*, AIR 1938 Bom 215.
2. AIR 1973 Andhra Pradesh 86.
3. See *Cross* v. *Lewis*, (1824) 2 B & C 686; *Moore* v. *Rawson*, (1824) 3 B & C 332.
4. *Palaniswamy Naicker* v. *Chinnaswami Naicker*, (1966) 1 MLJ 502 : 81 MLW 95.

of the dominant tenement. It is not necessary that it should be specifically mentioned in the transfer deed.[1] A plea of right of passage acquired by easement by prescription cannot be taken for the first time at the appellate stage.[2]

Acquisition of fishery rights by grant or prescription

Where exclusive right to fish in territorial waters within three miles of the shore is claimed as against the general public, the question may arise whether such a claim or right is opposed to public and, therefore, could not be supported or acquired either by grant or prescription through custom or immemorial user. That question, however, does not arise where two sets of villagers for the sake of preventing disputes among themselves have entered into a compromise whereby they have set apart exclusive areas defined in the memorandum of compromise in which each set of the villagers will have exclusive right to fish. There is no public policy involved in a private individual, who has as much right to fish in territorial waters, in agreeing with another, who has a similar right to fish in the same, that as between themselves they will have separate areas set apart for fishing either because of mutual convenience or because of a desire to avoid conflicts or disputes. In fact, such an arrangement would serve the ends of public policy rather than the same being opposed to it.[3]

Easements causing nuisance.—A right to create a public nuisance cannot be acquired by prescription[4] but a right to create a private nuisance is capable of being acquired by prescription. On the expiration of the period of twenty years the nuisance becomes legalised *ab initio*, as if it has been authorised in its commencement by a grant from the owner of the servient land.[5] In the case of nuisance by overhanging trees over the land of the neighbour any right to create such nuisance cannot be acquired merely by the non-objection of the previous owner of the neighbouring land.[6]

No right of easement can be acquired to flow dirty water

1. *Per* Field, J., in *Dolton* v. *Angus,* (1881) 6 App Cas 750.
2. *Thulahallikotra Basappa* v. *Pujari Rangappa*, (1996) 2 Kant. LJ 605 at 614.
3. *Periasami* v. *Kandappan*, AIR 1975 Mad, 239 (FB).
4. *Bherulal* v. *Mohan Singh*, AIR 1966 Raj 123 : 1960 Raj LW 497.
5. *Gopal Krishana* v. *Municipal Committee, Agra,* AIR 1958 M.P. 371 : 1958 M.P.C. 626 : 1958 M.PLJ 727.
6. *P. Sheikh Batcha Rowther* v. *N.R. Alavappan Servai,* AIR 1959 Mad 12.

towards neighbour's house which amounts to a nuisance.[1] In *Prabhu Narain Singh* v. *Ram Niranjan,*[2] Deoki Nandan, J., observed that a perusal of illustrations (f), (g), (h), (i) and (j) as also explanations to Section 7 show that there is no right by way of easement to discharge dirty water of the drain on another's land, so as to create a nuisance. "An easement of this kind is not contemplated by the Easements Act and I think properly so."

Right over land of neighbour.—An owner of tree does not acquire any right over the land of neighbour simply because the branches of his trees extended over the neighbour's land for any continuous length of time, the law does not countenance a prescriptive right to commit and continue a nuisance.[3]

Interpretation of expression "belongs to Government".—"Belongs to Government" in the last clause of Section 15 of the Act would clearly indicate that the land must belong to the Government when the right is claimed in a suit for the application of longer period of 30 years. When the provision is thus clear, there would be no justification to give a different meaning by interpretative device to extend the privilege exclusively available to the Government to a private party to whom the Government has assigned the said land. On assignment the interest of the Government is transferred to the assignee, and thereafter the property neither can have the character of Government land nor can have the privileges of Government land. Thus, if at the institution of the suit the servient tenement belonged to a private individual, the period of user to acquire easement by prescription is twenty years ending within two years immediately before the institution of the suit even though the predecessor-in-interest of the servient owner was the Government he can tack on the enjoyment while the servient tenement belonged to the Government for the said purpose.[4]

Easementary right by prescription.—In absence of specific pleadings, plaintiff is not entitled to claim right of easement of passage through land in dispute due to its continuous user.[5]

1. *Jag Narain* v. *Ram Dularey,* AIR 1979 All 71 at 74; *Swami Nath* v. *Sheoratan,* 1981 All W.C. 79; *Bansraj* v. *Ram Sahai,* 1981 All W.C. 582.
2. AIR 1983 All 223 at 224.
3. *Manikkam* v. *Kamala,* AIR 1987 Ker 72.
4. *Kesavan Velayudhan* v. *Kannan Kunjukutty,* AIR 1992 Ker 163.
5. *Smt. Savitri Devi* v. *Gauri Dutt,* AIR 2000 NOC 7 (HP).

Prescriptive right of easement in suit cart track not liable to be interfered with.—It was claimed by the plaintiff that suit cart track running between both survey numbers *viz.* one belonging to plaintiff and other to defendant and both parties were using suit cart track for more than sixty years to the knowledge of everybody. Defendant had taken the plea that the said cart track was running through only his land. There was report of Advocate-Commissioner and his oral evidence that cart track was running through both survey numbers. Held, that the case of defendants that suit cart track was running only in his survey number could not be accepted to be true. Therefore, finding that plaintiff had established his prescriptive right of easement in suit cart tract was not liable to be interfered with.[1]

No easementary right—Water flow onto land of neighbour.—Where plaintiff and respondent had purchased adjacent land and sale to both of them took place within two months, held that no person could have a right to have water from his property flow onto land of his neighbour. No such easementary right could be claimed in law. All that the appellants could claim was to see that water from the roof of his house was allowed to flow, onto his own land.[2]

Prescriptive right over a specific portion.—A decree was passed by the Trial Court on the basis of evidence on record holding that said portion was used by plaintiff and his predecessors as a way since time immemorial. Such decree was set aside by appellate Court assuming that such portion was part of public road in absence of such claim by the plaintiff. No other villager had claimed objection to use by plaintiff on ground that it was a public road. The defendant had himself admitted in oral evidence of the usage of portion by plaintiff.[3]

Easementary right of pathway—Reckoning of statutory period of 20 years.—Only a person who is in occupation of a hut of a homestead as defined in the Act can apply to the land tribunal for purchase of *'kudikidappu right'*. Therefore, the applicant has to satisfy the conditions precedent for grant of that right or confirmation of that right. Therefore, when such a declaratory relief is granted, it is a declaration of the right which relates back to the date on which he is in occupation of the hut or homestead, as the case may be.

1. *Periya Gounder* v. *Chinna Gounder*, AIR 2003 Mad 174.
2. *Saraswati* v. *S. Ganpathy*, AR 2001 SC 1844.
3. *Shekarappa Veerappa Harayabal* v. *Mohammad Sab Malik Sab Nadaf*, AIR 2002 Kant. 250.

Therefore, if a particular pathway is there in use, prior to the issuance of a purchase certificate, then it cannot be said to arise from the date on which the purchase certificate was issued if actually such user was there even from the date of occupation of the hut. In other words, if the plaintiffs are able to show that they are using the pathway even prior to the date on which the purchase certificate was issued to him, then they are certainly entitled to include those period also for the purpose of reckoning the 20 year period.[1]

No acquisition of right of easement by prescription.—The plaintiff and his predecessors were using water pond in the defendants' land for the last twenty years. Such permission was granted by the grandfather of the defendants. Held, that such permission was not binding upon his successors-in-interest. As the permission never matured into rights, hence plaintiff had not acquired any easementary right for use of water pond belonging to defendant.[2]

Entitlement to easement by prescription.—The field of defendant was situated on southern side of plaintiff's field and he could have access to his agricultural land only through the disputed way. User of way was for more than 30 to 40 years. Held, that as user was open, peaceful and without any obstruction for that period, hence, plaintiff could be said to have acquired right of easement by prescription.[3]

Right of access through prescription not tenable.—The plaintiff was proved to be using access to house as of right through property of defendants for more than 20 years. Moreover plaintiff had access to house on southern side which was being used by her for long time. Held, that claim as to the right of access through property of defendant was not tenable.[4]

Claim for easementary right of prescription could not be interfered with.—Specific plea of easementary right of prescription was taken by plaintiff. Issue was framed on basis of such specific pleadings and no objection was taken by defendant to framing of issue. It was found by trial court on basis of evidence that plaintiff was continuously using land as passage and for flow of rainwater from his shop for the last thirty years and decreed suit of plaintiff holding that he had

1. *Maddthil Radha* v. *M.P. Ramachandran*, AIR 2002 Ker 209.
2. *Punit Das* v. *Kanailal Das*, AIR 2001 Cal 110.
3. *Jivanlal* v. *Kishnarao D. Sathone*, AIR 2004 Bom 89.
4. *Justiniano Antao* v. *Bernandette B. Pereira*, AIR 2005 SC 236.

acquired easementary right by prescription. As findings given by Court were findings of fact, hence, could not be interfered with and plea taken for first time by defendant in second appeal that plaintiff had pleaded only customary right and had not pleaded easementary right was not tenable.[1]

Conditions necessary for the acquisition of a right of easement by prescription.—There are following seven ingredients of S. 15 of the Act : (1) There must be pre-existing easement which must have been enjoyed by the dominant owner; (2) the enjoyment must have been peaceable; (3) the enjoyment must have been as an easement; (4) the enjoyment must have been as of right; (5) the right must have been enjoyed openly; (6) the enjoyment must have been for a period of twenty years; and (7) the enjoyment for 20 years must have been without interruption.[2] The following conditions must be fulfilled for the acquisition of a right of easement by prescription :

(1) The right claimed must not be uncertain.

(2) The right claimed must have been enjoyed.

(3) It must have been enjoyed independently of any agreement with the owner or occupier of the land over which the right is claimed.

(4) It must have been enjoyed—

(a) peaceably,

(b) openly,

(c) as of right,

(d) as an easement,

(e) without interruption,

(f) for twenty years, or thirty years if the right is claimed against Government.

Of the last six sub-conditions, (b) and (c) are not necessary for easements of light and air or support. With this exception all the conditions and sub-conditions must be fulfilled before a right of easement is acquired. The Court does not recognize easement by illegal activity.[3]

They are proposed to be dealt with one by one as we

1. *Vipin Krishna Garg* v. *Shyam Lal Garg*, AIR 2004 All 386.
2. *Krishnan* v. *Nanukuttan*, ILR 1986 (1) Ker 526; *Badariya Madrassa Committee* v. *Antony Robert*, 2006 (2) KLT 636. See also *Sarnu* v. *Fagania*, 2007 (1) AWC 112 (UHC); *Dhaniya Bai* v. *Jiwan*, AIR 2003 M.P. 71.
3. *Ponnan* alias *Palaniappan* v. *Chinna Gounder (D) by LRs.*, AIR 2006 Mad 139.

proceed.

Easement of right of access by prescription.—If dominant heritage was being used for the purpose different from residential then it would not forfeit right of easement.[1]

Where the plaintiff claimed his easementary right to use pathway in the suit property but he failed to prove that he had been using suit pathway for about 65 years, he could not be entitled to decree on basis of prescription. More so while he had an alternate access to his property and there was no pathway in the suit property.[2]

Where the plaintiff could not prove his right to use suit pathway by prescription he would he would not be entitled to decree for the suit passage as the burden of proof was on him to show that he had been using the said passage for over 30 years to establish his right of using it by prescription.[3]

In the case of Government, thirty years enjoyment must be proved.—Where the plaintiff did not plead the user of Government land for 30 years or more he could not claim right of easement by prescription. Mere user of land for 20 years does not confer any easementary right by way of prescription.[4]

Easement, transfer of, on transfer of property.—When a property is sold it passes to the purchaser with all the rights and obligations. If the plaintiff has purchased the property with all the rights and obligations, then the right of easement would also stand transferred in his favour and he would be entitled to tack the right of easement.[5]

Easement of light and air temporary injunction, entitlement.—The plaintiff would be entitled to temporary injunction during pendency of suit restraining the defendant from raising further construction if it is depriving the plaintiff of light and air in everyday life.[6]

Easements relating to support—Right to support of buildings by adjacent and subjacent land.—The section enacts where support for one person's land, or things affixed thereto, has been peaceably received by another person's land subjected to artificial pressure, or by things affixed thereto, as

1. *Ram Charan* v. *Ram Asrey*, AIR 2008 M.P. 105.
2. *N. Boriah* v. *Nilgiri Coop Printing Press*, AIR 2008 Mad 69.
3. *N. Boraiah* v. *Pandurangan*, AIR 2008 (NOC) 1304 (Mad).
4. *Hans Raj* v. *Dewan Singh*, AIR 2007 (NOC) 2144 (Utr).
5. *Luhar Tulsidas Narsibhai* v. *Vrajlal Lalji Vaghela*, AIR 2007 Guj. 77 (81).
6. *Shashi Agrawal* v. *Usha Agrawal*, 2006 (3) MPLJ 146.

an easement without interruption, and for twenty years, the right to such support shall be absolute.

If necessary averments are not stated in the plaint, then the plaintiff cannot claim right of easement to lateral support.[1]

Easements relating to land appurtenant to Sugar Mill.—The land which was being utilised as land appurtenant to land of mill, would not vest in State. So the easement right available to sugar mill in respect of such land would not stand destroyed and would continue to be enjoyed by the mill.[2]

Easements of way—General.—To claim an easement by way of necessity, the plaintiff is required to plead that at some given point of time the two tenements were held by one person and owing to transfer or bequest of one of the tenements it became essential for the enjoyment of one tenement to have an easementary right over the other tenement. Where such a plea is not raised, the right of passage by way of easement of necessity cannot be claimed.[3]

In *M.M. Sahkari Sanstha Mariyadit* v. *Department of Fisheries, Maharashtra*,[4] where right of fishing it transpired that the practice was regular and continuous, creek used by project affected fisherman uniformly for purposes of fishing thereby making usage certain and not varied, their use for purposes of their own livelihood and not on industrial scale which made exploitation of their rights unreasonable, the customary rights of fisherman was established.

Acquisition by Prescription

In *Manisha Mahendra Gala & Ors.* v. *Shalini Bhagwan Avatramani & Ors.*,[5] rejected a plea for prescriptive easement because the pleadings merely stated the road was used "for the last many years." The Court ruled that vague phrases are insufficient; the claimant must specifically plead and prove the exact 20-year period ending within two years of the suit.

In *V.J. Mathew* v. *Surendran*,[6] Kerala High Courtc clarified the "Title Thereto" requirement. The Court held that to claim prescription under Section 15, the user must enjoy the right with the animus (intention) of holding a right, not

1. *Deo Kumar* v. *Kailash Chand*, 2008 (1) M.PLJ 123.
2. *State of U.P.* v. *R.B. Narain Singh Sugar Mill Ltd.*, AIR 2007 Utr. 87 (96).
3. *Satya Devi* v. *Sansar Chand*, 2006 (2) Shim LC 431.
4. AIR 2022 (NOC) 11 (Bom).
5. 2024 INSC 293.
6. 2025:KER:80618.

merely by permission or license.

In *Anand Kumar* v. *Anil Kumar*,[1] Delhi District Court (Upheld in recent appeals 2023-24) regarding Rights to Light and Air, the court ruled that Section 15 rights are not absolute on their own; they must be read with Section 33. A plaintiff must prove that the obstruction caused "substantial damage" rendering the property uninhabitable or unfit for business, not just that the light was reduced.

16. Exclusion in favour of reversioner of servient heritage.—Provided that, when any land upon, over or from which any easement has been enjoyed or derived has been held under or by virtue of any interest for life or any term of years exceeding three years from the granting thereof, the time of the enjoyment of such easement during the continuance of such interest or term shall be excluded in the computation of the said last mentioned period of twenty years' in case the claim is, within three years next after the determination of such interest or term, resisted by the person entitled [There is no proviso as to minority, idiocy, lunacy or other disability.] on such determination, to the said land.

Illustration

A sues for a declaration that he is entitled to a right of way over *B*'s land. *A* proves that he has enjoyed the right for twenty-five years. But *B* shows that during ten of these years *C* had a life interest in the land, that on *C*'s death *B* became entitled to the land, and that within two years after *C*'s death he contested *A*'s claim to the right. The suit must be dismissed, as *A*, with reference to the provisions of the section, has only proved enjoyment for fifteen years.

NOTES

The section is intended to protect the interests of reversioners whose lands may be burdened with easements by life estate holders or by person having an interest for a term exceeding 3 years during their term of possession. It lays down that in computing the period of 20 years for acquisition of

1. 2024/DHC/2865-DB.

easement rights, the period during which the land was in possession of a life estate holder or of a person having an interest for a term exceeding three years, shall be excluded provided that reversioner resists the claim to such an easement within three years of the determination of the interest of the limited estate holder.

17. Rights which cannot be acquired by prescription.—Easements acquired under Section 15 are said to be acquired by prescription, and are called prescriptive rights.

None of the following rights can be so acquired :

(a) a right which would tend to the total destruction of the subject of the right, or the property on which, if the acquisition were made, liability would be imposed.

(b) a right to the free passage of light or air to an open space of ground;

(c) a right to surface-water not flowing in stream and not permanently collected in a pool, tank or otherwise;

(d) a right to underground water not passing in a defined channel.

NOTES

Section 17 in clauses (a) to (d) defines the nature of those rights which cannot be acquired by prescription.

Clause (a).—Clause (a) lays down that easement rights which by their very nature tend to cause the total destruction of the subject matter of the right or of the property over which the liability is imposed cannot be acquired by prescription. The object, of this rule is to allow the servient owner to have full use and enjoyment of his tenement. No one can acquire a right of way, by prescription, over the servient tenement in every direction bcause that would altogether destroy the utility of the land to the servient owner but a right of way in particular direction can be acquired by prescription. A mere possibility of total destruction at some future date cannot be considered, the destructive effect of the enjoyment of the right must be such as to make itself felt within a reasoanble time.

Clause (b).—Section 15, clause (1) lays down that easement rights of light or air can be acquired for any *building* when such righs have been enjoyed peaceably, as an easement without interruption and for twenty years. Section 17 clause (b) lays down that such rights (right to the free passage of light or air) cannot be acquired by prescription for an open space of ground. It should be clearly understood that the dominant tenement alone should be building, the servient tenement may be a building or an open space. The reason for this restriction is that otherwise owners of continguous plots of lands which have remained unbuilt for 20 years would not be allowed to build at all because that would diminish their light.

A right to free passage of light or air to an open space of ground.—The rule of law enacted in clause (b) of this section, that an easement right in respect of light and air can be acquired only as appurtenant to certain definite apertures contained in the dominant tenement and not for any space of ground is an absolute one.[1] But the converse proposition that the servient tenement must also be a building is not necessary for it may be an open space.[2] The proposition laid down in clause (b) is in accord with the rule of English law and gives statutory recognition to a very salutary principle. The absence of such a rule would have tended to retard the growth of modern cities and would have possibly led to a crop of cases of having nothing as their object but to injure or annoy the neighbours.

Clause (c).—Right to surface-water flowing in a stream or permanently collected in a pool or tank can be acquired by prescription, but right to surface-water not flowing in a stream and not permanently collected in a pool or tank cannot be acquired by prescription.

From a plain reading of Section 17(c) it would appear that easement rights can only be acquired over surface-water if it is flowing in a stream, or if the surface-water is collected in a stream. The expression used is "collector" and not "collecting". Thus, easement rights can only be acquired over water which is already collected in a pool or a tank, and no rights are acquired over the collector of the same. Hence, no right of easement could be acquired over the surface-water till it reached the depression and, as such, the defendant was entitled to impound the surface-water or to divert it before it reached the depression. His or his predecessor's action in not impounding the water or diverting it for a long time would

1. *Roberts* v. *Macord,* (1832) 1 M & R 230; *Potts* v. *Smith,* (1868) 6 Eq. 311.
2. *Cable* v. *Bryant,* (1908) 1 Ch 259.

not create any right of easement over the surface-water as that is prohibited by Section 17. The right which cannot be acquired directly because of the provisions contained in Section 17, cannot be acquired indirectly as well. If it is held that only because the plaintiffs had acquired a right of easement over the water collector in the depression they had also acquired a right of insisting on the flow of surface-water in the depression, it would have to be held that the plaintiffs had acquired easementary rights over the surface-water as well. This conclusion cannot be reached as there is specfic prohibition in the Easements Act.[1]

The expression "stream" used in Section 17 should in the absence of any contrary intention be interpreted as is ordinarily understood by a common man and not in any technical manner. When one uses the word "stream", the idea conveyed is that the body of water flows through a defined channel, having a bed and banks on both the sides. A flow of excess rain water though in a body and in one direction, spread over a very large area in width without any bed or having any banks within which the flow is confined, cannot be treated as a "stream".[2]

A right to surface water not flowing in a stream and not permanently collected in a pool, tank or otherwise—Clause (c).—It has been held by the Nagpur High Court that the word "and" in this clause has been used by the Legislature in place of the word "or" and that it should be interpreted as such.[3]

Clause (d).—Right to underground water flowing in unknown and undefined channel cannot be acquired by prescription. The reason is that there being no visible or acertained means of knowing as to what extent, if at all, the accustomed supply of water alleged to have been received by the claimant during the prescriptive period was affected by that percolating water which is alleged to have been cut off by the other party, the right cannot be acquired by prescription.

Right to underground water—Clause (d).—As regards water flowing through a natural watercourse having a channel at once defined and known but which is underground, the owner of the soil under which the water flows can maintain

1. *Narsoo* v. *Madan Lal,* AIR 1975 MP 185.
2. *Narsoo* v. *Madan Lal* (Supra).
3. *Kalanath* v. *Wanarrao,* ILR 1937 N 13 : AIR 1937 N 310.

an action for diversion or obstruction if it took place under such circumstances as would have enabled him to recover if the watercourse had been wholly above ground.[1]

A right to draw water from a well is a right to underground water. Therefore, in view of the provisions of Section 17(d) a right claimed by the plaintiff to irrigate his field from the well situate in the defendant's land cannot be acquired as an easementary right by prescription.[2]

Right by prescription.—The plaintiff claimed to be using paint schedule property for drying fishing nets, dipping fishing boats and repairing them. Held, that finding of fact by the Courts that if claim of plaintiff was allowed, the entire property would become useful so far as defendants were concerned, could not be interfered with.[3]

Particular easements—Easements relating to water.—The law is settled that in respect of common well, the right to use of the co-owners is available. Where the use of water was not even from the common well but from private well belonging to the plaintiff, there would be absolutely no reason for the defendants to complain about conduct of the plaintiff at all on grounds that it indirectly affected right of co-owners[4]

18. Customary easement.—An easement may be acquired in virtue of a local custom. Such easements are called customary easements.

Illustration

(a) By the custom of a certain village every cultivator of a village land is entitled as such, to graze his cattle on the common pasture. *A*, having become the tenant of a plot of uncultivated land in the village, breaks up and cultivates that plot. He thereby acquires an easement to graze his cattle in accordance with the custom.

(b) By the custom of a certain town no owner

1. *Dikinson* v. *Grand Junction Canal Co.*, 1852 Exch. 282, 301; *Chasemore* v. *Richards*, (1859) 7 HLC 374, 384; *Black* v. *Ballymena Township Commissioners*, (1886) 17 LR Ir. 459; *Bradford Corporation* v. *Ferrand*, (1902) 2 Ch 655, 660; *Bleacher's Association Ltd.* v. *Chapel en-le-Firth R.D.C.*, 1933 Ch 356.
2. *Het Singh and others* v. *Amar Singh and others*, AIR 1982 Allahabad 468.
3. *Sreedharan* v. *Madanam*, AIR 2003 NOC 276 (Ker).
4. *Kuruppa Gounder* v. *Soundaram*, AIR 2007 Mad 175 (177).

or occupier of a house can open a new window therein so as substantially to invade his neighbour's privacy. *A* builds a house in the town near *B's* house. *A* thereupon acquires an easement that *B* shall not open new windows in his house so as to command a view of the portions of *A's* house which are ordinarily excluded from observation and *B* acquires a like easement with respect to *A's* house.

NOTES

Customary Easement.—A customary easement is not an easement in the true sense of that expression. It is not annexed to the ownership of a dominant tenement, and it is not exercisable for the more beneficial enjoyment of the dominant tenement; it is recognised and enforced as a part of the common law of the locality where it obtains. A customary easement arises in favour of an indeterminate class of persons such as residents of a locality or members of a certain community, and though not necessarily annexed to the ownership of land, it is enforceable as a right to do and continue to do something upon land or as a right to prevent and continue to prevent something done upon land. Sanction for its enforceability being in custom, the right must satisfy all the tests which a local custom for recognition by courts must satisfy.[1]

If by the exercise of a customary right in favour of an indefinite body of persons the property is the subject-matter of the *profit-a-prendre* is in danger of being destroyed the customary right will not be recognised.[2]

General.—The claim of a dominant owner for the beneficial enjoyment of his land to do and continue to do something or to prevent and continue to prevent something being done, in or upon, or in respect of the servient tenement, is a right which he can acquire under the other relevant sections of the Act, either by grant, express or implied, or by necessity or by prescription, and that such easement would clearly be different in nature from a customary easement provided for by his section, or a proprietor's or a citizen's right to use some public property, or a property belonging to himself and the rest of the community. If an easement as for instance, such as to pass over another's land, could also be brought

1. *State of Bihar* v. *Subodh Gopal Bose*, AIR 1968 SC 281.
2. *State of Bihar* v. *Subodh Gopal Bose*, (*supra*).

under this section, the provisions of Section 15 would be redundant. This section is not meant to be used in that way. Therefore, if a claim has to be established under Section 15, but it is not, the suit is bound to fail.

In *Narasappa* v. *Nanjappa*,[1] it was held that by merely describing a path as a *mamool* path, the dominant owner cannot escape the operation of Section 15, that if by a right to pass along a *mamool* path is meant a right to pass along a public way, or a pathway belonging to the village, a right which may be established by immemorial user, it would not really be an easement but a property right inherent in everyone in the village who will have a right to use it, and that the claim of a dominant owner to go over another's land for certain purposes, or generally, is a right which he can acquire under the other relevant sections of the Act, either by prescription or by necessity and would clearly be different in nature from customary easement provided for in this section, or a proprietor's or citizen's right to use a public path or a path belonging to himself and the rest of the community.

Custom.—A custom is a rule, which, in a particular family or a particular district, has, from long usage, obtained the force of law.[2] It is an usage by virtue of which certain persons belonging to a certain class in a certain locality are entitled to exercise certain rights against certain other persons of the same locality. In short, it is local common law. It is common law because it is not statute law. It is local law because it is the law of a particular place as distinguished from the general common law. According to Austin, it is a rule of conduct which governs to be observed spontaneously, not in pursuance of a law set by a political superior. [*Per* Jessel, M.R. in *Hammerton* v. *Honey*.][3]

The enjoyment of a right claimed to exist under an alleged custom must be enjoyed as of right, that is to say, all acts must be done under or by virtue of the custom. In order to establish the custom all acts must have been done without violence, without stealth or secrecy, or without leave or licence asked for or given either expressly or impliedly from time to time. No act which can be ascribed to a licence can ever support a claim of custom.[4]

1. AIR 1955 Mys. 62.
2. *Har Pershad* v. *Sheo Dayal*, 26 WR 55 (PC) : 3 IA 259.
3. (1876) 24 WR 603 (England).
4. Austin's Jurisprudence, Vol. 1, p. 23.

Customary easement and prescriptive easement distinguished.—Customary easements are acquired by virtue of local custom. Prescriptive easements are acquired on proof of peaceable enjoyment for twenty years. No fixed period of enjoyment is necessary for customary easements.

A customary easement belongs to those landowners of an ascertained class, caste or community who for the time being happen to own lands within that particular area or locality where the custom prevails. A prescriptive easement, on the other hand, is not limited to a particular locality it can be enjoyed wherever land can be found.

A customary easement must satisfy all the essentials of a custom, *viz.,* it must be ancient, reasonable, continuous and certain. But prescriptive easements need not be reasonable.

Customary easement and customary rights

A coustomary easement like all other easements is appurtenant to some dominant heritage and cannot exist without it. A customary right exists independent of any tenement. Right to burn Holi at a place or to bathe in a tank or to bury dead in a land are examples of customary rights because they exist independent of any tenement. In view of Section 2(b) customary rights are not affected by the Easements Act. A right to draw the water from a well can be customary right.[1]

A customary right is not easement. An easement belongs to a determinate person or persons in respect of his or their land. A fluctuating body like the inhabitants of the locality cannot claim an easement. Easements are private rights belonging to particular persons, while customary rights are public rights annexed to the place in general. It is again well settled that the customary right is also different from customary easement. An easement is always appurtenant to the dominant tenement and inseparably attached to it and cannot be severed from it.[2]

Customary right is recognised by courts only if the custom is reasonable, besides being ancient and certain. The question of reasonableness is to be decided with reference to the provisions contained in Article 15 of the Constitution. If a section of the public puts forward an exclusive right to the use of the public well, the proof must be on two points :

1. *Maheshwari Prasad* v. *Munni Lal*, AIR 1981 All 438.
2. *Ram Chandra Shah* v. *Abdul Hannan and others*, AIR 1984 Patna 313.

(i) that the well was not dedicated to the use of the general public but was dedicated to that section; and

(ii) that the user has been only by that section with instances and proof that the other members were excluded.[1]

Again, customary rights involving the interests of a locality are disallowed if they are unreasonable.[2] "Every prescription ought to have by common intendment, a lawful beginning; but otherwise it is of a custom; for that ought to be reasonable and *ex creta causa rationabili usitata*, but need not be intended to have a lawful beginning; as custom to have land divisible, or of the nature of gavelkind of borough-English, etc.".[3] The context shows that the statement applies to the minor local customs as well as to those given as instances, Cf. the judgment of the Lord Chancellor in *Dyce* v. *Hay*,[4] a case of copyhold customs, Lord Cranworth said : "In truth I believe that, when it is said that a custom is void because it is unreasonable, nothing more is meant than that the unreasonable character of the alleged custom conclusively proves that the usage, even though it may have existed immemorially, must have resulted from accident or indulgence and not from any right conferred in ancient times on the party setting up the customs". But it seems possible to keep the fiction of a right conferred out of the question, and to recognise the existence of local laws subject to a common law rule as to reasonableness. The rule was considered in *Goodman* v. *Mayor of Saltash*,[5] where the appellant's claim was affirmed not as a servitude, but as a trust or condition qualifying the title of the respondents.[6] As regards private rights involving only the interests of the owner of the dominant tenement on the one hand and the servient on the other, the rule as to

1. *Armugha Konar* v. *Narayana Asari*, 71 MLW 128 : AIR 1958 M 282 (*Palaniandi Tevan* v. *Puthiran Gonda Nandan*, ILR (1897) 20 M 389 and *Kuar Sen* v. *Manman*, ILR (1895) 17 All 87 distinguished).
2. *See* the judgments of Tindal, C.J., in *Tyson* v. *Smith*, (1828) 9 Ad. & E 406; and of Parker, J. in *Johnson* v. *Clark*, (1908) 1 Ch 311.
3. Gateward's Case, (1607) 6 Rep. 59b.
4. [(1852) 1 Macqueen 305; *Millichamp* v. *Johnson*, (1746) Willes 205n; *Blewett* v. *Tregonning*, (1835) 3 A & E 554; *Mounsey* v. *Ismay*, (1853) 1 H & C 729, subsequent proceedings 3 H & C 486; *Blackett* v. *Bradley*, (1862) 1 B.S. 940; *Sowerby* v. *Coleman*, 1867 LR 2 Exch. 96; *Warrick* v. *Queen's College*, (1840) 10 Eq. 105; *Hall* v. *Nottingham*, (1857) 1 Ex D 1. In *Salisbury* v. *Gladstone*, (1861) 9 HLC 692.
5. (1882) 7 App Cas 633 : 52 LJ QB 198.
6. Cf.; *Attorney-General* v. *Antrobus*, (1905) 2 Ch 188.

reasonableness requires to be stated more at length. It is settled first that a private easement must be an incident of a known and usual kind, and secondly, that a private easement cannot confer the exclusive use of a servient tenement. Beyond these two limitations, no question of reasonableness can arise where the title to an easement is based on express grant. It seems also probable that beyond the above limitations no question of reasonableness can arise where the title to an easement is based on prescription.[1]

A customary right exists independent of any dominant heritage and is vested in a defined case or community of a particular locality, as distinguished from individual for their sole benefit.[2]

It has been held by the Nagpur High Court that where the Mahomadans have been immersing their *tazias* at Muharram in two *ghats* of tank for such a length of time as to suggest that the usage has become the customary law of the place, they have a customary right to use the *ghats* for immersing their *tazias*.[3]

Where the plaintiffs as owners of cattle living in a particular village have been accustomed for a long period of time to make offerings when their cattle are afflicted by disease and those offerings are made at a particular "Isthan" in a room, it does constitute a right of the plaintiffs to continue to make those offerings and it is a customary easement under Section 18.[4]

Customary right of way.—When customary right of way is claimed, the onus is on the plaintiff to prove that the custom was ancient, invariable, certain and reasonable. Whether a customary right claimed is reasonable or not would depend on the facts and circumstances of each case. No hard and fast rule can be laid down. 'The fact that if the whole of the disputed land is allowed to be used as a *rasta* (way) it would result in complete extinction of the right of the owners would not by itself make the user unreasonable. Take, for instance, a right of way is claimed in respect of a path with a width of 1 foot which only a man can pass on foot. At the particular

1. *See,* however, the rule of reasonableness applied by Cozens-Handy, L.J., to a prescriptive claim to a *profit a prendre* in *Chesterfield* v. *Harris,* (1908) 2 Ch 410.
2. *Ram Nandan Singh* v. *Ram Kishan Lohar,* AIR 1958 Pat 571.
3. *Sabasha* v. *Baba Narayan Lokras,* AIR 1938 Nag. 177.
4. *Kanhai Singh* v. *Basdeo Sahai,* AIR 1939 All 387 : 185 IC 334 : 1939 ALJ 381.

locality the defendant has only that much of land. If the plaintiff's way of right is declared, evidently the right, title and interest of the defendant in respect of the whole land would be extinguished. The defendant cannot put it to any other user. It cannot be said on that ground that the right of way is unreasonable and must not be allowed.[1]

Customary right of privacy.—A customary right of privacy exists in Uttar Pradesh. This right would accrue to a person who builds a house on an open piece of land, the moment he builds the house. It is not acquired by prescription. This right of privacy is claimable by either party in connection with the infringement of privacy of either by the other.[2]

The right of privacy is a customary right based on purdah which entitled the owner of one property to compel the owner of another to modify the design or architecture of his property so that the women residing in the dominant tenement could be kept in purdah. The right is based on "natural modesty or human morality."

The custom of purdah prevailing in India has been recognised by courts in U.P. since almost a century. The question whether or not the purdah is in keeping with the social development of India would not be a matter for consideration in the law courts. The right of privacy of a purdanashin lady is still recognised, even though the concept of purdah may be gradually disappearing. If the law or the law courts recognise the right of privacy of an individual, that right is to be protected. If a pardanashin lady desires to observe purdah, she cannot be compelled to discard it and appear in public merely because it is outdated and not in consonance with the changing pattern of society from time to time. Privacy is also jealously guarded by even the most modern countries and it is not a privilege of only the pardanashin ladies. No one would like, especially in India, irrespective of the caste and creed to countenance their ladies while in their homes busy in the domestic routine of life being watched, observed, or stealthily stared by strangers. During summer most of the people including ladies, on account of oppressive heat, have to sleep out in the courtyard of the house. The Indian women have always been jealous of intrusion in their privacy in their homes. It is not always that

1. *Sridhar Pani* v. *Duryodhan Mahali*, AIR 1967 Orissa 77.
2. *Daropadi* v. *S.K. Dutt*, AIR 1957 All 48.

women inside their houses are clothed with the attire which they normally use while appearing in public. Therefore, privacy inside the house is a right of every woman and much more so for a woman who has inhibitions by custom or religious notions to appear in public and keeps herself in seclusion by observing purdah.[1]

The right of privacy being a customary right, it is always open to the Court to see whether the custom is, in the circumstances, reasonable and whether it was ceased to be enforceable by desuetude. Be that as it may, the customary right of privacy may be said to exist only in respect of the inner courtyard, and the inner parts of a house inhabited by women and cannot by any stretch, be said to exist in respect of the outer courtyard of a house which opens on the front street.[2]

Illustration (b).—It is clear from illustration (b) that in order to entitle the plaintiff to a decree for a mandatory injunction directing the defendant to close the window put up in his own property, the plaintiff must establish that there is such a customary right in the town where the properties are located that no owner or occupier of house can open a new window therein so as to substantially invade his neighbour's privacy. The plaintiff therefore, has to plead and prove that there is a custom in the town where the properties are situate that no owner or occupier of a house can open a new window therein so as to substantially invade his neighbour's privacy. He has further to establish that the plaintiff has enjoyed such customary right of privacy and that there is an infringement or a threat to the infringement of such a right.[3]

The owner of a property is entitled to open window in the walls located in his property, so long as there is no infringement of the right of others. A right to open a window in one's own property need not in so many words be conferred in the title-deed under which a person acquires the property.[4]

Right of privacy—Nature of the right.—In India, specially in the territories where Mahommedan population abounds and women are kept in strict *purdah,* this right is

1. *Ganeshi Lal* v. *Mst. Rasool Fatima*, AIR 1977 All 118; *Gokal Prasad* v. *Radho*, (1988) ILR 10 All 358; *Nihal Chand* v. *Mst. Bhagwan Dei*, AIR 1935 All 1002 and *Bhagwan Das* v. *Parmeshwar*, 1971 AWR 474.
2. *Diwan Singh* v. *Inderjeet*, AIR 1981 Allah. 342.
3. *Deepchand* v. *Hansraj*, AIR 1971 Mysore 322.
4. *Deepchand* v. *Hansraj* (supra).

very much valued. In England, a right of privacy is not recognised as capable of acquisition as an easement[1] though an action for the invasion of privacy may be maintained on the basis of a covenant contained in a deed whereby the defendant undertakes not to build so as to invade the privacy of the plaintiff.[2] But in India, such right has always been recognized as a valuable right[3] and the Legislature, by inserting illustration (b) to Section 18 has only given legislative recognition to a long-standing right.[4] A customary right of privacy accrues by custom to a person who builds on an open piece of land, the moment he builds the house. It is not ordinarily acquired by prescription, and it does not cease on the acquisition of land.[5] A right of privacy is negative easement inasmuch as it prevents the servient owner from building on his own land so as substantially to interfere with the privacy of the occupants of the dominant heritage. It is continuous in the sense that it does not require any act of the dominant owner for its continuance.[6] But it is non-apparent.[7] It is capable of acquisition by covenant,[8] or custom,[9] or even perhaps by prescription,[10] in the localities where it is recognized as a substantial right appertaining to buildings.

The Calcutta case of *Sri Narain Chowdhury* cited above was followed by the Patna High Court in *Kesho Sahu* v. *(Mst.)*

---

1. Goddard, p. 117, citing Kindersley, V.C. in *Turner* v. *Spooner,* 30 LJ Ch 803; *Brown* v. *Flower,* (1911) 1 Ch 219; *In re* Penny and South Eastern Ry. Co., 7 E & B 660; Gale (1986), p. 27.
2. *Per* Hall, V. C., in *Lord Manners* v. *Johnson,* 1 Ch D 680.
3. *Sheonath* v. *Ali Hussain,* 1 ALJ 118; *Gokul Prasad* v. *Radho,* 10 All 358.
4. Whiteley Stock's Anglo-Indian Codes, Vol. I, p. 881; *Abirchand Gulabchand Jain* v. *Manik Ramnarain, Tailor,* 1978 M.PLJ 204 at 206.
5. *Daroupady Debi* v. *S. K. Dutt,* AIR 1957 A 48.
6. *See* Section 5 of the Indian Easements Act, *ante.*
7. *See* Illus. (d) to Section 5, *ubi sup.*
8. *Lord Manners* v. *Johnson,* 1 Ch D 680.
9. See *Komathi* v. *Gurunadha Pillai,* 3 Mad HC 141; *Gokul Prasad* v. *Radho,* 10 All 358; *Mohammad Abdur Rahim* v. *Birju Sahu,* 5 BLR 676 : 14 WR 103.
10. Calcutta High Court favours the acquisition of a right of privacy by prescription. See *Mohammed Abdur Rahim* v. *Birju Sahu,* 5 BLR 676 : 14 WR 103; *Sheikh Gulam Ali* v. *Gazi Mahomed Zahur Alam,* 6 BLR App 76; *Kalee Pershad Shaha* v. *Ram Pershad Shaha,* 18 WR 14; *Sri Narain Chaudhary* v. *Jadoonath Chaudhry,* 5 CWN 147; *Mahomed Shabbir* v. *Mahomed Jawad,* 15 IC 270.

Muktakiman,[1] In *Kashinath* v. *Ramjiwan*,[2] the Lahore High Court had refused to grant injunction to the plaintiff because he had failed to show any pre-existing or well established right of privacy. Even if such a custom as to right of privacy is held to be proved, an injunction cannot be granted unles it is established that there has been a substantial infringement of the right of privacy.[3]

There is no such thing as natural right of privacy recognised anywhere in India,[4] and it is only in the Bengal Presidency where the right has been recognised as capable of acquisition by prescription as an easement,[5] all the other High Courts holding it to be only a customary easement arising by virtue of a local custom.[6]

In the case of *Deepchand* v. *Hansraj Sait,*[7] Justice, V. S. Malimath, observed that there is no such thing as a natural right of privacy recognised by law anywhere in India. It is only a customary easement arising by virtue of a local custom. As provided by Section 18 of the Indian Easements Act, 1882, an easement may be acquired in virtue of a local custom, Illustration (b) to Section 18 of the Indian Easement Act makes

1. 10 Pat 280 : AIR 1931 Pat 212 : 135 IC 163.
2. AIR 1933 Lah. 847 : 148 IC 224.
3. *Abirchand Gulabchand Jain* v. *Manik Ramnarain Tailor,* 1978 M.PLJ 204 at 207.
4. *Komathi* v. *Gurunadha Pillai,* 3 Mad HC 141; *Sayyad Asaf* v. *Ammea Bibi,* 18 Mad 160; *Manaklal Motilal* v. *Mohanlal Narotumdas,* 44 Bom 496; *Chintala Krishnamurty* v. *Uppala Rajlingam,* AIR 1980 AP 69 (72, 73) : 1980 LS (AP) 80; *Ghul Md. Phalwan* v. *Aziz Sheikh,* AIR 1976 J & K 49 : 1976 Kash LJ 51.
5. See *Mohamed Abdur Rahim* v. *Birju Sahu,* 5 BLR 676 : 14 WR 103; *Sheikh Gulam Ali* v. *Gazi Mahomed Zahur Alam,* 6 BLR (App) 76; *Kalee Pershad Shaha* v. *Ram Pershad Shaha,* 18 WR 14; *Sri Narain Choudhry* v. *Jadoonath Choudhary,* 5 CWN 147; *Mahomed Shabbir* v. *Mahomed Jawad,* 15 IC 270.
6. *Mani Shankar* v. *Tikaram,* 5 Bom HC (ACJ) 42; *Kurvarji* v. *Bal Javar,* 6 Bom HC (ACJ) 143; *Keshva* v. *Ganpat,* 8 Bom HC (ACJ) 87; *Srinivas* v. *Reid,* 9 Bom HC (ACJ) 266; *Manjaldas* v. *Jiwan Ram,* 23 Bom 675; *Gokul Prasad* v. *Radho,* 10 All 358; *Abdul Rahman* v. *D. Emile,* 16 All 69; *Abdul Rahman* v. *Bhagwan Das,* 19 All 582; *Komathi* v. *Gurunadha Pillai,* 3 Mad HC 141; *see* also 6 IC 398; *Fazal Haq* v. *Fazal Haq,* AIR 1928 All 201; *Bhagwan Dass* v. *Parmeshwar,* 1971 AWR 474; *Basai* v. *Hasan Raza Khan,* AIR 1963 All 340; *Diwan Singh* v. *Inderjeet,* AIR 1981 All 342 : 1981 All WC 533 : (1981) 7 All LR 469; *Chintala Krishnamurty* v. *Uppala Rajlingam,* AIR 1980 AP 69 : 1980 LS (AP) 80; *Ghul Md. Phalwan* v. *Aziz Sheikh,* AIR 1976 J. & K. 49 : 1976 Kash. LJ 51; *Abir Chand Gulab Chand Jain* v. *Manik Ram Narain Tailor,* 1978 MPLJ 204.

it clear that a right of privacy can be acquired as a customary easement. In order to entitle the plaintiff to a decree for a mandatory injunction directing the defendant to close the window put up in his own property, the plaintiff must establish that there is such a customary right in the town where the properties are located that no owner or occupier of house can open a new window therein so as to substantially invade his neighbour's privacy. The plaintiff therefore, has to plead and prove that there is a custom in the town where the properties are situate that no owner or occupier of a house can open a new window therein so as to substantially invade his neighbour's privacy. He has further to establish that the plaintiff has enjoyed such customary right of privacy and that there is an infringement or a threat to the infringement of such a right.

Right to neighbour's property to repair partition wall

A right to repair boundary wall from his neighbour's side can only be considered as a customary easement and must be exercised at such a time and in such a manner as not to cause any inconvenience to the neighbour.[1]

Mohammedans' right to bury dead.—The right of Mohammadans of a village to bury dead in another man's land is a customary right which can be established by immemorial user.[2]

Right of pasturage.—A right of pasturage by villagers can be claimed as a customary right.[3]

Customary rights and res judicata.—Ordinarily adjudications of questions of title or rights and granting declaratory relief consequent upon such adjudication are not undertaken in a writ petition under Article 32 of the Constitution and such a petition is usually entertained for enforcement of existing or established title or rights or infringement or encroachment thereof. But where enforcement of customary right to perform religious rights, practices, observances and functions on plots which have already been adjudicated by decisions of competent civil Courts in earlier litigation is claimed, the Court would entertain writ petition and consider it on merits. Whatever reliefs the petitioners are

1. *S. Mudaliar* v. *P. Mudaliar*, AIR 1956 Mad 577.
2. *Ramzan Momin* v. *Desrath Raut*, AIR 1953 Pat 138.
3. *N.G. Dutta* v. *K.C. Banerjee*, AIR 1952 Cal 108.

entitled legally would be granted to them.

It is well settled that Section 11 of Civil Procedure Code is not exhaustive of this general doctrine of rule of *res judicata*. The section is not exhaustive with respect to an earlier decision on the general principle of *res judicata*, any previous decision on a matter in controversy, decided after full contest or after affording fair opportunity to the parties to prove their case, by a Court competent to decide it, will operate as *res judicata* in a subsequent suit. "It is not necessary that the Court deciding the matter formerly be competent to decide the subsequent suit or that the former proceeding and the subsequent suit have the same subject matter. The nature of the former proceeding is immaterial." It was *held* that the customary right of the Shia community to perform religious rites was established by earlier decree of a Court and would operate as *res judicata* in subsequent proceedings.[1]

Right of way.—It was held that the right of using the edges (mainds) of each other's fields for going to their respective fields by the agriculturists is a customary right of easement and not a right of easement which is to be acquired either by prescription or by necessity.[2]

No right flowing from a custom.—Court of law does not know of cases where the plaintiff claims a right flowing from a custom is or can be himself the progenitor of the custom. From the nature of things, a custom is something the originator of which is known to none by certainty. Ex-hypothesis, therefore, plaintiff cannot claim to have started a custom. He may start a practice but the practice cannot lead to the legal consequence to which a custom leads.[3]

19. Transfer of dominant heritage passes easement.—Where the dominant heritage is transferred or devolves, by act of parties or by operation of law, the transfer or devolution shall, unless a contrary intention appears, be deemed to pass the easement to the person in whose favour the transfer or devolution takes place.

1. *Ghulam Abbas* v. *State of U.P.*, AIR 1981 SC 2198 at pp. 2202-2208, 2212, 2213 : 1981 Cr. LJ 1835 following; *Gulabchand Chotalal Parikh* v. *State of Bombay*, AIR 1965 SC 1153.
2. *Rup Chand* v. *Sh. Daulatu*, AIR 1992 H.P. 6.
3. *Smt. Radha Krishna Kandolkar* v. *Tukaram Pundalik Homkhandi*, AIR 1991 Bom 119.

Illustration

A has certain land to which a right of way is annexed. *A* lets the land to *B* for twenty years. The right of way vests in *B* and his legal representative so long as the lease continues.

NOTES

This section lays down that a transfer or devolution of a property which may be due to act of parties or by operation of law, will convey to the person in whose favour the transfer or devolution takes place all those easements which are annexed or are appurtenant to the heritage transfered, unless a contrary intention appears. If nothing is mentioned in the instrument of transfer, all easements enjoyed before the transfer will pass to the transferee and in this respect this section enjoins upon the transferor to have the transfer deed drafted very carefully to avoid future litigation.

Various ways in which easements may be acquired

(1) **By grant.** *Example.*—A is a tenant of B's land for twenty years. A has right to transfer his interest under the lease. A may impose an easement on the land to continue during the time that the lease exists. (Section 8).

(2) **By necessity.**—*Example.*—On severance of a piece of land into two portions it may be absolutely necessary to have a right of way over one portion for reaching the other portion. (Section 13).

(3) **By quasi-necessity.**—Easements which may be necessary (not absolutely necessary) for enjoying the land as it was enjoyed before severance. (Section 13).

(4) **By prescription.** (Section 15).

(5) **By custom.** (Section 18).

(6) **By transfer of dominant heritage.**—Because by transfer of an heritage, easements attached to it also pass to the transferee unless a contrary intention appears.

(7) **Easements may be acquired by immemorial user.**

(8) **Easements may be acquired by legislative enactment.**

Section 19 covers all cases of transfer or devolution of property.—Section 19 is most comprehensive and covers all cases of transfer or devolution of property, by an act of parties or by operation of law, whether voluntary as in the case of voluntary sale[1] mortgage,[2] lease[3] etc., or involuntary as in the case of execution sale[4] foreclosure, etc. whether *inter vivos* as by gift, endowment or after death as by inheritance, survivorship or bequest. It is not necessary to mention the transfer of easement with dominant heritage to the purchaser in the sale deed.[5]

Severance of dominant tenement.—If a severance of the dominant tenement takes place, all its easements which are attached to the tenement, and not to the person of the owner, will attach to the severed portions.[6] It is obvious, however, that by such severance, no right is acquired to impose an additional burden on the servient tenement.[7] However, numerous the occupants of the severed tenements may be, they must still confine themselves within the limits of the right existing at the time of severance.

Effect of transfer of servient heritage.—As the benefit of an easement passes with the dominant tenement into the hands of every subsequent owner of that tenement, similarly the burden of it passes with the servient tenement to every person into whose occupation the servient tenement comes[8] and in the latter case even though a contrary intention appears.

Proof of easement by grant.—In the present matter, there was acquisition of easement by grant by predecessor-in-interest of plaintiffs over suit passage as apparent from deed of conveyance. The defendants had acquired property long after predecessor-in-interest of plaintiffs. Use of passage had never been discontinued. Factum

---

1. *Nubeen* v. *Bhoobun*, 15 WR 526; *Govind* v. *Haji*, (1885) B.P.J. 20.
2. *Vishnu* v. *Rango*, 18 B 382.
3. *Amjudee Begum* v. *Ahmed Hussain*, 6 WR 314.
4. *Huree Madhub* v. *Hem Chunder*, 22 WR 522.
5. *Gundali Basavaniyappa* v. *G.S. Basavaraja*, (1996) 1 Civil Court Cases 303 at 306 (Karn).
6. *Harris* v. *Drewe*, (1831) 2 B & Ad. 164; *Codlin* v. *Johnson*, (1829) 9 B & C 933, and *Newcomen* v. *Coulson*, (1877) 5 Ch D., 141 (as to right of way); *Midland Ry* v. *Gribble*, (1895) 2 Ch 827, where the way was erected for the purpose of affording communication between the two tenements while in the same hands. And cf. as to Commons, *Tyringham's case*, (1584) 4 Rep. 36b; *Wyat Wild's cases*, (1610) 8 Rep. 78b.
7. *Bower* v. *Hill*, (1835) 1 Bing. N.C. 549. Compare the Scottish case of *Menzies* v. *Macdonald*, (1856) 2 Jur. (NS) 575.
8. *Leech* v. *Schweder*, 9 Ch App 474 (475).

of user by plaintiff coupled with documentary evidence had unmistakably substantiated easement by grant. Therefore, concurrent findings of fact that no easement by grant was created was improper.[1]

---

1 *Nirmal Das* v. *Panchanan Banerji*, AIR 2001 Cal 37.

CHAPTER III

INCIDENTS OF EASEMENTS

20. Rules controlled by contract or title.—The rules contained in this chapter are controlled by any contract between the dominant and servient owners relating to the servient heritage, and by the provisions of the instrument or decree, if any, by which the easement referred to was imposed.

Incidents of customary easements.—And when any incident of any customary easement is inconsistent with such rules nothing in this chapter shall affect such incident.

NOTES

Section 20 lays down that rules contained in Chapter III of the Easements Act are not of universal application but will apply only when a contract between the parties or a decree which created or imposed an easement right, fails to define, limit or to regulate by its expressed or implied provisions the extent or scope of the user permitted under its terms. But where the contract between the parties or the decree of the court clearly defines the way in which the easement right is to be exercised or the burden over the servient heritage is to be imposed, the rules laid down in this chapter would have no application. By virtue of Section 20 if there is anything in the agreement between the dominant and servient owners then the other sections of that Chapter (i.e., Sections 20 to 31) will have no operation.[1]

21. Bar to use unconnected with enjoyment.—An easement must not be used for any purpose not connected with the enjoyment of dominant heritage.

Illustrations

(a) *A*, as owner of farm *Y*, has a right of way

1. *Balram Das Goswami* v. *Puran Chandra Rath*, AIR 1975 Orissa 88.

over *B*'s land to *Y*. Lying beyond *Y*, *A* has another farm *Z* the beneficial enjoyment of which is not necessary for the beneficial enjoyment of *Y*. He must not use the easement for the purpose of passing to and from *Z*.

(b) *A*, as owner of a certain house, has a right of way to and from it. For the purpose of passing to and from the house, the right may be used, not only by *A* but by the members of his family, lodgers, servants, workmen, visitors and customers; for this is a purpose connected with the enjoyment of the dominant heritage. So, if *A* lets the house, he may use the right of way for the purpose of collecting the rent and seeing that the house is kept in repair.

NOTES

A easement right exists for the beneficial use of a dominant tenement and it cannot be enjoyed for purposes unconnected with the enjoyment of the dominant tenement.

A right to free passage of light and air is merely a right to prevent the servient owner from causing discomfort to the dominant owner by laying obstructions thereto. It does not entitle the dominant owner to create new rights by using his heritage for extraordinary purposes.[1]

A misuser of an easement by the dominant owner does not necessarily result in a forfeiture of the easement, or authorise the servient owner to obstruct it but the dominant owner becomes liable for damage resulting from a misuser of the easement, and an injunction.[2]

22. Exercise of easement—Confinement of exercise of easement.—The dominant owner must exercise his right in the mode which is least onerous to the servient owner; and when the exercise of an easement can without detriment to the dominant owner be confined to a determinate part of the servient heritage, such exercise shall, at the request of the servient owner, be so confined.

Illustrations

(a) *A* has a right of way over *B*'s field. *A* must

1. *David Sasoon & Co.* v. *Edulje Dinshaw*, 1 IC 961.
2. *See* Section 31 of the Act.

enter the way at either end and not any intermediate point.

(b) *A* has a right annexed to his house to cut thatching grass in *B*'s swamp. *A*, when exercising his easement, must cut the grass so that the plants may not be destroyed.

NOTES

Section 22 lays down that every easement right should be exercised in a way which is 'least onerous' to the servient owner. Where the exercise of the easement right can be confined to a determinate part of the servient tenement without any detriment to the dominant owner, the dominant owner shall do it at the request of the servient owner. The reason is that an easement right imposes a burden on the servient heritage and it is but reasonable that the dominant owner should be enjoined not to increase the burden by indiscriminate use of his right, e.g., A has a right of way over B's field. A must enter the way at either end and not at any intermediate point because that would make the whole servient tenement useless for the owner.

"Least onerous mode of enjoyment."—The least onerous mode of enjoyment of his right by the dominant owner is that which might be expected from the full owner of the servient tenement himself had he any occasion to enjoy the same right. The test of conduct of the dominant owner is what a reasoable man would do under similar circumstances on his own land.

Remedies for an excessive or improper user.—If the owner of an easement exceeds his rightful user or does anything which would, after long user, produce an increased right, the servient owner may, in all cases obstruct or prevent the excessive user or new mode of enjoyment, if he can do so without obstructing the rightful user.[1] Section 31, *post* confers on a servient owner the right of obstruction in the case of excessive user. But if the obstruction or the prevention of the excessive user or new mode of enjoyment involves the obstruction of rightful user also he should seek the aid of a law Court for restraining the dominant owner from such excessive user or new mode of enjoyment and if instead of doing so, he stops such user or enjoyment himself, thereby

1. Goddard, p. 349 citing *Greenslade* v. *Halliday*, 6 Bing. 379; *Esa Abbas* v. *Jacob Harron*, 4 IC 425.

obstructing the rightful user also, he is liable for damages to the dominant owner,[1] and cannot plead justification on the ground of the excessive user or new mode of enjoyment by the dominant owner. Besides as excessive user can only be obstructed by the servient owner on his own land he cannot enter the dominant tenement, or do anything there to prevent the user. If he does so he would be liable for trespass.[2]

23. Right to alter mode of enjoyment.—Subject to the provisions of Section 22, the dominant owner may, from time to time, alter the mode and place of enjoying the easement, provided that he does not thereby impose any additional burden on the servient heritage.

Exception.—The dominant owner of a right of way cannot vary his line of passage at pleasure, even though he does not thereby impose any additional burden on the servient heritage.

Illustrations

(a) *A* the owner of a saw-mill, has a right to a flow of water sufficient to work the mill. He may convert the saw-mill into a corn-mill, provided that it can be worked by the same amount of water.

(b) *A* has right to discharge on *B*'s land the rain water from the eaves of *A*'s house. This does not entitle *A* to advance his eaves if, by so doing, he imposes a greater burden on *B*'s land.

(c) *A*, as the owner of a paper-mill, acquires a right to pollute a stream by pouring in the refuse liquor produced by making in the mill-paper from rags. He may pollute the stream by pouring in similar liquor produced by making in the mill-paper by a new process from babmoos, provided that he does not substantially increase the amount, or injuriously change the nature of the pollution.

(d) *A*, a riparian owner, acquires as against the lower riparian owners, a prescriptive right to pollute a stream by throwing sawdust into it. This does not

1. *Greenslade* v. *Halliday*, 6 Bing. 379.
2. Goddard, pp. 349-50; *see* also Section 31, infra, and *Tapling* v. *Jones*, 11 HLC 290.

entitle *A* to pollute the stream by discharging into it poisonous liquor.

NOTES

An easement right exists for the enjoyment of his tenement by the dominant owner. Section 23 lays down that the dominant owner is free to alter the mode and place of enjoying the easement from time to time provided he does not thereby impose any additional burden on the servient heritage. The only exception has been made in the case of a right of way, in which case the enjoyer cannot change his line of passage at his pleasure, even though the change may not impose any additional burden on the servient heritage.

It should also be clear that it is the duty of every dominant owner not only to avoid placing by altered mode of user any additional burden on the servient heritage but further to exercise his right even under the altered circumstances in the way "least onerous to the servient owner". In other words, the dominant owner while altering the mode and place of enjoying the easement is not only to see that by his action he is not imposing any additional burden on the servient tenement but he should also see that by his altered mode of enjoyment he is not placing any such burden on the servient heritage which can be avoided.

Since an easement constitutes a restriction on the right of property of the servient owner, the dominant owner can make no alteration in the dimensions, location, or use of the easement which would increase such restrictions, or make the condition of the servient tenement worse except with the previous consent of the servient owner. Mere matters of convenience do not justify such alterations. Thus, the dominant owner cannot construct a concrete pavement over a way without the consent of the servient owner, even though such improvement would benefit the latter's property.[1]

On the other hand, there is nothing in the nature of an easement, apart from an express prohibition, which prevents all changes during the course of its enjoyment. So long as the use is confined to the purposes under which the easement was acquired or created without increasing the burden on the servient tenement, the dominant owner may make changes that do not impair or otherwise affect its substance, and may effect such alterations as would render it effectual.[2]

1. *Lorene* v. *Swiderski*, 156 A 465.
2. *Graham* v. *Philox*, (1984) 2 All ER 643 (655).

Right of eavesdroppings.—The right of eavesdroppings will not be lost by raising the house. The occupier of a house who has a right to have the rain-water fall from the eaves of it upon another man's land cannot by spouts discharge it upon such land in a body.[1]

The defendant had a right to discharge water from thatched roof to the plaintiff's roof. He pulled down his house and built a three stories pucca house with spouts on his roof to discharge water on the plaintiff's land. *Held*, that the burden on the plaintiff's land was increased within the meaning of Section 28.[2]

24. Right to do acts, to secure enjoyment.—The dominant owner is entitled, as against the servient owner, to do all acts necessary to secure the full enjoyment of the easement; but such acts must be done at such time and in such manner as, without detriment to the dominant owner, to cause the servient owner as little inconvenience as possible; and the dominant owner must repair, as far as practicable, the damage (if any) caused by the servient heritage.

Accessory rights.—Rights to do acts necessary to secure the full enjoyment of an easement are called accessory rights.

Illustrations

(a) *A* has an easement to lay pipes in *B*'s land to convey water to *A*'s cistern. *A* may enter and dig the land in order to mend the pipes, but he must restore the surface to its original state.

(b) *A* has an easement of a drain through *B*'s land. The sewer with which the drain communicates is altered. *A* may enter upon *B*'s land and alter drain, to adapt it to the new sewer, provided that he does not thereby impose any additional burden on *B*'s land.

(c) *A*, as owner of certain house, has a right of way over *B*'s land. The way is out of repair, or a tree is blown and falls across it. *A* may enter on *B*'s land,

1. *Noor Bux* v. *Abdul Samad*, 1957 MPC 279.
2. *Damodar Das* v. *Tilak Chand*, 13 ALJ 791.

repair the way or remove the tree from it.

(d) *B*, as owner of certain field, has a right of way over *B*'s land. *B* renders the way impossible. *A* may deviate from the way and pass over the adjoining land of *B*, provided that the deviation is reasonable.

(e) *A*, as owner of a certain house, has a right of way over *B*'s field, *A* may remove rocks to make the way.

(f) *A* has an easement of support from *B*'s wall. The wall gives way. *A* may enter upon *B*'s land and repair the wall.

(g) *A* has an easement to have his land flooded by means of a dam in *B*'s stream. The dam is half swept away by an inundation. *A* may enter upon *B*'s land and repair the dam.

NOTES

Accessory rights.—Rights to do acts necessary to secure the full enjoyment of an easement are called accessory rights. They are sometimes called "Accessory easements" or "Secondary easements". A dominant owner is free to do all such act on the servient tenement as are accessory to secure the fullest possible enjoyment of the easement, but he cannot act in a manner as to impose a greater burden on the servient tenement. He must take all possible precautions to see that he exercises his acts at such time and in such manner that least inconvenience is caused to the servient owner. If by the exercise of an accessory right some damage is caused to the servient owner, the dominant owner must repair as far as possible the damage so caused.

Nature and extent of accessory rights.—The nature and extent of the accessory rights vary with the nature and extent of the easement to which they are accessory, and rest upon the terms of the grant by which the easement is created or on the user which gives rise to it. Thus, a person, who has a right of easement to lay pipes on another's land to convey water to his cistern, has also a right to dig the land and mend the pipe.[1] A person having right of way has the accessory right to take necessary steps to level the pathway or to prevent

1. *Imperatrix* v. *Vanmali*, 22 B 525; *Pomfret* v. *Ricroft*, 1 Saund 223; see *Goodhart* v. *Hyett*, (1883) 50 LT 95 : 25 Ch D 182; *see* Illustration (a).

erosion.[1] Similarly, if a person has an easement of drain through another's land to a sewer and the position of the sewer is altered by order of some public authority so that the old drain does not fit in with the new sewer, he has a right to enter upon the servient tenement and alter the drain so as to adapt it to the new sewer.[2] He is also entitled to supervise and cleanse the drain from time to time as the necessity arises.[3] A dominant owner was allowed to convert a *kachha* drain into a *pucca* one at his cost, flowing on servient tenement.[4] So a person having an easement of support from another's wall is entitled to enter the land of such other person and repair the wall if it gives way.[5] So a person who has a right of way on another's land has also the right to keep the way in repair[6] and remove obstacles[7] and in case an obstruction is laid by the servient owner so as to render it impassable, he has also a right to deviate from the way and pass over the adjoining land of the servient owner provided he does not thereby cause unreasonable and unnecessary loss to the servient owner.[8]

Nature and extent of accessory rights.—In terms of right of way or right of access, the appellant cannot seek new grant to use vehicles in the holy road under the pretext of reasonable purposes.[9]

25. Liability for expenses necessary for preservation of easement.—The expenses incurred in the constructing works, or making repairs, or doing any other act necessary for the use or preservation of an easement, must be defrayed by the dominant owner.

NOTES

The servient owner is under no personal obligation to do

1. *Anchan, O.S.* v. *Grace W. Enthat*, AIR 1982 Kant. 14 : (1981) 1 Kant. LJ 250 : 1981 Civ. LJ 282.
2. *Finlinson* v. *Porter*, 32 LT 391; *See* Illustration (b).
3. *Rameshwar* v. *Kunj Behari*, 4 C 644; *Sultani* v. *Ram Saran*, 1900 PR 49.
4. *Gajadhar* v. *Bhai Khan*, 1979 All LJ 538.
5. *Colebeck* v. *Girdlers Co.*, 34 LT 350; *Gerrard* v. *Cooke*, 2 B & P (NR) 109; *Taylor* v. *Whitehead*, 2 Doug. KB 745; *Ingram* v. *Morecraft*, 33 Beav. 49; *see* Illustration (f).
6. *See* Illustration (c).
7. *See* Illustrations (e) and (f).
8. Goddard, p. 396; *see* Illustration (d); *Laxman* v. *Tukia*, 44 IC 868 (N); *Hawkins* v. *Carbines*, 27 LJ Exch. 44; *Dawes* v. *Hawkins*, 8 C.B.N.S. 848.
9. *Loordhu Mary* v. *Bishop of Tanjore Society*, AIR 2007 Mad 98 (1010).

anything for the convenient enjoyment by the dominant owner of his easement right, unless the servient owner binds hiself by an express agreement to do so. It is in the interest of the dominant owner to preserve all those things which are necessary for the enjoyment of his easement right and therefore he should spend for them also. Because "he who has the use of a thing ought to repair it."

26. Liability for damage from want of repair.—Where an easement is enjoyed by means of an artificial work, the dominant owner is liable to make compensation for any damage to the servient heritage arising from the want of repair of such work.

NOTES

If the enjoyment of an easement right is to be had by means of an artificial work, the dominant owner is under a duty to keep the work in proper repair so as not to cause damage to the servient tenement. If for want of repair of the work, some damage is caused to the servient tenement, the dominant owner is bound to compensation for the same.

27. Servient owner not bound to do anything.—The servient owner is not bound to do anything for the benefit of the dominant heritage, and he is entitled, as against the dominant owner, to use the servient heritage in any way, consistent with the enjoyment of the easement; but he must not do any act tending to restrict the easement, or to render its exercise less convenient.

Illustrations

(a) *A* as owner of a house, has a right to lead water and send sewage through *B*'s land. *B* is not bound, as servient owner, to clear the watercourse or scour the sewer.

(b) *A* grants a right of way through his land to *B*, as owner of a field. *A* may feed his cattle on grass growing on the way, provided that *B*'s right of way is not thereby obstructed; but he must not build a wall at the end of his land so as to prevent *B* from going beyond it, nor must he narrow the way so as to render the exercise of the right less easy than it was at the date of the grant.

(c) *A*, in respect of his house, is entitled to an easement of support from *B*'s wall. *B* is not bound as servient owner to keep the wall standing and in repair. But he must not pull down or weaken the wall as to make it incapable of rendering the necessary support.

(d) *A*, in respect of his mill, is entitled to a watercourse through *B*'s land. *B* must not drive stakes so as to obstruct the watercourse.

(e) *A*, in respect of his house, is entitled to a certain quantity of light passing over *B*'s land. *B* must not plant trees so as to obstruct the passing to *A*'s windows of that quantity of light.

NOTES

The servient owner is under no personal obligation to do anything for the benefit of the dominant owner. He is free to use his tenement in any way he likes provided it is not inconsistent with the enjoyment of his easement by the dominant owner. The servient owner is prohibited from doing anything which may render the easement incapable or more difficult of enjoyment. Thus where A, in respect of his house, is entitled to an easement of support from B's wall, B is not bound as servient owner to keep the wall standing and in repair. But he must not pull down or weaken the wall so as to make it incapable of the necessary support.

28. Extent of easements.—With respect to the extent of easements and the mode of their enjoyment, the following provisions shall take effect.

Easements of necessity.—An easement of necessity is co-extensive with the necessity as it existed when the easement was imposed.

Other easements.—The extent of any other easement and the mode of its enjoyment must be fixed with reference to the probable intention of the parties, and the purpose for which the rights were imposed or acquired.

In the absence of evidence as to such intention and purpose—

(a) **Right of way.**—A right of way of any one kind does not include a right of way of any other kind.

(b) **Right to light or air acquired by grant.**—The extent of a right to the passage of light or air to a certain window, door or other opening imposed by a testamentary or non-testamentary instrument, is the quantity of light or air that entered the opening at the time the testator died or the non-testamentary instrument was made.

(c) **Prescriptive right to light or air.**—The extent of a prescriptive right to the passage of light or air to a certain window, door or other opening is that quantity of light or air which has been accustomed to enter that opening during the whole of the prescriptive period irrespective of the purposes for which it has been used.

(d) **Prescriptive right to pollute air and water.**—The extent of a prescriptive right to pollute air or water is the extent of pollution at the commencement of the period of user on completion of which the right arose; and

(e) **Other prescriptive rights.**—The extent of every other prescriptive right and the mode of its enjoyment must be determined by the accustomed user of the right.

NOTES

Section 28 lays down certain rules for determining the extent of easements and the mode of their enjoyment.

Right of easement.—'A' gifted a house to defendant and a certain extent of land to the south of the plaintiff leaving a *gali* (lane) between the house gifted to defendant and the land gifted to plaintiff. In the deed of gift executed in favour of the plaintiff, it was expressly recited that there were windows, *jalis & parnalas* of the house gifted to defendant opening into the adjacent land and therefore for the enjoyment of the windows. *Jalis & parnalas* a strip of land was left out as a *gali*. In order to avoid any future trouble, 'A' took the further step of transferring the *gali* to the defendant. The plaintiff started raising constructions on the land gifted to him. He opened doors and windows into the *gali*. As his privacy was being invaded by the opening of the doors and windows into the *gali* the defendant put up a wall in the *gali*. Thereupon the plaintiff claiming a right of easement filed a suit to restrain the defendant from raising any wall which would obstruct this right to light and air through doors and windows opened by into the *gali*. *Held* that there was no grant of easement by implication in favour of the plaintiff and the defendant could put up the wall.[1]

Easement of necessity.—An easement of necessity is co-extensive with the necessity as it existed when the easement was imposed. It cannot be enlarged beyond the requirement of absolute necessity known to the grantor at the time of the grant. It is a settled law both in India and England that a easement of necessity cannot be converted into an easement of convenience, which might change its character frequently according to the whims and needs of the dominant owner.

In the case of an easement other than an easement of necessity the mode of its enjoyment must be fixed with reference to the probable intention of the parties, and the purpose for which the right was imposed or acquired.

Framing of issues.—In a suit for easementary rights the plaintiff claimed right of way on disputed property. Two defendants claimed ownership over the disputed land. There was no need to frame issue as to who is real owner. The issue framed by trial court and finding given by first appellate court on said issue was liable to be set aside.[2]

Right to light and air.—In suit for damages for obstruction of easement of light and air the dominant owner (plaintiff) must prove that there has been diminution in the quantity of light and air which used to enter his house during the whole of the prescriptive period and that such diminution has made the occupation of the house uncomfortable or unsuitable for carrying on his business as beneficially as he was doing before. Mere diminution in the quantity of light and air does not give cause for action.

Section 28 which confers the right of easement has to be read with Section 33 of the Act which indicates the extent and the limitation under which the right of easement is enjoyed. Indeed if Section 28 is completely divorced from the scope of Sections 33 and 35 then the two sections would run contradictory to each other and this will be against the rule

1. *Mst. Kamla & others* v. *Bhanwarlal Vaid & others*, AIR 1985 SC 473.
2. *Krishna* v. *Shiv Lal*, 2011 AIR CC 828 (829) (HP).

of harmonious interpretation of statutes. Section 28 merely indicates in what measure a right of easement of light or air can be acquired but how that right is to be actually enforced when disturbed is laid down in Sections 33 and 35 of the Act.

An injunction can be granted by the Court where the plaintiff claims that his right of easement is disturbed, only when the plaintiff is able to show that there has been a sufficient diminution of his right to receive light and air and that such diminution has caused sufficient damage or amounts to actionable nuisance so as to materially affect the physical comfort and health of the plaintiff.[1] On an analysis of Sections 28, 33 & 35, the Allahabad High Court has held in all the above three cases that the plaintiff must establish a substantial injury or deprivation of his right sufficient to render the use and occupation of his house inconvenient or uncomfortable according to the ordinary requirements of mankind. These cases do lay down in clear terms that it is not enough to allege and prove that there has been a reduction in the quantum of air and light in the physical sense by the acts complained of by the plaintiffs. The plaintiff must further prove that the curtailment of right has been so substantial as to render a comfortable living or use of the residence of course judged by ordinary notions impossible.[2]

In this regard there is a good case of *Uthramma C.K. Basanti Thampurithy* v. *M. Krishna Pannikar*,[3] In this case, right to use a land of a particular community as a burial ground for years (from the immemorial) has been considered as a customary right by the Kerala High Court.

Easement of rain water drainage.—If the defendant claims an easement to drain rain water by making a hole in the plaintiff's wall, then he has to prove acquisition of that easement, otherwise the plaintiff can stop him by way of injunction.[4]

Extent of right to light or air acquired by grant.—If the plaintiff has been receiving light and air through his two ventilators for over the statutory period and has thus acquired

1. *Kasturi Lal* v. *Krishan Chand*, AIR 1971 JK 27; *Ram Narayan Ram* v. *Ram Dhani Ram*, 1973 AWR (HC) 173, *Suraj Narain* v. *Kalyan Das*, AIR 1929 Allahabad 430 and *Shambhu Prasad* v. *Mahadeo Prasad*, AIR 1933 Allahabad 493.
2. *See* also *Chapsi Bhai Dhanji Bhai Daud* v. *Purushottam*, AIR 1971 SC 1878; *Smt. Phulwati Devi* v. *Munna Lal*, AIR 1982 Allahabad 20.
3. AIR 1998 Kerala 149.
4. *Sabu Yela Anjnayulu* v. *U. Laxman*, AIR 2006 (NOC) 660 AP.

easementary right, he is entitled to get light and air through the said ventilators though he might be getting enough light and air by other means.[1]

But there is something in the instrument itself, as to the extent and mode of enjoyment, the terms of the deed, and not this rule, will be the proper guide fixing such extent and mode of enjoyment, as the rule applies only when there is no evidence as to the intention of the parties and the purpose for which the right was created.[2]

Questions as to the extent of right to light or air which has been acquired by grant, have been of rare occurrence and there is but little authority on the subject. [*See* Goddard, p. 357.] The reason perhaps is that the extent is usually provided for by the deed and there is seldom an occasion for dispute. Besides, these rights are more frequently acquired by prescription or as quasi-easement under Section 13 by an implied reservation than by an express grant. Opinion of Mellish, L.J., in *Kelk* v. *Pearson*,[3] that the nature and extent of right to light acquired by grant, express or implied, is precisely the same as if the rights were acquired by prescription, has not been accepted by the Indian Legislature as good law. Hence, a separate provision has been made in clause (c) for determining the extent of the rights acquired by prescription. It has also been doubted in England and the recent authorities appear to doubt its accuracy.[4]

Extent of prescriptive right to light and air.—Clause (c) of Section 28 vests in the owner of the dominant tenement a right to claim that he must receive his prescriptive share of light or air through the defined passage.[5]

The use of the words "window, door or other opening" in clause (c) shows that the Indian law, unlike the English law[6] expressly regards a door as an opening for the passage of light. Therefore, according to the Indian law, the prescriptive right to light and air can be acquired even through a door.[7]

---

1. *Santhannagiri Ramayya* v. *Narsinhapuram Narayana Chetty*, AIR 1968 Andh Pra 151.
2. See *Ganga Charan Dhar* v. *Satkrit Lal Dey*, 133 IC 214 : A.I.R 1932 Cal 118 : 53 CLJ 604.
3. 24 LT 890.
4. *See* Goddard, p. 357.
5. *Shanker* v. *Dattaraya*, 131 IC 429 : AIR 1931 Nag. 80.
6. *See* Halsbury's Laws of England, 4th Ed., Vol. 14, p. 110, Para. 228 and Gale on Easements, 13th Ed., p. 220.
7. *Veerappa Mallappa* v. *Nagappa Jakirappa*, A.I.R 1965 Mys. 292.

Whatever the nature of the aperture, it defines the area which is to be kept free over the servient tenement. However, it does not permit dominant owner to open new door for air and light.[1]

The right of air is co-extensive with the right to light. The principle, therefore, is that easements acquired by ancient light or air is not measured by the amount of light, and air enjoyed during the period of prescription. The owner of the dominant tenement obtains a right to so much of it as will suffice for the ordinary purposes of inhabitancy or business according to the ordinary notions of mankind having regard to the locality and surroundings. He does not obtain by his easement a right to all the light or air which he has enjoyed.[2] There is no infringement of the right, unless what is done amounts to a nuisance.[3]

Section 28 of the Act is not to be taken in isolation, but must be read along with the provisions of Sections 33 and 35. From such a combined reading it follows that the diminution of a person's right of easements becomes actionable not merely from the fact of disturbance but also because it has caused substantial damage to him. No damage, however, is substantial in cases of infringement of an easement of light unless (1) it is likely to injure the plaintiff by affecting the evidence of the easement or materially diminishes the value of the dominant heritage, or (2) materially interferes with the physical comfort of the plaintiff, or (3) prevent him from carrying on his accustomed business on the dominant heritage as beneficially as he had done previous to the institution of the suit. Further according to Explanation III, the inter-damage in the case of disturbance of an easement of air is only such as it interferes with the physical comfort of the plaintiff though it may not be injurious to his health.[4]

Even in cases where a plaintiff complains of invasion of the right to light acquired by easement, Sections 28, 33 and 35 of the Easements Act shall be kept in view and read

1. *K.S. Kamal* v. *Surinder Kumar*, (1995) 2 Sim. LJ 1278 at 1280 (1995) 1 Punj LR 470 (P & H).
2. *Bunsidhar* v. *Matru Mal*, 1959 Pat LR 92 : 1959 BLJR 311 : AIR 1959 Pat 517; *Umrao Kunwar* v. *Ram Pyari*, ILR (1959) 9 Raj 602 : AIR 1959 Raj 235.
3. *Bunsidhar* v. *Matru Mal*, AIR 1959 Pat 517; *Shiv Pratap Singh* v. *Prem Narain*, 1978 All LJ 304 : 1978 All WC 87; *Bhulawati Devi* v. *Munna Lal*, (1982) Civ LJ 98 (All); *(Smt.) Laxmibai* v. *(Smt.) Kashibai Pannranga Salagaonkar*, AIR 1983 NOC 57 (Kant) : (1982) 1 Kant LJ 229; *Chandranadivelue Chettiar* v. *Vadappa Chetty*, (1975) 1 Mad LJ 401 : 77 LW 99.
4. *Devinder Kumar* v. *Chatro Devi*, AIR 1966 Punj 502.

together. When so read, interference with light and air which is not substantial does not give a cause of action to a person entitled to the right. To determine whether an act which is complained of as being of nuisance is strictly so or not is to be judged by the ordinary standards of persons residing in the neighbourhood and the criterion would be the ordinary physical comfort of human existence according to plain, sober and simple notions obtaining amongst people and not according to the elegant and dainty modes and habits of living. It is not the standard of a petulant, cynical, hypersensitive or fastidious person that should furnish a guide but of a person who expects to enjoy the ordinary comforts of decent and healthy life in the local area where he resides. It is possible that some inconvenience or discomfort may be caused but it must be of a substantial character to warrant legal interference. Injury complained of must be material.[1]

Easement of necessity.—Where aggrieved party could not prove that disputed path was creating any disturbance for him, it was held that no case of easement was made out.[2]

Deprivation of easementary rights of air and light.—The plaintiff and defendant's houses were adjacent to each other. Finding of fact was recorded by trial Court that extension of balcony on first floor by defendant had deprived easementary rights of air and light to house of plaintiff. Held that defendant would not be entitled to take advantage of interlocutory orders passed by Court in miscellaneous application for grant of police aid. The fact that unauthorised construction of defendant was subsequently regularised would not in any way alter the situation. Therefore, plaintiff was entitled to mandatory injunction directing removal of portion of balcony.[3]

Injunction.—Although a decree for permanent injunction is not transferable against purchaser, from the judgment-debtor because injunction being *personam* does not transfer with land, a transferee judgment-debtor has to follow the decree respecting the decree-holder's easementary right, same as his predecessors were bound by the decree.[4]

Easement by grant, inference of.—The parks, roads,

1. *Krushna Kishore* v. *Sankarsan*, AIR 1974 Ori. 89 (FB) (G.K. Misra, C.J.); following *Cawashah Bomaji Parakh* v. *Prafulla Nath Rudra*, AIR 1941 Nag. 364; *Ismail* v. *Venkatanarasimbulu*, AIR 1936 Mad 905.
2. *Durga Pada Mukherjee* v. *Ambujakshya Ganguli*, AIR 1993 Cal 125.
3. *Samdani Begum* v. *Dil Mohammed Khan*, AIR 2004 AP 272.
4. *Ramchandra Deshpande* v. *Lakshmana Rao Kulkarni*, AIR 2000 Kant. 298.

staircases, parking places, water reservoirs or facilities and sewer lines left in lay out plans are easements by grant by the colonizers, which cannot be appropriated by them at a later date claiming ownership rights.[1]

Rights and liabilities of the owner of the soil.—Where sale deed executed in favour of defendant is not produced, a presumption could be drawn that there was no recital relating to easement in sale deed.[2]

Extent and mode of enjoyment.—Considered with reference to their extent and mode of user, there are various kinds of rights of way; for a right of way may be general in its character that is usable for all purposes; or it may be a limited right, as a right of way for carriages but not for carts, or for horses and not for carriages; or it may simply be a footway.[3]

When there is a prohibition in using the vehicles in the holy road all along, which is also not granted to the appellants under Ex A1, they cannot seek alteration or addition or changes user thereof. Moreover, the respondents also cannot grant any such right to the appellants to use the vehicles through the holy road. Hence, in terms of right of way or right of access, the appellant cannot seek new grant to use vehicles in the holy road under the pretext of reasonable purpose.[4]

29. Increase of easement.—The dominant owner cannot, by merely altering or adding to the dominant heritage, substantially increase an easement.

Where an easement has been granted or bequeathed so that its extent shall be proportionate to the extent of the dominant heritage, if the dominant heritage is increased by alluvion, the easement is proportionately increased and, if the dominant heritage is diminished by diluvion, the easement is proportionately diminished.

Save as aforesaid, no easement is affected by any change in the extent of the dominant or the servient heritage.

---

1. *Tara Devi* v. *G. Raj Shekhar*, 2006 (65) ALR 352.
2. *Sabbu Yella Anjaveylu* v. *Uppari Lakshmanna*, AIR 2006 (NOC) 660 (AP).
3. Goddard, pp. 375, 376.
4. *Loordhu Mary* v. *Bishop of Tanjore*, AIR 2007 Mad 98.

Illustrations

(a) *A*, the owner of a mill, has acquired a prescriptive right to divert to his mill part of the water of a stream. *A* alters the machinery of his mill. He cannot thereby increase his right to divert water.

(b) *A* has acquired an easement to pollute a stream by carrying on a manufacture on its banks by which a certain quantity of foul matter is discharged into it. *A* extends his works and thereby increases the quantity discharged. He is responsible to the lower riparian owners for injury done by such increase.

(c) *A*, as the owner of a farm, has a right to take, for the purpose of manuring his farm, leaves which have fallen from the trees on *B*'s land. *A* buys a field and unites it to his farm. *A* is not thereby entitled to take leaves to manure this field.

NOTES

An easement is a burden of the servient heritage. Section 29 lays down that the dominant owner cannot increase this burden by altering or adding to the dominant heritage unless an easement right has been granted or bequeathed with the superadded condition that the extent of the easement right would vary in proportion to the increasing or decreasing size of the dominant heritage. In other words, the extent of an easement cannot vary to suit the convience of the dominant or the servient owner unless there is a contract to the contrary.

It is well settled that in the absence of a contract to the contrary, the scope or extent of the easement right cannot be increased or decreased to suit the convenience either of the dominant or the servient owner.[1]

Section 29 deals with the law as to the increase of an easement. The first paragraph embodies the universal rule that the dominant owner cannot by increasing or altering the

1. *K. Komuraiah* v. *G.S. Rani*, (1997) 1 Andh LT 239; *United Land Co.* v. *Great Eastern Railway Co.*, (1875) 10 Ch App 586 : 33 LT 292 : 44 LJ Ch 568; *Phillimore* v. *Watford Rural Council*, (1913), 2 Ch 434 : 77 J.P. 453 : 109 LT 616; *Newcomen* v. *Coulson*, (1877) 5 Ch D 133; *Suresh Chandra Biswas* v. *Jogendar Nath Sen*, 58 IC 854 : 32 CLJ 27 : 24 CWN 896; *Hans Raj* v. *Malawa Mal*, 69 IC 406 : AIR 1924 Lah. 387; *Ram Chandra Das Dalal* v. *Bholanath Hati*, AIR 1929 Cal 350.

dominant heritage, substantially increase an easement. "It is well settled that no man can impose a new or increased restriction or burden on his neighbour by his own act, and for this reason an owner of an easement cannot, by altering his dominant tenement, increase his right."[1]

Thus, for instance, where the defendants were using from time immemorial certain area as a pond for water storage for irrigating their lands, and in order to increase its capacity for storage of more water increased the height of the surplus escaped weir to a substantial extent with the consequences that the plaintiff's lands higher up were inundated rendering them unfit for cultivation for a considerable time, it was held that there was a good cause of action, as the act of the defendants in increasing the storage capacity amounts to a substantial increase within the meaning of this section.[2]

30. Partition of dominant heritage.—Where a dominant heritage is divided between two or more persons, the easement becomes annexed to each of the shares, but not so as to increase substantially the burden on the servient heritage: provided that such annexation is consistent with the terms of the instrument, decree or revenue proceedings (if any), under which the division was made, and, in the case of prescriptive rights, with the user during the prescriptive period.

Illustrations

(a) A house to which a right of way by a particular path is annexed is divided into two parts, one of which is granted to *A*, the other to *B*. Each is entitled in respect of his part, to a right of way by the same path.

(b) A house to which is annexed the right of drawing water from a well to the extent of fifty buckets a day is divided into two distinct heritages, one of which is granted to *A*, the other to *B*, *A* and *B* are each entitled in respect of his heritage, to draw from the well fifty buckets a day; but the amount drawn by both must not exceed fifty buckets a day.

1. *Suresh Chandra Biswas* v. *Jogendra Nath Sen*, 58 IC 854 : AIR 1920 Cal 268.
2. *Sellappa Goundan* v. *Subramanya Goundan*, 78 MLW 337.

(c) *A*, having in respect of his house an easement of a light, divides the house into three distinct heritages. Each of these continues to have the right to have its windows unobstructed.

NOTES

Where a dominant tenement is divided into two or more parts, easement right attach to each severed portion, provided no additional burden is imposed on that servient heritage. Thus, where an easement right allows drawing fifty buckets of water every day from the servient well and the dominant tenement is partitioned into two, the occupiers of both the portions can draw fifty buckets daily and not more after partition.

Easement are rights appertaining to the property as a whole for the benefit of which they are exercised, and not to any part of it or to any individual owner thereof. If such property is partitioned into two or more shares an easement which was hitherto enjoyed for the benefit of the whole will continue to be so enjoyed for the benefit of each part, if such enjoyment does not throw an additional burden on the servient heritage.[1]

In case of partition, the person holding each portion of the property is entitled to such easements of necessity which he enjoyed before the partition unless the deed of partition provided otherwise.[2]

The process of partition does not vest in the new owners of the several properties a right to place any additional burden on the servient heritage. They are entitled to enjoy their several rights in such a manner that the effect of their joint enjoyment may not exceed the maximum lawful limit of the right. However numerous may be the occupants or their severed tenements, they must confine themselves in the exercise of their easements right within the limits or the rights existing at the time of severance.[3]

31. Obstruction in case of excessive user.—In the case of excessive user of an easement, the

1. *Newcomen* v. *Coulson*, 36 LT 385; *see* also *Midland Ry.* v. *Gribble*, (1895) 2 Ch 827; *Nathabhai Dhirajram* v. *Bal Hansagavri*, 36 Bom 379; *Ram Prashad* v. *Court of Wards*, 21 WR 152.
2. *Garuda Satyanarayana* v. *Grandhi Venkatachalapathi Rao*, AIR 1969 Andh Pra 131; *see* also *Ersad Ali* v. *Muhammad Yakub Khan*, AIR 1969 Orissa 201 : (1968) 34 Cut. LT 835.
3. *Menzies* v. *Macdonalds*, (1856) 2 Jur (NS) 575.

servient owner may, without prejudice to any other remedies to which he may be entitled, obstruct the user, but only on the servient heritage: Provided that such user cannot be obstructed when the obstruction would interfere with the lawful enjoyment of the easement.

Illustration

A, having a right to the free passage over *B*'s land of light to four windows six feet by four, increases their size and number. It is impossible to obstruct the passage of light to the new windows without also obstructing the passage of light to the ancient windows. *B* cannot obstruct the excessive user.

NOTES

If the dominant owner exceeds his limit in the exercise of his easement right, the servient owner, without prejudice to any other remedy to which he may be entitled, is free to obstruct the excessive user, provided he does so on his own tenement only and provided the obstruction does not interfere with the lawful exercise by the dominant owner of his easement right.

It is one of the principal rights of property to protect it from injury caused by others by committing nuisance or any other tortious acts. Easements are only legalised wrongs to the property of others and if a person having a right to an easement exceeds the limit to which the new law authorises him to act in exercise of his right, he is a wrong doer and all his acts done in excess of such limit are wrongs which the person whose property is affected thereby can either redress himself or seek the help of a law Court for such redress. But the right to protect one's property also involves a duty that in protecting one's property, one should not act in such a way as to interfere with or injure the lawful rights of others. Section 31 embodies these principles.[1] It authorises the servient owner to obstruct the excessive user provided he can do so without committing trespass on the dominant tenement and without interfering with the lawful enjoyment of the easement.

There is an *obiter dictum* of the Nagpur High Court,[2] that even where the windows of the dominant tenement are

1. *K. Komuraiah* v. *G.S. Rani*, (1997) 1 Andh LT 239.
2. *Shankar* v. *Dattatraya*, AIR 1931 Nag. 80 : 131 IC 429.

enlarged, the servient owner cannot so obstruct as to diminish the light and air that entered originally. This should be taken subject to qualification.

The remedy provided by the section is in addition to other remedies, for instance, a suit for injunction or damages, to which the servient owner may be entitled under other provisions of the Act. It is really one of the ordinary rights of ownership available either before the acquisition of the easement by what is technically known as "interruption" or after the acquisition of the easement when the limits of the right are exceeded.

CHAPTER IV

THE DISTURBANCE OF EASEMENT

32. Right to enjoyment without disturbance.—The owner or occupier of the dominant heritage is entitled to enjoy the easement without disturbance by any other person.

Illustration

A, as owner of house, has a right of way over *B*'s land. *C* unlawfully enters on *B*'s land, and obstructs *A* in his right of way. *A* may sue *C* for compensation not for the entry, but for the obstruction.

NOTES

An easement right is a *right in rem,* i.e., a right available against the whole world. Therefore, if a dominant owner is obstructed in the exercise of his right either by the servient owner or by any other person, the dominant owner has a right of suit against the obstructing party.

Disturbance—What amounts to?—Whether a particular act causes disturbance of a right of easement, is a question of fact to be determined in each case with reference to the nature of the act, the nature of the easement and the circumstances connected with enjoyment of such easement as well as with the doing of such act.

Any act which tends to interfere with or obstruct or inconvenience or diminish the enjoyment of the right is sufficient to cause disturbance to it although it does not cause total obstruction thereof. But as in the case of excessive user, a user is not excessive unless it materially adds to the burden on the servient heritage, so in the case of disturbance of an easement, no obstruction amounts to an actionable disturbance unless it materially diminishes the enjoyment of such easement or more accurately materially diminishes the benefit to the dominant heritage. As in the case of excessive user, any user which if not obstructed would, on expiry of the prescriptive period, have entitled the dominant owner to claim a greater right, would be excessive, so in the case of disturbance of an easement, any obstruction which if not objected to, would, in course of time, result in the diminution or total annihilation of the right, is a sufficient disturbance. But for the purpose of this Chapter the disturbance of an easement must be taken to refer to some act done on the servient tenement, [For if it is caused by an act done on the dominant tenement, such act itself amounts to trespass and, therefore, actionable whether the easement is disturbed or not.] which disturbs the enjoyment of an easement as such and not the enjoyment of some inchoate right.[1] But if the disturbance is caused by a person who does not own or occupy the servient tenement,[2] or by such owner or occupier not by a voluntary act to obstruct the enjoyment but by negligence,[3] the fact that the right of easement is still inchoate or that the disturbance is only temporary, is immaterial.

33. Suit for disturbance of easement.—The owner of any interest in the dominant heritage or the occupier of such heritage may institute a suit for compensation for the disturbance of the easement or of any right accessory thereto; provided that the disturbance has actually caused substantial damage to the plaintiff.

Explanation I.—The doing of any act likely to injure the plaintiff by affecting the evidence of the easement, or by materially diminishing the value of the dominant heritage, is substantial damage within the meaning of this section and Section 34.

Explanation II.—Where the easement disturbed is a right to the free passage of light passing to the opening in a house, no damage is substantial within the meaning of this section, unless it falls within the First Explanation or interferes materially with the

1. *Bridewel Hospital Governors* v. *Ward Lock, Bowden & Co.*, 62 LJ Ch 270; *Greenhalgh* v. *Brindley*, (1902) 2 Ch 324; *Dhuman Khan* v. *Muhammad Khan*, 19 All 153; *Jootoor* v. *Vanamala*, 5 MLJ 24 (25).
2. *Jefferies* v. *Williams*, 3 Exch. 792; *Bibby* v. *Carter*, 28 LJ Exch. 182; *Dhuman Khan* v. *Muhammad Khan*, 19 All 153; *Jootoor* v. *Vanamala*, 5 MLJ 24 (25); but see *Davies* v. *Williams*, 16 QB 546; *Anantha Desikachariar* v. *Viswanatha*, 30 IC 989 (Mad).
3. *See* Peacock, p. 170.

physical comfort of the plaintiff or prevents him from carrying on his accustomed business in the dominant heritage as beneficially as he had done previous to instituting the suit.

Explanation III.—Where the easement disturbed is a right to the free passage of air to the openings in a house, damage is substantial within the meaning of this section if it interferes materially with the physical comfort of the plaintiff, though it is not injurious to his health.

Illustrations

(a) *A* places a permanent obstruction in a path over which *B* as tenant of *C*'s house, has a right of way. This is substantial damage to *C*, for it may affect the evidence of his reversionary right to the easement.

(b) *A*, as owner of a house, has a right to walk along one side of *B*'s house. *B* builds a verandah overhanging the way about ten feet from the ground, so as not to occasion any inconvenience to foot-passengers using the way. This is not substantial damage to *A*.

NOTES

Section 33 provides that the owner of any interest in the dominant heritage may institute a suit for the disturbance of the easement provided that the disturbance has actually caused substantial damage to the plaintiff. Under Explanation II read with Explanation I to the section, where the disturbance pertains to the right of free passage of light passing through the openings of the house, no damage is substantial unless the interference materially diminishes the value of the dominant heritage. Where the disturbance is to the right of the free passage of air, damage is substantial if it interferes materially with the physical comfort of the plaintiff.[1]

The words "affecting the evidence of the easement" used in Explanation I would not apply to the disturbance of an easement regarding right to the free passage of air or light. Illustration 'a' seems to indicate that this part would apply to

1. *Chapsibhai Dhanjibhai Daud* v. *Purshotam*, AIR 1971 SC 1878.

the easement of right of way.[1]

The Second and Third Explanation to Section 33 make it clear that no interference with free passage of light and air is actionable unless such interference is of substantial character. An injunction to restrain the disturbance of an easement cannot be granted where substantial damage is not proved to have been caused.[2] In other words, the person complaining of disturbance of right of easement must show not only there has been disturbance of the right but also that such disturbance has actually resulted in substantial damage to him.[3]

Decree for removal of obstruction by closing window proper.—Plaintiff had filed suit for temporary injunction on ground that staircase constructed by defendant was obstructing window of kitchen of plaintiff. Some space was available between plaintiff's window and staircase of defendant. Two doors for kitchen in dispute, one was opening in chowk, other door was opening in another room. Ventilator was only available source of air and light against said window. Decree for removal of obstruction by closing said window was proper as facts were showing substantial diminution of air and light by closure of said window.[4]

In *Mrs. Bhulvati Devi and others* v. *Munnalal*,[5] it has been said that unless the plaintiff proves that the construction work of the defendant will prevent him from using his house comfortably or will cause him material damage or he will be deprived of his rights, till then the injunction should not be issued.

34. When cause of action arises for removal of support.—The removal of the means of support to which a dominant owner is entitled does not give rise to a right to recover compensation, unless and until substantial damage is actually sustained.

1. *Vaghela Vakhatsinh Agarsinh* v. *Parmar Lalji Khodidas*, AIR 1975 Gujarat 109.
2. *Ram Narayan Ram* v. *Dhani Ram*, 1973 AWR 134 at 174, relying on *Suraj Narain* v. *Kalyan Das*, AIR 1929 All 430 and *Wali Mohammad* v. *Batuk*, 1936 AWR 525; *Prem Devi* v. *Sohan Lal*, AIR 1989 NOC 176 (Raj).
3. *K.S. Kamal* v. *Surinder Kumar*, (1995) 2 Sim. LJ 1278 at 1280 : (1995) 1 Punj LR 470 (P & H).
4. *Rajendra Singh* v. *Har Kanwar*, AIR 2005 Raj 127.
5. AIR 1982 All 20.

NOTES

Substantial injury when caused

(1) When the alleged wrongful act is likely to affect the evidence of the easement right itself.

(2) When the alleged wrongful act materially diminishes the value of the dominant tenement.

(3) In the case of an easement right to the free passage of light, in addition to the above two conditions, a substantial injury is caused if the alleged interruption of the free passage of the light and air : (a) interferes materially with the physical comfort of the plaintiff, or (b) prevents him from carrying on his accustomed business in the dominant heritage as beneficially as he had done prior to the obstruction.

(4) In the case of an easement right to the free passage of air, damage is substantial if the alleged disturbance interferes materially with the physical comfort of the plaintiff even though it may not be injurious to his health.

(5) In the case of an easement of right of support, no right of action accrues on removal of the means of support unless substantial damage is actually sustained by the dominant owner. A servient owner is free to make any excavation he likes on his land and he cannot be held liable, unless the land of the dominant owner subsidies.

Infringement of easement right of light and air—What constitutes

To constitute an infringement of an easement of light and air there must be a substantial privation of light and air enough to render the occupation of mankind and (in the case of business premises) to prevent the plaintiff from carrying on his business as beneficially as before.

Sections 33 and 34 set out the circumstances under which a suit for compensation for disturbance of an easement may lie. Section 33 provides that the owner of any interest in the dominant heritage or the occupier of such heritage, may sue for a disturbance of easement if it has caused him substantial damage. Such damage includes the doing of any act likely to injure the plaintiff by affecting the evidence of the easement or by materially diminishing the value of the dominant heritage.[1] In the case of easement of light, it also includes the

1. *Whitley Stoke's Anglo-Indian Codes,* Vol. I, p. 885, Explanation I to Section 33.

doing of any act which interferes materially with the physical comfort of the plaintiff or prevents him from carrying on his accustomed business in the dominant heritage as beneficially as he had done previous to the institution of the suit. In the case of easement of air damage is substantial even if it only interferes materially with the physical comfort of the plaintiff notwithstanding the fact that it is not injurious to his health. The law as it stood, before the passing of the Easements Act both in England and in India, was that though a suit for disturbance of a right to light would lie on the ground of material interference with only the physical comfort of the plaintiff without showing any injury to his health, in the case of easement of air such suit was not maintainable until the obstruction amounted to a nuisance or was injurious to health.[1]

It is clear from Explanation II to Section 33 that damage to free passage of light would not be substantial unless (1) it is such as to diminish the value of dominant heritage; (2) it interferes with physical comfort; and (3) prevents the carrying on of the accustomed business in the dominant heritage. It is also clear from Explanation III to Section 33 that the damage would be substantial if it interferes materially with physical comfort of the plaintiff though not injurious to his health.[2]

An infraction of an easement of light and air becomes actionable only when the obstruction amounts to a nuisance. Whether the owner of the dominant heritage has sufficient light and air through his old windows is a question of fact and should be decided having regard to the comfortable use and enjoyment of his house. The right of the easement of light and air cannot be said to be infringed unless the interference amounts to nuisance.[3]

In England, questions relating to easements of light and air are governed by the principles enunciated in the well-known case of *Colls* v. *Home and Colonial Stores*,[4] and that law in fact does not contemplate an easement of air as separately from that of light. Under the present Act, however, the easement of air is separately provided for and the question of quantity of air is free from the limitation of the principles laid down in *Colls'* case.

---

1. *Bagram* v. *Khettranath*, 3 BLR OC 18.
2. *Devinder Kumar* v. *Chatra Devi*, AIR 1966 Punj 502.
3. *Ligory Minezes* v. *J.C. Lobo*, AIR 1970 Mys. 76 : (1969) 2 Mys. LJ 92.
4. 1904 AC 179 : 90 LT 687 : 73 LJ Ch 484.

In India, as has been observed in certain cases,[1] an easement to the free passage of air to a building is more valuable than an easement of light and requires greater protection. The Act accordingly allows a suit for the obstruction of the free passage of air where it interferes materially with the plaintiff's physical comfort, although it is not injurious to his health.[2] Section 34 relates to the disturbance of the right of support.

It was laid down in the undernoted cases[3] that in case of a natural right even a trivial infringement is actionable. Section 34 which deals with a right of support enacts an exception to the rule. It enacts that unless substantial damage is actually sustained by the dominant owner by removal of the means of support to which he is entitled, he cannot institute a suit for compensation. The section, however, does not take away the right to sue for injunction.

Easement of support.—Unlike other easements but as in the case of a natural right of support, an easement of support is not limited in its extent and enjoyment to the neighbouring tenement alone but extends to the whole column of earth or structure which is necessary to support the dominant tenement, whether it forms only one estate or is divided into several estates.[4] But when the right is acquired by implication of law on a severance of tenements, the estoppel by contract, which binds the parties, does not extend to third persons, hence, except in the case of ancient buildings for which right is acquired by prescription by the grantor himself before he makes the grant, neither the grantor nor the grantee can, of course, claim an easement of support against the estate of a third party by virtue of such grant. In other respects the rules which determine the extent and mode of enjoyment of easements generally also apply to the easement of support and need not be repeated here.[5]

35. Injunction to restrain disturbance.—Subject to the provisions of the Specific Relief Act, 1877, Sections 52 to 57 (both inclusive)] an injunction

1. *Madhoosoodun* v. *Bissonath*, 15 BLR OC 361 (367-68); *Thodamlal* v. *Jesomal*, 19 IC 483 (Mad); *Ammani Ammal* v. *Ranganayaki Ammal*, AIR 1926 Mad 898.
2. *Whitley Stoke's Anglo-Indian Codes*, Vol I, p. 885.
3. *Wood* v. *Waud*, (1894) 3 Ex 748, 772, 789, 799; *Subramania Ayyar* v. *Ram Chandra Rau*, 1 Mad 335.
4. *Corporation of Birmingham* v. *Allen*, 6 Ch D 284.
5. *Dalton* v. *Angus*, 6 App Cas 740 at pp. 752, 779.

may be granted to restrain the disturbance of an easement—

(a) if the easement is actually disturbed when compensation for such disturbance might be recovered under this Chapter;

(b) if the disturbance is only threatened or intended—when the act threatened or intended must necessarily if performed disturb the easement.

NOTES

The courts might issue injunctions in the following two cases in accordance with the provisions of the Specific Relief Act.

(1) When the easement is actually disturbed and a suit for compensation can be lawfully maintained by the dominant owner against the wrongdoer.

(2) Where the disturbance is only threatened or intended but the threatened or intended act is such that it is bound to cause disturbance to an easement if it is allowed to be performed.

Whether injunction can be issued on opening of windows and doors.—If a person opens windows or ventilators in his own wall but facing towards the adjoining land belonging to another person, then unless by doing so he invades the privacy or any other pre-existing and well established right vested in his neighbour, the latter canot force him to close aperture. But when a man opens a door in another man's land he interferes with the right of the latter to use that land without obstruction because the existence of the door would naturally enable the former to pass over the land or to trespass into it. If the person in whose land, the door is opened sits silent and does not take any action for closure of the door, after the lapse of twenty years the opener of the door might come forward with the plea that he had acquired an easement either of light or of right of way over the neighbour's land and this would certainly subject the owner of the land to a great hardship or it may lead to an irreparable injury. In such a case mandatory injunction can be issued directing the door to be closed. The argument that the owner of the land can take any other steps for closing the door such as building a wall in front of it, ignores the fact that this would compel the person concerned to incur expense which he might not be able to bear or which he may not like to bear if left to himself.[1]

Issue of injunction for construction on party wall.—It would not be correct to say that each of the tenants-in-common of the party wall is owner of the moiety to the wall on his side in absence of a partition by metes and bounds. The party wall cannot be treated as a wall divided longitudinally into two strips, one belonging to each of the neighbouring owners and both the neighbours are entitld to the use of the whole width of the wall. The construction of a new wall by one neighbour (A) on half the width of the wall without the permission of the other neighbour (B) is unwarranted, and the other neighbour (B) can ask for pulling it down. If he (B) does not do so but makes use of the moiety of the wall constructed by the other neighbour (A), the neighbour (B) cannot be said to have encroached upon A's wall and A is not entitled to have the constructions made by B on the party wall demolished nor is he entitled to get any perpetual injunction in this respect.[2]

Right to privacy

When the right to privacy is established, the plaintiff complaining of the infringement of the right should not be calld upon to prevent the infringement by shutting up of or screening the doors or windows of his own house, that is, by doing something at his own cost. The infringer should be required by an injunction to stop the infringement.[3]

When the right to privacy is established an injunction for closure of window can be granted. The opening of a door in one's own wall differs from opening a window. The law is uniform in the point that a neighbouring owner is not entitled to object a person from opening windows in his own wall and if he is aggrieved the only course open to him is to construct a wall in his own site obstructing the windows.[4]

No injunction for closing the windows on the ground that they are overlooking into his outer courtyard on the ground of invasion of his right of privacy can be granted especially when there is a lane of five feet width separating both the houses and not overlooking the inner courtyard.[5]

1. *Kaur Sani* v. *Birinder Kaur*, AIR 1971 Punjab 439.
2. *Jagan Nath* v. *Kachhulal*, AIR 1971 Rajasthan 112.
3. *Mt. Jaraoo* v. *Shiv Nath Byas*, AIR 1949 All 308.
4. *Agha Mohd.* v. *Wahiddino*, AIR 1948 Sind 36.
5. *Diwan Singh* v. *Inderjeet*, AIR 1981 All 342.

Right to privacy is not generally recognised as an easement and it is not recognised throughout India. It is confined to certain localities by usage or custom. It may be acquired by prescription also. Though a right of privacy is held to be proved, an injunction cannot be granted unless it is established that there has been substantial infringement of the right.[1]

When the right to privacy is not established, no suit for injunction is maintainable.[2]

There is no right of privacy in the Madras province and the remedy open to him is only to build on his ground to shut out the view from the side of the other side. The invasion of right of privacy in south cannot be prevented by grant of an injunction.[3]

The right of privacy is mostly confined to north India. But every infringement of the right of privacy is not actionable. It must be proved that there has been a substantial and material infringement of privacy and that it is actionable and then only an injunction restraining such infringement would be granted. The right of privacy cannot be carried to an oppressive length.[4]

An injunction cannot be granted for protecting the right of privacy as a customary easement since at the present day the *purdah* system is not in vogue.[5]

Invasion of privacy by opening a window overlooking another man's land is not recognised by law as a wrongful act giving rise to a cause of action for the issue of perpetual injunction.[6]

When the plaintiff seeks injunction against violation of a right of privacy, he should plead the right of privacy in the plaint. If the females of the family do not observe *purdah* no such claim can possibly be made. Whether the claim is based on custom or on prescription should be clearly stated.[7]

If there is no customary right to privacy, when an owner opens a window, the neighbour cannot have an injunction for protection of his privacy. It is for him to erect a wall on his

1. *Abirchand* v. *Manik Ramanarain*, 1978 MPLJ 204.
2. *Narain Chowdary* v. *Jodoo Nath*, 5 CWN 147.
3. *Sayyad Azuf* v. *Amerbujji*, ILR 18 Mad 163.
4. *Diwan Singh* v. *Inderjeet*, AIR 1981 All 342.
5. *Bsai* v. *Hasan Raza Khan*, AIR 1963 All 340.
6. *Agha Mohamed Hussain* v. *Elias*, ILR (1947) Ker 64.
7. *Krishnamurthy* v. *Rajlingam*, AIR 1980 AP 69 at 72.

own land.[1]

A right to privacy can be established by proof of prescription agreement or usage and in such a case it can be protected by grant of an injunction.[2]

Substantial damage

A person complaining the disturbance of his right has to show not only that there has been a disturbance of an easement but also has to prove that the disturbance has resulted in damage which is substantial. No damage would be substantial unless : (a) it is likely to injure the plaintiff by affecting the evidence of the easement materially diminishing the value of the dominant heritage, or (b) it interferenes with the physical comfort of the plaintiff, or (c) prevents him from carrying on his accustomed business in the dominant heritages as beneficially as had done before the filing of the suit.[3]

Removal of the raised portion of the party wall

A "party wall" means the dividing wall between two tenements or buildings but the precise easements claimed on a party wall would depend on the circumstances of the particular case. It is a wall belonging to the adjoining owners both owning their peculiar rights of easements over it. In case one co-owner raises the height of the wall without the consent of the other, the other co-owner is entitled for joint possession, or damages or injunction to remove the raised wall.[4]

Entitlement of a party for injunction

In suit for injunction on the ground of infringement of prescriptive right to light and air from certain window and ventilators, the plaintiff can get injunction if he is able to prove substantial damage.[5]

The easement of light and air that is acquired by prescription is not measured by the amount of light and air enjoyed during the period of prescription and an obstruction to the same cannot be said to be an infringement of that right unless it amounts to a nuisance. Though there is some domination of light and air, but it is not such as to cut off the entire light and air thus amounting to a nuisance, the person

1. *Abdul Sattar* v. *Chhaji Lal*, AIR 1973 All 538.
2. *Md. Abdoor Rahiman* v. *Bijor Sahoo*, 14 WR 103.
3. *Devinder Kumar* v. *Chatro Devi*, AIR 1966 Punj 502.
4. *Purshottam* v. *Madhavaji*, (1973) 4 Guj LR 194.
5. *Nemichand (dec) LRs.*, v. *Basantilal*, 1997 AIHC 2906 (Raj).

is not entitled for an injunction.[1]

Under the provisions of Section 38 of the Specific Relief Act, where a defendant invades or threatens to invade the plaintiff's right to or enjoyment of the property, the Court is entitled to grant perpetual injunction when injunction is necessary. Section 7, illustration (i) of the Indian Easements Act speaks of the right of the owner of the upper land to throw natural water on the lower land. The owners of the lower lands can take steps for discharge of water from their lands in any manner they like, provided such channel is not sufficient nor unsuitable for the purpose so as to interfere with the natural flow of water from the lands on higher level. If there is interference to such rights, a suit for injunction can be filed.[2]

The right to let water from the eaves so as to fall on the neighbour's site, however, can be acquired only as an easement. When such a right has been exercised for 16 years, though not for 20 years, the exercise of that right need not be restrained by an injunction.[3]

No injunction can be granted restraining interference with a right of way over a land when the defendants have a right of using the land for construction purposes.[4]

When a Municipal Board has wrongly cut off water supply, an injunction can be granted against them for the restoration of water supply.[5]

The owner of a house wanted to open a door in his wall but was prevented by the public as a public urinal existed outside which he wrongfully demolished by opening the door. The public cannot in such a case be restrained by injunction as they have acted within their rights.[6]

A is the joint owner of a well along with B and C The well water is to be utilised for irrigation of the joint lands of A, B and C A wants to use the well water for irrigating lands separately owned by him. This is obstructed by B and C. A cannot obtain an injunction for he has no right to use the water of the joint well for irrigation of his separate lands.[7]

1. *Thimmaraju* v. *Sita Ramchandar*, 1957 ALT 855 : (1958) I An WR 78.
2. *Dhanapati Beg* v. *Narain Das*, 75 CWN 590.
3. *Tulasamma* v. *Nandula Buchiarmiah*, AIR 1949 Mad 826 : (1949) 1 MLJ 314 : (1949) MWN 153.
4. *Jagdish* v. *Ram Saran*, AIR 1978 All 311.
5. *Municipal Board, Agra* v. *Kanhaiya Lal*, (1944) ALW 487.
6. *Jagdish Prasad* v. *Ram Saran*, AIR 1978 All 311.
7. *Mahadev* v. *Umaraj*, AIR 1977 All 283 following; *Shivaramma Pillai* v. *Marihami Pillai*, (1970) 1 MLJ 376 : AIR 1971 Mad 230.

Sections 22, 23 and 24 of the Easements Act embody the rule that though the claimant to an easementary rights is entitled to full protection, there must be an adjustment with the right of the servient owner also that the least inconvenience is caused to the other. When it is possible to retain a part of the new construction that would not come in the enjoyments of the easements as before, demolition of the entire construction should not be ordered.[1]

Delayed action disentitles a person for injunction

If a plaintiff having a right to object to windows, kept quiet until the entire construction was over, it is a fit case where the Court should exercise its discretion in favour of the defendant by refusing to grant injunction.[2]

Maintainability of injunction

Even in a case where a person has acquired a right of easement, an action for damages or injunction is not maintainable unless the injury complained is material.[3]

Injunction restraining reduction in the width of lane

Where the house of the plaintiff is abutting a lane that was being used by the plaintiff and several others for ingress and egress from their houses, if part of the width of the lane is reduced by sale, the plaintiff can bring a suit for an injunction asking them not to reduce the width of the lane.[4]

Injury to easement should be material for seeking injunction

The injury to an easement should be material before an action lies for damages or for injunction.[5]

Obstruction to the view of the road from one's building or place of business does not *per se* give right for obtaining injunction unless the obstruction affects his right of access or otherwise causes damages to his building. The obstruction must cause pecuniary loss to the plaintiff.[6]

1. *Ram Narain* v. *Gangadhar*, AIR 1975 All 248.
2. *Dhannu Lal* v. *Bansidhar*, AIR 1929 Pat 349.
3. *Krishna Kishore Bal* v. *Shankarason Samal*, AIR 1974 Ori 89.
4. *Kedarnath Sah* v. *Narendra Prasad*, AIR 1974 Pat 359.
5. *G.V. Rama Murthy* v. *Senapati*, AIR 1980 Ori 101; *Krishna Kishore Bal's Case,* AIR 1974 Ori 89 (FB).
6. *Dulichand* v. *Bhairondas*, AIR 1973 Raj 96.

Explanations to Section 38 of the Easement Act clearly define the nature and extent of the right of easement and provide that the easement can be disturbed only if the value of the dominant heritage is materially diminished or if the damage is substantial so as to materially affect the physical comfort and health of the dominant owner. Under the circumstances, Section 35 of the Easements Act cannot be read in isolation and must be read in conjunction with Section 33 because both these sections deal with the same subject, namely, the question of grant of injunction where there is a disturbance of easement.[1]

An injunction under clause (a) would indirectly call for consideration of all criteria of substantial interference as mentioned in Section 33 of the Easements Act. But that does not mean that in a suit for injunction under clause (b) would be granted, even, if the threatened disturbance is trival and would not cause any substantial damage. To obtain an injunction, the threatened disturbance should not be trival; it must cause substantial damage.[2]

Injunction restraining obstruction in use of the easementary rights

Section 35 of the Indian Easements Act indicates how the easement is to be actually enforced when the easement is disturbed. When the plaintiff is able to show that there has been sufficient disturbance of his right to easement and that it has caused sufficient damage amounting to actionable nuisance, then an injunction may be granted.[3]

Where a person acquires by grant a right to land, part of which is to be kept as a passage for Muslims going to a mosque near, he has something more than an easementary right of passage. He can maintain a suit for a permanent injunction to keep open the means of ingress and egress to and from the mosque and for removal of a door causing obstruction thereto even after the expiry of two years from the date of obstruction.[4]

Under Section 35 of the Indian Easements Act, injunction may be granted to restrain disturbance of an easement subject to the provisions of the Specific Relief Act. An injunction will not be granted, if the injury can be compensated in money.

1. *Kasturilal* v. *Krishan Chand*, AIR 1971 J & K 27.
2. *Manoharlal* v. *Bheerulal*, AIR 1975 Raj 31.
3. *Kasturi Lal* v. *Krishan Chand*, AIR 1971 J & K 27.
4. *Syed Manzoor* v. *Hakim Lal*, AIR 1980 All 389.

Grant of mandatory injunction is a discretionary relief and the discretion has to be exercised judiciously. The Court must consider the balance of conveniences and whether the injury is irreparable. After the closure of the windows, if the plaintiff is getting sufficient light from other sources, injunction has to be refused.[1]

A person who is in occupation of a room, though he is not owner of it, can file a suit for injunction when there is an obstruction to the light and air coming to the room from window. The suit cannot be dismissed on the ground that the owners of the house are not made parties to the suit.[2]

Throwing into the public drain offensive products from a factory may be restrained by an injunction at the instance of an occupier of property who is thereby specially injured.[3]

Sections 15, 28 and 33 to 35 of the Easements Act provide the mode of action to be taken when there is disturbance to an easement; (1) an interference which does not result in substantial damage do not give any cause of action [Ch. VIII. Sy 10] [Ch. VII. Sy Section]; (2) there may be cases where substantial damage may result but will not give a cause of action for obtaining injunction; and (3) an interference that materially affects the utility of the dominant tenement that injunction alone is the appropriate relief.[4]

Damages and injunction are two remedies alternative in character given in respect of the same wrong, namely, an infraction of the legal right by way of an easement and such an infraction takes place only when the deprivation is such as to amount to a nuisance. According to Section 35 of the Easements Act, an injunction may be granted to restrain the disturbance of an easement where the disturbance is only threatened or intended, when the act threatened or intended much necessarily, if performed, disturb the easement.[5]

In the case of an easement of light and air it is not necessary that the dominant owner should be conscious of his right every moment. If he establishes that he enjoyed the light and air over the statutory period, then he is entitled for an injunction.[6]

---

1. *V.N. Chandravela Chetty* v. *Varadappa Chetty*, (1975) 1 MLJ 401.
2. *Alifannessa* v. *Ali Akbar*, AIR 1958 Assam 83.
3. *Galstaun* v. *Doonialal Seal*, ILR 32 Cal 697.
4. *Ebrahimji* v. *Badrudin*, AIR 1951 Sau 46.
5. *Bhushanam* v. *Umapathi*, AIR 1935 Mad 870.
6. *Unrao Kanwar* v. *Ram Pyari*, AIR 1959 Raj 235.

Where the windows and openings were there overlooking a courtyard for more than 20 years, the person acquires right to light and air by prescription and it is a fit case where permanent injunction should be granted restraining the defendant from obstructing the windows and openings over the courtyard by raising a wall on his land.[1]

Where there is a decree in favour of a person to use water from a tank, the Court will grant an injunction restraining the owner of the tank if he obstructs the filling of tank by water on the ground that the stagnant water in the tank is breeding weeds and insects, especially when the person having the easementary right offers to clear the weeds from the tank.[2]

When there is interference that materially affects his right of easement to water, an injunction should be granted.[3]

In a case where the plaintiff has enjoyed the right of easement of flow of rain water from his house for more than 40 years, he is entitled for an injunction restraining others from obstructing the same. But in granting the relief the Court should not put unnecessary restriction on the other side.[4]

The upper riparian owner of a natural stream is not entitled to exclusive use of the water in the natural stream and he is not entitled for an injunction restraining the lower riparian owner to built up a bund across the natural stream and diverting the water for purpose of irrigating his lands.[5]

Each owner through whose land a river passes has a right to make use of the water, but it is subject to similar rights of the other owners. If a owner erects acquanduct so as to affect other owners thereby causing injury to them, an injunction may be granted restraining him from constructing the dam.[6]

The owner of the higher land has got a right to let the water from his land to the lower land in a natural flow. If there is any obstruction for the same he can ask for the help of a court by injunction.[7]

The owner of dominant tenement is entitled to the uninterrupted quantity of light which is necessary for his comfortable use of the house, through the ventilators. It is to

1. *Ammani Ammal* v. *Ranganayaki Ammal*, AIR 1926 Mad 898 : 51 MLJ 304.
2. *Aut Behary* v. *Rameswar*, AIR 1917 Cal 636 : 35 Ind Case 40.
3. *Ebrahimji* v. *Badruddin*, AIR 1951 Sau 46.
4. *Ram Lal* v. *Makhan Lal*, AIR 1919 Oudh 43.
5. *K. Anantha* v. *K.M. Ganapathy*, AIR 1981 Ker 102.
6. 1910 Ind Cas 181.
7. 8 Ind Cases 456.

be judged according to ordinary notions of the mankind. If the obstruction complained of amounts to nuisance, he is entitled for a mandatory injunction for removal of the obstruction. Where certain ventilators alone were obstructed, and the obstruction did not interfere with the supply of air and light to the plaintiff, no mandatory injunction should be issued.[1]

Where a person from whose property a structure has projected, acquires a right of easement to such projection by prescription but has not acquired any such right on the space below it or above it, the adjacent owner is entitled to build above and below the projection. But he cannot make any construction on the projection itself. If the adjacent owner tries to construct any structure touching in the projection, he can be prevented by way of an injunction from doing so. But if the proposed structure does not touch the projection, he cannot be prevented from constructing the same.[2]

To justify the grant of an injunction the threatened interference must disturb the material comfort of the petitioner. The light or air coming from other sources has to be taken into consideration.[3]

The owner of a dominant tenement does not get by his easement a right to all the light and air he enjoyed during the period of prescription. He is entitled to only so much of light that is sufficient for a comfortable use according to the ordinary notions of the locaity. Unless it amounts to a nuisance there would be no infringement to the receipt of the ancient lights. The claim to receive light and air from the windows and ventilators stands on a different footing. It is not sufficient to show that there is a reduction in the light that is received; unless it is shown that occupant has become uncomfortable, he will not get an injunction.[4] When the owner of a tenement has acquired a right of easement of light and air by prescription, he is entitled to a quantity of light or air sufficient for use of ordinary purposes of inhabitancy and business in the tenement according to the ordinary notions of mankind. The actual user will neither increase nor diminish the right. In such cases the actual question is whether obstruction would amount to nuisance. Unless, it amounts to nuisance, he is not entitled for an injunction.[5]

1. *Walaiti Ram* v. *Gopiram*, AIR 1935 Lahore 75.
2. *Pazhaniandi Bakthar* v. *Co-operative Urban Bank*, AIR 1963 Mad 155.
3. *Md. Zaman Khan* v. *Malik Umar Hayat Khan*, AIR 1936 Lah 792.
4. *Shiv* v. *Prem*, 1978 AWC 87.
5. *Lali Mohan* v. *Samirendra Kumar*, AIR 1977 Cal 174.

Though, a dominant owner has an easementary right to project the eves of his building over the servient tenement and discharge water, if the defendant raises his building and wants to throw additional burden on the servient tenement the plaintiff is entitled for an injunction.[1]

A neighbour claiming easementary right of light and air has a right to file a suit for restraining his neighbour from raising any construction contrary to the building bye laws. If the defendant opposite party is not restrained from raising of construction over the disputed land it may be difficult later on to get the construction demolished. The defendant has no legal right to raise construction against building bye laws of Municipal Council, while the plaintiff being a neighbour of defendant opposite party has every right to file a suit for permanent injunction restraining the defendant from raising construction against the building bye laws.[2]

Where the plaintiff sought to restain the defendant from carrying on construction obstructing his right of light and air, in order to make out a prima facie case necessary for granting temporary injunction, the plaintiff need not establish his title and it was sufficient if he can satisfy that the disputed open land should be preserved in its present condition until the question of his alleged right of light and air is finally disposed of. Such questions can be disposed of only in the suit after its trial.[3]

If the plaintiffs are entitled to easement right, they ought to have initiated the suit for easement right and they ought not to have let in evidence before the trial court for their right as co-owners, and as they have not chosen to elect the nature of their claim before the trial Court now they cannot be permitted to withdraw the suit for filing a fresh suit on the very same cause of action.[4]

When a plaintiff in a suit for declaration of his right to use the way establishes the terminal from which and to which the way runs, he is entitled to get the relief prayed for.[5]

Though the claimant is entitled to the full use of his right of way, if an adjustment can be made it will be granted by Court. If the claimant can use the way without complete

1. *Ayoob Ismail* v. *Mahomed*, AIR 1915 Sind 12 : 28 IC 169.
2. *Tejkaran* v. *Sushil Kumar*, 1996 AIHC 3064 (Raj).
3. *Tejkaran* v. *Sushil Kumar*, 1966 AIHC 3064 (Raj).
4. *Soma Naicker* v. *Veluchamy*, (1995) MLJ 108 at 109.
5. *Achhel Mahoto* v. *Harichand*, AIR 1976 Pat 5.

demolition of the structure obstructing the way the Court can order partial demolition of it alone.[1]

Injunction restraining obstruction in the right of way

A suit for an injunction to restrain the defendant from obstructing the ingress and egress of the plaintiff to a building through a gate and to direct to remove the chainlock put on the gate is a suit for land.[2]

The use of a public way is not in the nature of an easement, but the right to use the public highway is an incident of the public right over it. When the plaintiff claims that his house abutted on the public way and claims a right of egress and ingress through the door fixed in the northern wall abutting the public highway, that can be declared and injunction granted.[3]

When defendant raised construction on the public road which completely blocked his ingress and egress to the public road it amounted to a nuisance and the person is entitled to file a suit for its demolition and injunction.[4]

When the Municipality has constructed a wall on the public road within ten feet of his house thus depriving the plaintiff from enjoying the basic rights and amenties it raises the presumption for an injunction.[5]

If any obstruction is placed by any person or authority of public way which affects the ingress and egress, it must be presumed that special damage is caused to the owner of the house. When a defendant raised a construction on the public road and completely blocked the door of the plaintiff's house which abutted on the public way it cannot be said that no inconvenience, and, therefore, special damage is not caused to the plaintiff. It amounts to public nuisance and the public is entitled to a suit for demolition and consequential injunction.[6]

In a suit for declaration of his right to use the cart track over another's land and for an injunction, the fact that the defendant claims that of the two ways available the track that goes through his land is very inconvenient in rainy season is

1. *Ram Narain Choubey* v. *Gangadhar Choubey*, AIR 1975 All 248.
2. *Praveen Kumar* v. *VIIth Additional District Judge, Meerut*, AIR 1994 All 153 (157, 158).
3. *Ranjit Singh* v. *Ramnath Singh*, AIR 1976 All 417.
4. *Bhagwanti* v. *Jiuti*, AIR 1975 All 341.
5. *Shanker Dayal* v. *Stat*, AIR 1973 All 310.
6. *Bhagwanti* v. *Jiuti*, AIR 1975 All 341.

not enough to establish plaintiff's right in the track.[1]

The case of a person opening a door so that the passage goes into the neighbour's land is different from opening a window in his own wall. An injunction restraining the defendants from opening doors in their walls so that they can walk into the land of neighbour may be granted.[2]

Easement is a necessity to a tenement and it is not possible to claim easement as a right in gross. Without there being no dominant tenement in existence there cannot be any easement. Legal easement must ensure to the benefit of the dominant tenement. An easement with regard to a right of way need not be contiguous to the dominant tenement. When a wall is constructed across a right of way, an injunction may be granted for its removal.[3]

A right of passage over a vacant space may be claimed as an easementary right. This can be protected by an injunction restraining the owner of the vacant site from doing any act that would interfere with the plaintiff's reasonable enjoyment of that open site for effectuating his right of passage.[4]

The owner of the house adjoining the public way has every right to open any number of doors in his wall, but if there was public urinal in the public place the owner has no right to remove the long-standing urinal and use it for his passage and injunction can be granted against the public not to object the owner of the house from removing the urinal.[5]

When admittedly, on one side of the plaintiff's wall there was a public road and a urinal, though ordinarily the plaintiff is entitled to open any number of doors in his wall or remove the wall completely, but he has no right to pass over the land of others ajoining the wall. When the object of the opening of the door was to pass over the public land where previously a urinal existed, if the public objected the plaintiff from passing over the land which was being used by the public it cannot be said that the use of the public is wrongful or that an injunction cannot be granted.[6]

Plaintiff cannot sue for an injunction prohibiting the

1. *Seetharamappa* v. *Appaiah*, 1961 ALT 262 : AIR 1962 AP 84.
2. *Pabia* v. *Badia*, AIR 1957 Raj 175.
3. *Fatiklal* v. *Klipad*, 82 CWN 607.
4. *Chander Bhan* v. *Pehlad*, AIR 1988 Delhi 177.
5. *Jagdish Prasad* v. *Ram Saran*, AIR 1978 All 311.
6. *Jagdish Prasad* v. *Ram Saran*, AIR 1978 All 311.

defendant from discharging dirty water into a lane when the lane is not the property of the plaintiff.[1]

Injunction restraining the projection of eaves

The plaintiff's eaves projected over defendant's roof which rested on a common wall for more than thirty years. The defendant sought to raise the wall and remove the eaves. It was held that he could be restrained by injunction from doing so.[2]

Grant of injunction without proof of damage

Once the disturbance of an easement is established, injunction can be granted without proof of damage.[3]

Injunction when can be refused

In a suit seeking relief to permanent injunction restraining the defendants from enforcing their way through the disputed plot when the plaintiffs failed to prove their exclusive possession over the plots, injunction was refused.[4]

A person has a right to use his own property in any manner he likes and when it has been shown that opening of ventilators infringed the right of any one no perpetual injunction directing him to close the ventilators can be granted.[5]

If the defendant has a right to construct a terrace and make use of it, would be ineffectual to grant an injunction restraining the opening of a window in the wall.[6]

The apprehension that the defendant may acquire a right of easement of light and air after 20 years, if their windows remain open, is no ground for preventing the defendants by injunction from enjoying their property by opening windows.[7]

Damages in lieu of injunction

When the plaintiff has established a clear right to an easement, the Court should not award damages to him against

1. *Diwan Singh* v. *Indeerjeet*, AIR 1981 All 342.
2. *Nasarbhai* v. *Munshi Badruddin*, ILR 16 Bom 535.
3. *Sarab Lall* v. *Sheshwar*, AIR 1972 Pat 490.
4. *Chander Bhan* v. *Pehlad*, AIR 1988 Delhi 177.
5. *Dhanya Kumar Jain* v. *Rajendra Prasad*, AIR 1978 All 469.
6. *Krishnamurthy* v. *Rajlingam*, AIR 1980 AC 69 at 72.
7. *Ganesh Prasad* v. *Bashdeo*, ILR 16 Luck 686 : AIR 1941 Oudh 442 : 194 IC 73.

his wish in lieu of an injunction.[1]

Unless it is established that the interference complained of results in substantial injury to the person and that compensation is not an adequate relief, then only an injunction will be issued. To get an injunction the plaintiff should establish substantial reduction in the receipt of light so as to render his occupation of the house uncomfortable according to the normal standards of living.[2]

When the Court finds that there is an infringement of a right of easement but that there is no jurisdiction for granting an injunction, it can direct an enquiry into the question of damages though the plaint does not contain a prayer for the award of damages in the alternative.[3]

Mandatory injunction for restoration of easementary rights

In a case where the defendant arbitrarily and deliberately kept the level of his *kotha* such as to allow flow of water from his site into the plaintiff's site, the plaintiff cannot be forced to accept the compensation. The user made by the plaintiff may mature into a right of easement in the course of a time. Under the circumstances grant of a mandatory injunction is the proper remedy.[4]

The right of owner of land adjoining the highway to go upon the highway from any point on their land is a private right distinct from his right to use the highway as a member of public. If the right to access is obstructed by anyone, the owners of the land abutting the highway are entitled to maintain action for the injury, whether the obstruction does or does not constitute a public nuisance. Hence, where the plaintiff's right to such access is completely obstructed by the defendants by putting up a wall, they are entitled for a mandatory injunction directing the defendants to remove the wall when there is no proof that they had abandoned their right of access to public highway on the side or the wall.[5]

Under Section 35 of the Easements Act, an injunction may be granted subject to the provisions of the Specific Relief Act.

1. *Esa Abbas* v. *Jacob*, ILR 33 Mad 327; *Syed Shaful Hasan* v. *Syed Mukhtar Hasan*, (1947) OWN 616 : 2 DLR 635.
2. *Veerappa* v. *Nagappa*, AIR 1965 Mys 292.
3. *Kalliandas* v. *Tulsidas*, ILR 23 Bom 786; *Krishnan Pillai* v. *Kilashathammal*, AIR 1928 Mad 810; *Nasarbhai* v. *Munshi Badruddin*, ILR 16 Bom 533.
4. *Natha Singh* v. *Sanwalia*, AIR 1971 Raj 241 : 1971 Raj LW 169.
5. *Damodara Naidu* v. *Thirupursundari Ammal*, AIR 1972 Mad 386 at 387, 388.

Usually, an order of injunction is not granted when the injury can be compensated by money. Granting of mandatory injunction is a discretionary relief and such a discretion has to be exercised judiciously. While granting a mandatory relief the Court has to take into account the balance of convenience and consider whether the granting of mandatory injunction is the only relief that can remedy the mischief and not the grant of compensation. Where the plaintiff has the alternative relief which is more than sufficient, then a mandatory injunction should not be granted.[1]

Once the easement right is established, there is no scope for issuing a mandatory injunction to put an end to the mode of enjoyment which has given rise to the easement.[2]

Section 35 of the Indian Easements Act provides when an injunction may be granted in the case of easements and clause (b) refers to a mandatory injunction and clause (b) refers to a perpetual injunction. Further, injunctions are neither prohibitory nor mandatory. The prohibitory injunction puts a stop to some matter that is in progress by restraining the further action and a mandatory injunction issues an order to undo a thing that has been done. Sections 33 and 35 of the Easements Act enact in clear terms that a person is not entitled for injunction or damages in every case of interference with an easement. The explanation appended to Section 33 makes it clear when action can be taken in case of interference with an easement. Unless the interference in case of light and air is substnatial, no action can be taken. Unless there is actionable interference, no injunction can be granted.[3]

When the plaintiff seeks an injunction restraining the opening of a door and for "other reliefs", the defendant may be directed to remove the door if it is opened pending the suit though there is no specific prayer for such a relief.[4]

Where the door is opened with a view to secure a passage for ingress and egress wrongfully over to plaintiff's land, the invasion of the plaintiff's rights would be such that pecuniary compensation would not afford adequate relief and a negative injunction would only be futile leading to interminable litigation. In such a case a mandatory injunction may be

1. *V.N. Chandravaivelu* v. *Varadappa Chettiar*, (1975) 1 MLJ 401 : 81 MLW 49.
2. *Dehajabhai* v. *Hiralal*, AIR 1936 Bom 3 : 160 IC 62.
3. *Wali Mohammad* v. *Batuk*, 1936 AWR 525.
4. *Magan Lal* v. *Chotu Lal*, ILR 26 Bom 136.

granted to close the door.[1]

When there is unjustifiable invasion of plaintiff's right and acquiescence on his part would enable the defendant to acquire a prescriptive easement for discharge of water over the plaintiff's land, a mandatory injunction may be issued and the plaintiff cannot be required to accept compensation in lieu of the injunction.[2]

When the building constructed by the defendant is in contravention of the municipal rules, and also caused obstruction to the light and air to the plaintiff's building, the plaintiff is entitled for mandatory injunction in his favour for demolition of the offending construction.[3]

In a suit for a mandatory injunction for demolition of a portion of the house which is infringing the plaintiff's easement to light, the owner of the offending house is a necessary party. If he is not made a party, the suit is liable to dismissal.[4]

Free flow of light and air.—It was held that questions such as reasonableness of the conduct of the defendant, extent of harm, nature of the locality, utility of the defendant's conduct, abnormal sensitivity, temporary injury, malice are all the factors that have to weigh the mind of the Court while assessing strict liability in nuisance. Defendant in his evidence has admitted that plaintiff and his ancestors have been getting light and air through the windows fixed to two rooms which are used as kitchen and *pooja* on western portion of the plaintiff's house from the open space where defendant is intending to put up septic latrines. This establishes that plaintiff has an interest in the land in question and is the sufferer.[5]

Easementary rights and passages.—Commissioner was appointed where construction of wall by defendant blocked the right of ingress and egress to specified portion of property. The commissioner made suggestion to provide passage for ingress and egress to disputed portion. Interim order was passed directing the defendants to remove wall forthwith and permit access to plaintiff through main gate of property.[6]

Grant of injunction.—When reduction in light and air

1. *Pabia* v. *Badia*, AIR 1957 Raj 175.
2. *Nath Singh* v. *Sanwalia*, AIR 1971 Raj 241.
3. (1970) 2 Andh LT 193.
4. *G.V. Ram Murthy* v. *Senapati*, AIR 1980 Ori 101.
5. *Narayana Rao* v. *R. Narasinga Rao (deceased by LR's)*, AIR 1995 Kant. 11.
6. *Jaskirat Datwani* v. *Vidyawati*, AIR 2002 SC 2180.

in physical sense is not proved so substantial as to render comfortable living impossible, the same cannot be considered to constitute an infringement warranting the grant of injunction.[1]

Easements relating to way.—In a suit for permanent injunction restraining the defendant and her family members from interfering with use of public road. The plaintiff, however, failed to establish existence of public road which he described under the plaint schedule and alleged acts of defendant's interference. Injunction could not be granted.[2]

36. Abatement of obstruction of easement.—Notwithstanding the provisions of Section 24, the dominant owner cannot himself abate a wrongful obstruction of an easement.

NOTES

A dominant cannot himself abate a wrongful obstruction of his easement right.

---

1. *A.V. Kuppuswamy Iyer* v. *S.K. Subramanian*, AIR 1998 Mad 268.
2. *Narayanappa* v. *Anandamma*, AIR 2007 Kar. 1 : 2006 AIHC 3826 (Kar).

CHAPTER V

THE EXTINCTION, SUSPENSION AND REVIVAL OF EASEMENT

37. Extinction by dissolution of right of servient owner.—When, from a cause which preceded the imposition of an easement the person by whom it was imposed ceases to have any right in the servient heritage, the easement is extinguished.

Exception.—Nothing in this section applies to an easement lawfully imposed by a mortgagor in accordance with Section 10.

Illustrations

(a) *A* transfers Sultanpur to *B* on condition that he does not marry *C*. *B* imposes an easement on Sultanpur. Then *B* marries *C*. *B*'s interest in Sultanpur ends, and with it the easement is extinguished.

(b) *A*, in 1860, let Sultanpur to *B* for thirty years from the date of the lease. *B*, in 1861, imposes an easement on the land in favour of *C*, who enjoys the easement peacefully and openly as an easement without interruption for twenty-nine years. *B*'s interest in Sultanpur then ends, and with it *C*'s easement.

(c) *A* and *B*, tenants of *C*, have permanent transferable interest in their respective holdings. *A* imposes on his holding an easement to draw water from a tank for the purpose of irrigating *B*'s land. *B* enjoys the easement for twenty years. *A*'s rent falls into arrear and his interest is sold. *B*'s easement is extinguished.

(d) *A* mortgages Sultanpur to *B* and lawfully

imposes an easement on the land in favour of *C* in accordance with the provisions of Section 10. The land is sold to *D* in satisfaction of the mortgage debt. The easement is not thereby extinguished.

NOTES

When the person who imposed an easement over the servient tenement ceases to have any interest in the servient tenement due to causes which preceded the imposition to the easement, the easement is extinguished. But an easement imposed by a mortgagor after the mortgage will not be extinguished unless its effect is to render the mortgage security insufficient.

38. Extinction by release.—An easement is extinguished when the dominant owner releases it, expressly or impliedly, to the servient owner.

Such release can be made only in the circumstances and to the extent in and to which the dominant owner can alienate the dominant heritage.

An easement may be released as to part only of the servient heritage.

Explanation I.—An easement is impliedly released—

(a) where the dominant owner expressly authorizes an act of a permanent nature to be done on the servient heritage, the necessary consequence of which is to prevent his future enjoyment of the easement, and such act is done in pursuance of such authority;

(b) when any permanent alteration is made in the dominant heritage of such a nature as to show that the dominant owner intended to cease to enjoy the easement in future.

Explanation II.—Mere non-user of an easement is not implied release within the meaning of this section.

Illustrations

(a) *A*, *B* and *C* are co-owners of a house to which an easement is annexed. *A*, without the consent of *B* and *C*, releases the easement. This release is effectual only as against *A* and his legal representative.

(b) *A* grants *B* an easement over *A*'s land for the beneficial enjoyment of his house. *B* assigns the house to *C*. *B* then purports to release the easement. The release is ineffectual.

(c) *A* having the right to discharge his eavesdroppings into *B*'s yard, expressly authorises *B* to build over his yard to a height which will interfere with the discharge. *B* builds accordingly . *A*'s easement is extinguished to the extent of the interference.

(d) *A*, having an easement of light to a window, builds up that window with bricks and mortar so as to manifest an intention to abandon the easement permanently. The easement is impliedly released.

(e) *A* having a projecting roof by means of which he enjoys an enjoyment to discharge eavesdroppings on *B*'s land, permanently alters the roof, so as to direct the rainwater into a different channel and discharge it on *C*'s land. The easement is impliedly released.

NOTES

This section lays down the law as to extinction by release. A release may be express or it may be implied from circumstances which are set out in the Explanation. Explanation II declares that mere non-user of an easement is not an implied release within the meaning of this section. This provision should be distinguished from the provisions of Section 47 which lays down the law as to the extinction of an easement by non-user for a particular period. Under Section 38, a non-user even for a period shorter than that laid down in Section 47, *viz.*, twenty years, may cause the extinction, of an easement if it is accompanied by such circumstances that an implied release or abandonment of the right may be inferred from them. Though a mere non-user may not imply a release under Section 38, yet if it is continued for a period of twenty years it may *per se* cause the extinction of discontinuous easement under Section 47. The circumstances laid down in Explanation I as to when an easement may be impliedly released should again be distinguished from certain other circumstances which are tantamount to release by conduct of the dominant owner estopping him from claiming the rights which are not wholly covered by the section. Properly speaking, they are within the domain of the law of estoppel rather than within the law of easement. For instance, *A* has a right of way over *B*'s land. He discontinues the enjoyment of the right. *B* believing that *A* has abandoned the right builds on his land blocking up the way altogether. *A* stands by and sees the building in progress but makes no protest. His right of way is extinguished and by his conduct he is estopped from claiming it. This is a release by conduct not covered by Section 38. Again, if this non-user continues for twenty years, the right is extinguished by mere non-user under Section 47 even though no other circumstances intervene. Certain confusion on this point which is noticed in certain text-books on the law of easement is due to the oversight of the distinctions noted above.

An easement exists for the enjoyment of the dominant heritage by the dominant owner and hence a dominant owner is quite free to release an easement expressly or impliedly and a servient owner cannot insist that the dominant owner must exercise his easement right. But the release of an easement by the dominant owner can be only to the extent to which he can alienate his interest in the dominant heritage.

Non-user.—Mere non-user of an easement right cannot amount to abandonment unless non-user is accompanied by acts which shows unequivocally an intention to abandon the right. The reason is that right might not be enjoyed by the dominant owner for a long time simply because he finds no occasion to exercise his right. Non-user of a way may be explained by showing that the owner had, for the time being, no occasion to use it by having other and more convenient means of enjoying his land, but then adverse possession coupled with non-user may raise a presumption of release.

Mere non-user does not amount to abandonment of right. The correct law is, that if a non-user for certain period is proved, it is further to be seen whether the non-user was due to an obstruction laid down by the servient owner, or due to the abandonment of the intention to enjoy it on the part of the dominant owner, or because no occasion arose for the exercise of the right, or because, though the occasion arose for dominant owner, during this period other and more convenient means to enjoy his property being available to him, he did not stand in the need of exercising the right claimed. In the first two of contingencies mentioned above, the continuity shall be deemed to be broken, but, in the last two contingencies, it will remain unaffected, as mere non-user is not abandonment.[1]

Partial release.—An easement may be released in part and a partial abandonment will not amount to an abandonment of the whole unless the part reserved is not sufficient for the continuance of the right. [*See* Peacock, 3rd Ed., p. 537 as to Negative Easements. The principle applies with greater force to positive easements as well.] For instance, if a person has a right of way over a number of tenements and he abandons his right in one of them, if he cannot enjoy the right over the other tenements without passing over the tenement in which he has abandoned his right, his right to the way is lost, but if he can do so, he is entitled to enjoy it on the other tenements notwithstanding such abandonment.[2] So in the case of ancient lights received from two directions the abandonment in one direction does not amount to an abandonment in the other direction also though the amount of light received from the latter is very small in quantity.

39. Extinction by revocation.—An easement is extinguished when the servient owner in exercise of a power reserved in this behalf, revokes the easement.

40. Extinction on expiration of limited period or happening of dissolving condition.—An easement is extinguished where it has been imposed for a limited period or acquired on condition that it shall become void on the performance or non-performance of a specified act and the period expires or the condition is fulfilled.

NOTES

When an easement is imposed for a limited period or is acquired on condition that it shall become void on the performance or non-performance of a specified act, then such an easement would be extinguished on the expiration of the limited period or on the fulfilment of the contingent condition.

---

1. *Heeralal* v. *Ramjeevan*, AIR 1989 Raj 1,6,7,8, para 13, 14, 17, 18.; Relying on *Koylash Chandra* v. *Sonatan*, (1881), ILR 7 Cal 132.
2. *Bailey* v. *Holborn*, 110 LT 574; *see* also *Scott* v. *Pape*, 31 Ch D 554; *Colls* v. *Home & Colonial Stores*, 90 LT 687. See *Varadarajulu Chettiar* v. *Muthukannu Ammal*, AIR 1966 Mad 158 as to the effect of partial abandonment.

41. Extinction on termination of necessity.—An easement of necessity is extinguished when the necessity comes to an end.

Illustration

A grants *B* a field inaccessible except by passing over *A*'s adjoining land. *B* afterwards purchases a part of that land over which he can pass to his field. The right of way over *A*'s land which *B* had acquired is extinguished.

NOTES

Easements of necessity are those easements which are *absolutely necessary* for the enjoyment of the dominant heritage. When the absolute necessity ceases and the dominant heritage can be enjoyed without such easement, the easement extinguishes. Where A grants a field to B inaccessible except by passing over A's adjoining land and B subsequently purchases a piece of land over which he can pass to his land, B will cease to have any right of way over A's land which is no longer necessary owing to a purchase of another piece of land by B.

42. Extinction of useless easements.—An easement is extinguished when it becomes incapable of being at any time and under any circumstances beneficial to the dominant owner.

NOTES

When an easement ceases to be of any benefit to the dominant owner under any circumstance and places an unnecessary burden on the servient tenement, the easement extinguishes.

43. Extinction by permanent change in dominant heritage.—Where, by any permanent change in the dominant heritage the burden on the servient heritage is materially increased and cannot be reduced by the servient owner without interfering with the lawful enjoyment of the easement, the easement is extinguished, unless—

(a) it was intended for the beneficial enjoyment of the dominant heritage, to whatever extent the easement should be used; or

(b) the injury caused to the servient owner

by the change is so slight that no reasonable person would complain of it; or

(c) the easement is an easement of necessity.

Nothing in this section shall be deemed to apply to an easement entitling the dominant owner to support of the dominant heritage.

NOTES

Where due to a permanent change in the dominant heritage the burden of the servient heritage is materially increased and cannot be lawfully reduced by the servient owner, the easement right itself is extinguished.

Where the owner of a house had a right to discharge water from one privy in his house into the drain of another's house, and he subsequently built a new privy in the house and connected that up with the drain, *held*, that the burden could be reduced without difficulty to its original limits by the drain from the new privy being blocked or cut away, and the easement was not extinguished.[1]

Exceptions

(1) When the extent of the easement right is co-extensive with the increased needs of the dominant tenement, the easement is not extinguished.

(2) Where the additional burden on the servient tenement is of such a triffing nature that no reasonable person would complain of it, then also the easement would not be extinguished.

(3) Where the easement in question is an easement of necessity.

(4) Where the easement is an easement of right of support. It is not lost simply because the dominant owner by making some permanent alterations in the dominant tenement causes to be placed on the servient tenement an additional burden.

How extinction of easement is effected?

Reading Sections 23 and 43 of the Easements Act together it can easily be inferred that the enjoyment of the easement can be extinguished only when the position of the place where the easement is enjoyed, is permanently altered in a manner so as to impose an extra burden on the servient heritage. If

1. *Rameshwar Dayal* v. *Maharaj Charan*, 20 ALJ 202.

by closing verandah and converting it into a room no extra burden is imposed on the servient heritage in the enjoyment of the easementary right which became ripe by prescription, the owner of the servient heritage cannot claim that the easementary right has extinguished.[1]

Permanent change in the dominant heritage.—In order that extinction may be caused under this section there should be a permanent change in the dominant heritage, so that an intention to abandon may be inferred.[2] If the change is only of a temporary character, no such intention can be inferred and hence no extinction follows such change, even though the burden on the servient heritage may be materially increased. To effect a permanent cessation of a right, there must be an act of a permanent character. In England, it may be taken to be a general rule that any alteration of a dominant tenement of such a nature, that the tenement or the mode of user of an easement, is substantially changed in character, or that the burden on the servient tenement is materially increased, will cause the extinction or suspension of an easement unless the easement was intended for the benefit of the dominant tenement to whatever purpose it should be applied or in whatever manner the easement should be used.[3] The substitution of the phrase "permanent change" in this section for "substantial change" of English law is significant and many cases of English law which proceed on that ground are of doubtful authority in the territories governed by the Indian Easements Act.[4] Under this section unless the change is permanent, the right is not extinguished. It does not appear even to become suspended for the time a temporary change lasts inasmuch as no provision for such suspension has been made in this chapter. The only remedy for such change appears to be by a suit for damages or for injunction for the removal of such temporary cause. What amounts to a permanent

1. *Chaturbhuj* v. *Ramjeevan*, AIR 1976 Raj 162.
2. *Ankerson* v. *Connelly*, (1906) 2 Ch 544; *Liggins* v. *Inge*, 7 Bing. 682.
3. Goddard, Law of Easements, p. 370, citing *United Land Co.* v. *Great Eastern Railway Co.*, 33 LT 292; *Newcomen* v. *Coulson*, 36 LT 385.
4. *Allan* v. *Gomme*, 11 Ad. & El. 759; *Henning* v. *Burnet*, 8 Exch 187; *South Metropolitan Cemetery Co.* v. *Eden*, 16 CB 42; *Bower* v. *Hill*, 2 Bing NC 549; *White* v. *Grand Hotel*, (1913) 1 Ch 113; *Williams* v. *James*, 16 LT 664 : *Wimbledon* v. *Dixon*, 33 LT 679; *Taff Vale Railway Co.* v. *Gorden Canning*, 100 LT 845; *Great Western Railway Co.* v. *Talbot*, (1902) 2 Ch 759; *Milner's Safe Company Ltd.* v. *Great Northern and City Railway Co.*, (1907) 1 Ch 208; *Clarke* v. *Somersetshire Drainage Commissioner*, 59 LT 670.

change is a question of fact to be determined with reference to the circumstances of each case. [Innes Easements, p. 95.] Excessive user is only one element in determining this question, another element being the increase of burden on the servient heritage.

Extinguishment of easement.—Taking into consideration Section 23 and Section 43 of the Act together it can easily be inferred that the enjoyment of the easement can be extinguished only when the position of the place where the easement is enjoyed, is permanently altered in a manner so as to impose an extra burden on the servient heritage.[1]

44. Extinction on permanent alteration of servient heritage by superior force.—An easement is extinguished where the servient heritage is by superior force so permanently altered that the dominant owner can no longer enjoy such easement :

Provided that where a way of necessity is destroyed by superior force, the dominant owner has a right to another way over the servient heritage, and the provisions of Section 14 apply to such way.

Illustrations

(a) *A* grants to *B*, as the owner of a certain house, a right to fish in a river running through *A*'s land. The river changes its course permanently and runs through *C*'s land. *B*'s easement is extinguished.

(b) Access to a path over which *A* has a right of way is permanently cut off by an earthquake. *A*'s right is extinguished.

NOTES

Where the servient tenement is permanently altered by a *superior force* in such a way that the dominant owner can no longer enjoy his easement right, the easement is extinguished. But an exception has been made in case of an easement of way of necessity, in which case the dominant owner has a right to a fresh way of necessity.

Section 44 relates to extinction of easementary right because of permanent alteration of servient heritage by superior force. Where ridge channel and well are brought into existence by the defendant and not by any superior force

1. *Chaturbhuj* v. *Ramjeevan*, AIR 1976 Raj 162 (Tyagi, J.).

Section 44 has no application.[1]

An easement of way of necessity forms an exception.—An easement of way of necessity being absolutely necessary for the use and enjoyment of the dominant heritage is looked upon with favour to guarantee the use of the property in the dominant tenement and a right is given to the dominant owner to have another way over the servient heritage if the former is destroyed by such change or has become permanently incapable of enjoyment. Such subsequent way must be set out by the servient owner and on his default the dominant owner may set it out himself.[2] But as the servient owner is not bound to keep it in repairs in the absence of a contract to the contrary, the mere fact that the way has become impassable for want of repairs does not entitle the dominant owner to a substituted way.

45. Extinction by destruction of either heritage.—An easement is extinguished when either the dominant or the servient heritage is completely destroyed.

Illustration

A has a right of way over a road running along the foot of a sea-cliff. The road is washed away by a permanent encroachment of the sea. *A*'s easement is extinguished.

NOTES

Before Section 45 can be attracted there must be complete destruction of the dominant or the servient heritage.

Cause of destruction.—It is immaterial whether such destruction is brought about by *vis major* or is due to some act of man. Though the servient owner cannot be compelled to reconstruct the servient heritage so as to make it serviceable for the dominant heritage,[3] yet if the destruction is due to his wilful act or even omission, in certain cases he may be held liable to the dominant owner for the damages caused to him by such destruction.[4]

Partial destruction—Effect of.—If destruction is only partial and the part left undestroyed is sufficient for the

1. *Chanti China Venkatareddy* v. *Kurasani Koti Reddy*, AIR 1967 Andh Pra 81 : (1966) 2 Andh WR 80 : (1966) 2 Andh LT 177.
2. *See* Section 14, *ante*.
3. *See* Section 27, *ante*.
4. *See* Commentaries under Section 27, *supra*.

enjoyment of the right though partially or with some inconvenience or with certain restrictions provided such enjoyment does not throw additional burden on the servient heritage,[1] or does not amount to the creation of a substantially new right,[2] the easement is not extinguished.[3] But if the partial destruction makes the enjoyment of the easement impossible at any time and under any circumstances the easement is extinguished. In the case of a way of necessity if the land or building on which the way exists is destroyed totally so that no portion of the servient tenement remains on which a substituted way may be claimed the right is lost by such destruction, but if a portion of the servient tenement still remains on which a way may be carved out, it may be claimed under the proviso to Section 44.

46. Extinction by unity of ownership.—An easement is extinguished when the same person becomes entitled to the absolute ownership of the whole of the dominant and servient heritages.

Illustrations

(a) *A*, as the owner of a house, has a right of way over *B*'s field. *A* mortgages his house, and *B* mortgages his field to *C*. Then *C* forecloses both mortgages and becomes thereby absolute owner of both house and field. The right of way is extinguished.

(b) The dominant owner acquires only part of the servient heritage; the easement is not extinguished except in the case illustrated in Section 41.

(c) The servient owner acquires the dominant heritage in connection with a third person; the easement is not extinguished.

(d) The separate owners of two separate dominant heritages jointly acquire the heritage which is servient to the two separate heritages; the easements are not extinguished.

1. Cf. *Ankerson* v. *Connelly*, (1907) 96 LT 681.
2. Cf. *Clarke* v. *Somersetshire Drainage Commissioners*, 59 LT 670.
3. *Framji Shapurji* v. *Framji Edulji*, 7 Bom LR 352 (356) : 30 Bom 319; *Yosef David Varulekar* v. *Moses Solomon Talkar*, AIR 1931 Bom 490 : 33 Bom LR 1114; see *Varadarajulu Chettiar* v. *Muthu Kannu Ammal*, AIR 1966 Mad 158.

(e) The joint owners of the dominant heritage jointly acquire the servient heritage; the easement is extinguished.

(f) A single right of way exists over two servient heritages for the beneficial enjoyment of a single dominant heritage. The dominant owner acquires one only of the servient heritages. The easement is not extinguished.

(g) *A* has a right of way over *B*'s road. *B* dedicates the road to the public. *A*'s right of way is not extinguished.

NOTES

No one can have an easement right over his own property. Therefore where the same person becomes entitled to the *absolute ownership* of the whole of the dominant and the servient heritages, the easement is extinguished.

Before there can be any extinguishment, there must be a merger of the seveint and dominant tenements so as to result in the single ownership of both. It cannot be said that there is such a merger of the two tenements in a case where the owner of the dominant tenement acquires the right of a co-sharer in the servient tenement. In such a case there is no extinguishment but merely a suspension of the right of easement which will revive on partition between the co-sharers.

An easement may be revived after it has been extinguished by the union of the dominant and servient tenements in one owner, by their subsequent severance, provided the easement is apparent, continuous and essential to the enjoyment of the dominant tenement.

47. Extinction by non-enjoyment.—A continuous easement is extinguished when it totally ceases to be enjoyed as such for an unbroken period of twenty years.

A discontinuous easement is extinguished when for a like period it has not been enjoyed as such.

Such period shall be reckoned, in the case of a continuous easement, from the day on which its enjoyment was obstructed by the servient owner, or rendered impossible by the dominant owner, and in the case of a discontinuous easement, from the day on which it was last enjoyed by any person as dominant owner :

Provided that if, in the case of a discontinuous easement, the dominant owner, within such period, registers under the Indian Registration Act, III of 1877, a declaration of his intention to retain such easement, it shall not be extinguished until a period of twenty years has elapsed from the date of the registration.

Where an easement can be legally enjoyed only at a certain place, or at certain times, or between certain hours, or for a particular purpose, its enjoyment during the said period at another place, or at other times, or between other hours, or for another purpose, does not prevent its extinction under this section.

The circumstances that during the said period, no one was in possession of the servient heritage, or that the easement could not be enjoyed or that a right accessory thereto was enjoyed, or that the dominant owner was not aware of its existence, or that he enjoyed it in ignorance of his right to do so, does not prevent its extinction under this section.

An easement is not extinguished under this section—

(a) where the cessation is in pursuance of a contract between the dominant and servient owners;

(b) where the dominant heritage is held in co-ownership, and one of the co-owners enjoys the easement within the said period; or

(c) where the easement is necessary easement.

Where several heritages are respectively subject to rights of way for the benefit of a single heritage, and the ways are continuous, such rights shall, for the purpose of this section, be deemed to be a single easement.

Illustration

A has, as annexed to his house, rights of way from the high road thither over the heritages *X* and *Z* and the intervening heritage *Y*. Before the twenty years expire, *A* exercises his rights of way over *X*. His rights of way over *Y* and *Z* are not extinguished.

NOTES

An easement right is extinguished by a twenty year period of non-user. In other words, an easement can only be extinguished if it is not utilied for 20 years. Where 20 years had not elapsed from the alleged date of disuse till the date of the institution of the suit, easement of customary right is not extinguished.[1]

Non-enjoyment when dominant heritage is held by a life or limited owner.— Whether non-enjoyment during the period the dominant tenement is held by a life or limited owner, affects the rights of the remainderman or reversioner seems also to be a moot question and there appear to be no decided cases on the point. The analogy of the acquisition of right by prescription does not apply in this case as there are no provisions similar to those contained in Section 16, made by the Legislature in connection with non-enjoyment. Besides clause (2), paragraph 6 of Section 47 provides that the mere disability of the claimant to enjoy the right does not save it from extinguishment. Hence, the circumstances that during the whole or any part of such period of twenty years the dominant tenement is *held* by a life or limited owner is immaterial and the fact that the remainderman or reversioner could not enjoy the right during such period does not save it from extinction.[2]

Continuous ways through several servient heritages.—A way to a dominant heritage which passes through several servient heritages constitutes only one right of easement for the purposes of this section and the enjoyment of the right over one of such heritages is sufficient to save the right from extinction over the other heritages also.[3] But for these provisions contained in the last paragraph of Section 47

1. *Maheshwari Prasad* v. *Munni Lal*, AIR 1981 Allah 438.
2. But *see* Section 38 *supra* which provides that a release by a person who holds only a limited interest does not affect the rights of the remainderman or reversioner. Hence, though a life-tenant cannot effect release which would extend beyond his life yet he can extinguish the right by his mere forbearance to enjoy it.
3. *See* Illustration (f) to Section 47.

such right would be extinguished by partial non-enjoyment which is not the intention of the Legislature.[1]

Right of access to highway.—Where a man has abutted road, he is entitled to enforce his right in spite of the fact that there is some space available between the offending constructions, suit filed after six years of construction is not barred by limitation.[2]

Continuous easements when extinguished by non-enjoyment.—An easement is extinguished when it totally ceases to be enjoyed as such for an unbroken period of twenty years. Where there was no occasion to exercise such right, the right itself would not amount to extinction of such right.[3]

48. Extinction of accessory rights.—When an easement is extinguished, the rights (if any) accessory thereto are also extinguished.

Illustration

A has an easement to draw water from *B*'s well. As accessory thereto, he has right of way over *B*'s land to and from the well. The easement to draw water is extinguished under Section 47. The right of way is also extinguished.

NOTES

Where an easement is extinguished, the rights accessory thereto are also extinguished because accessory rights are those rights which are necessary to secure the full enjoyment of an easement and when the principal right, *viz.*, the easement right is extinguished, rights to enjoy such right will automatically go.

49. Suspension of easement.—An easement is suspended when the dominant owner becomes entitled to possession of the servient heritage for a limited interest therein, or when the servient owner becomes entitled to possession of the dominant heritage for a limited interest therein.

NOTES

Easement rights are suspended when the two tenements happen to be in possession of the same person but they revive

1. *See* Whitely Stokes' Anglo-Indian Codes, Vol. I, p. 887, Statement of Objects and Reasons.
2. *Bharathamantha Desiya Sangam* v. *Roja Sundaram*, AIR 1987 Mad 183.
3. *Bhaurao A. Kasar* v. *Vinod R. Kasar*, 2006 (2) Bom CR 201.

when the unity of possession comes to an end.

Suspension by a trespass.—Section 49 declares that the right is suspended when there is unity of possession due to the same person being entitled to it by virtue of a limited interest in both the heritages. The Legislature here appears to have very advisedly excluded the unity of possession due to an encroachment or trespass which is possessed without any interest at all.[1]

Such possession, before it ripens into a full right of ownership, by adverse claim, is only a very precarious right, and can be put to an end at any moment. Hence, there is no unity of possession as required by Section 49 during such period. But if it ripens into full ownership, Section 46 applies and the right is extinguished. Hence, the omission of suspension by encroachment by the Indian Legislature.

Difference between the English and the Indian law.—Section 47, as has been already noted, is a departure from English law. The provision in paragraph 3 of Section 51 is only a corollary to Section 47. Hence, though in English law, a right suspended is not extinguished by any length of such suspension,[2] in India, under this Act, such suspension continued for an unbroken period of twenty years causes extinction of the right.[3]

50. Servient owner not entitled to require continuance.—The servient owner has no right to require that an easement be continued; and, notwithstanding the provisions of Section 26, he is not entitled to compensation for damage caused to the servient heritage in consequence of the extinguishment or suspension of the easement, if the dominant owner has given to the servient owner such notice as will enable him, without unreasonable expense, to protect the servient heritage from such damage.

Compensation for damage caused by extinguishment or suspension.—Where such notice has not been given the servient owner is entitled to

1. *See* Whitley Stokes' Anglo-Indian Codes, Vol I, p. 887, Statement of Objects and Reasons.
2. *Thomas* v. *Thomas*, 2 Cr. M. & R 34 : *Simper* v. *Foley*, 5 LT 669; *see* Halsbury's Laws, of England, 4th Ed., Vol. 14, p. 62.
3. *Kandhanath* v. *Chemboli*, 16 IC 375 (Mad).

compensation for damage caused to the servient heritage in consequence of such extinguishment or suspension.

Illustration

A, in exercise of an easement, diverts to his canal the water of *B*'s stream. The diversion continues for many years, and during that time the bed of the stream partly fills up. *A* then abandons his easement, and restores the stream to its ancient course. *B*'s land is consequently flooded. *B* sues *A* for compensation for the damage caused by the flooding. It is provided that *A* gave *B* a month's notice of his intention to abandon the easement, and that such notice was sufficient to enable *B*, without unreasonable expense to have prevented the damage. The suit must be dismissed.

NOTES

An easement right exists for the benefit of a dominant owner and he is free to enjoy his right or not and the servient owner cannot insist that the enjoyment of an easement be continued. But before a dominant owner discontinues his easement he must give a notice of his intention to do so to the servient owner, otherwise the servient owner would be entitled to compensation for the loss caused to him by the discontinuance of the dominant owner's enjoyment of his easement right.

How are easements extinguished? State the circumstances under which easements can be revived.

Easements are extinguished in the following ways :—

(1) By the dissolution of the right of servient owner in his heritage except when it is imposed by a mortgagor in accordance with Section 10. (Section 37).

(2) By release by the dominant owner expressly or impliedly. It may be released as to part only of the servient heritage. (Section 38).

(3) By revocation by the servient owner in exercise of a power reserved by him in this behalf. (Section 39).

(4) On expiration of the limited period, if it is for a fixed period or on fulfilment of the contingent condition,

if it is contingent. (Section 40).

(5) On termination of necessity, if it is an easement of necessity. (Section 41).

(6) By its being useless. (Section 42).

(7) By permanent change in the dominant heritage, if the burden on the servient tenement is thereby increased and cannot be reduced by the servient owner without interfering with the lawful enjoyment of the easement. (Section 43).

(8) By the permanent alteration of the servient tenement by superior force. (Section 44).

(9) By the complete destruction of either heritage dominant or servient. (Section 45).

(10) By unity of ownership, i.e., when the same person becomes entitled to absolute ownership of both the heritages. (Section 46).

(11) By non-enjoyment for a period of 20 years. (Section 47).

Easement can be revived in the following ways :—

(1) If it is a suspended easement it revives when the cause of suspension is removed before the right is extinguished by 20 years' non-enjoyment.

(2) If it is extinguished under Section 16 by unity, of ownership it is revived if the grant or bequest by which the unity of ownership was produced is set aside by a decree of a competent court except in the case of an easement of necessity which is revived when the unity ceases from any other cause.

(3) If it is extinguished because of destruction of either heritage, it is revived when the destroyed heritage is restored or rebuilt on the same site before expiry of 20 years.

51. Revival of easements.—An easement extinguished under Section 45 revives : (a) when the destroyed heritage is, before twenty years have expired, restored by the deposit of alluvion; (b) when the destroyed heritage is a servient building and before twenty years have expired such building is rebuilt upon the same site; and (c) when the destroyed heritage is a dominant building and before twenty years have expired, such building is rebuilt upon the same site and in such a manner as not to impose greater burden on the servient heritage.

An easement extinguished under Section 46 revives when the grant or bequest by which the unity of ownership was produced is set aside by the decree of a competent Court. A necessary easement extinguished under the same section revives when the unity of ownership ceases from other cause.

A suspended easement revives if the cause of suspension is removed before the right is extinguished under Section 47.

Illustration

A, as the absolute owner of field *Y*, has a right of way thither over *B*'s field *Z*. *A* obtains from *B* a lease of *Z* for 20 years. The easement is suspended so long as *A* remains lessee of *Z*. But when *A* assigns the lease to *C*, or surrenders it to *B*, the right of way revives.

NOTES

When does a suspended easement revive?—An easement suspended by unity of possession revives, if the cause of suspension is removed before the right is extinguished under Section 47. The illustration makes it clear beyond all doubt that, if such unity of possession is continued for a period of twenty years, the easement is destroyed altogether, and does not revive on severance of such possession after such period.[1] But an easement is only suspended when there is unity of possession of the two tenements and it is due to either the servient or the dominant owner's holding only a limited or life interest in the other tenement so that it is an ascertained fact that there will be severance of possession on the ceasing of such interest. If the unity of possession is due to the transfer of absolute ownership in the two tenements to one and the same person, the right is extinguished and not suspended and revives at any time when such transfer is set aside by a decree of a competent Court. As has been already noticed, suspension by encroachment is not recognised by the Act.[2] Hence, unity of possession due to a trespass by the owner of either heritage on the other does not suspend the right, though it may cause

1. *Kandhanath* v. *Chemboli*, 16 IC 375 (Mad) : (1913) MWN 95.
2. *See* Section 49, *ante*.

the extinction of the right when after the lapse of the prescriptive period his possession as trespasser ripens into that of an absolute owner. [*See* Section 46, *ante.*] and in the latter case the right will not revive at any time even if such unity of possession ceases inasmuch as neither paragraph 2 nor paragraph 3 of Section 51 applies to such cases.

The right of easement was held to have been revived by estoppel where the appellant had by his conduct permitted the respondents to believe that they would have the right to irrigate, upon their repairing the well and the respondents acting upon that permission had repaired the well. The appellant under Section 115 of the Evidence Act was estopped from repudiating respondents' right of easement.[1]

---

1. *Anatha* v. *Ganu*, AIR 1931 Bom 417 : 45 Bom 80.

CHAPTER VI

LICENCES

52. "Licence" defined.—Where one person grants to another, or to a definite number of other persons, a right to do or continue to do, in or upon the immovable property of the grantor, something which would, in the absence of such right, be unlawful, and such right does not amount to an easement or an interest in the property, the right is called a licence.

NOTES

What is a licence.—A license is a personal right granted to a person to do something upon immovable property of the grantor, and does not amount to the creation of an interest in the property itself. It is purely a permissive right and is personal to the grantee. It creates no duties and obligations upon the person making the grant and is, therefore, revocable except in certain circumstances expressly provided for in the Act itself. The licence has no other effect than to confer a liberty upon the licensee to go upon the land which would otherwise be unlawful.[1]

In the decision of the Supreme Court in *Associated Hotels of India Ltd.* v. *R.N. Kapoor*,[2] Subba Rao, J., after quoting Section 52 stated thus :

> Under the aforesaid section, if a document gives only a right to use the property in a particular way or under certain terms while it remains in possession and control of the owner thereof, it will be a licence. The legal possession, therefore, continues to be with the owner of the property, but the licensee is permitted to make use of the premises for a particular purpose. But for the permission, his occupation would be unlawful. It does not

1. *Mohammad Khan* v. *Ramanarayan Misra*, AIR 1956 Orissa 16).
2. AIR 1959 SC 1262.

create in his favour any estate or interest in the property. In *Mrs. M.N. Clubwala* v. *Fida Hussain Saheb*,[1] it is stated—

In the case before us, however, while it is true that each stall-holder is entitled to the exclusive use of his stall from day today it is clear that he has no right to use it as and when he chooses to do so or to sleep in the stall during the night after closure of the market or enter the stall during the night after 11 P.M. at his pleasure. He can use it only during a stated period everyday and subject to several conditions. These circumstances, coupled with the fact that the responsibility for closing the stalls, disinfecting them and of closing the market in which the stall are situate is placed by the Act, the regulations made thereunder and the licence issued to the landlords, is on the landlords, would indicate that the legal possession of the stalls must also be deemed to have been with the landlords and not with the stall-holders. The right which stall-holders had was to the exclusive use of the stalls during the stated hours and nothing more. Looking at the matter in a slightly different way it would seem that it could never have been the intention of the parties to grant anything more than a licence to the stall-holders. The duties cast on the landlord by the Act are onerous and for performing those duties they were entitled to free and easy access to the stalls. They are also required to see to it that the market functioned only within the stated hours and not beyond them and also that the premises were used for no purpose other than of vending combustibles. A further duty which lay upon the landlords was to guard the entrance to the market. These duties could not be effectively carried out by the landlord by parting with possession in favour of the stall-holders by reason of which the performance by the landlords of their duties and obligations could easily be rendered impossible if the stall-holders adopted an unreasonable attitude. If the landlords failed to perform their obligations they would be exposed to penalties under the Act and also stood in danger of having their licences revoked. Could in such circumstances the landlords have ever intended to part with possession in favour of the stall-holders and thus place themselves at the mercy of these people? We are,

1. AIR 1965 SC 610.

therefore, of the opinion that the intention of the parties was to bring into existence merely a licence and not a lease and the word 'rent' was used loosely for "fee".

The decision in AIR 1959 SC 1262 is followed in later decisions of the Supreme Court in *Qudrat Ullah* v. *Municipal Board, Bareilly*,[1] and in *Board of Revenue* v. *A.M. Ansari*.[2]

The essential features of a licence.—The following constitute the essential features of a licence :

(1) A licence is not connected with the ownership of any land, but creates only a personal right or obligation,[3] hence, it cannot be assigned.[4]

(2) It is purely permissive right arising only by permission, express or implied, and not by adverse exercise or in any other way,[5] hence, it is generally revocable at the will of the grantor.[6]

(3) It only legalises a certain act which would otherwise be unlawful and does not confer any interest in the property itself in or upon or over which such act is allowed to be done.[7]

The amount paid by a licensee is only licence fee. Mere payment would not create any interest in the property. Licence creates no interest in the property.[8] Where a deed provides that licensee would be entitled to use premises but will have no right, title or interest to possess premises and the license fee is payable per day, it was held that the intention of parties was to create licence and not lease.[9]

As a grant generally forms the basis of transfer of an interest in immovable property, of an easement, or of a licence pure and simple as well as of licence coupled with a grant of an interest in immovable property, in each case where a grant is alleged it is to be seen whether the right granted thereby

1. AIR 1974 SC 396.
2. AIR 1976 SC 1813.
3. *Hill* v. *Tupper*, (1863) 2 H & C 121; *Sundrabai* v. *Jayawant*, 23 Bom 397, 400; *Mohammad Khan* v. *Ram Narayan*, AIR 1946 Orissa 156; *see* notes under "Nature of the right".
4. *See* Section 56, *post*.
5. *See* Section 52, *post*.
6. *See* Section 62, *post*.
7. *Head* v. *Hartley*, 42 Ch D 461.
8. *Mayabhai Jamalbhai* v. *Karimbhai Mohammadbhai*, AIR 1967 Guj. 16.
9. *M/s Hind Trading* v. *M/s Didi Modes*, AIR 1993 Delhi 301 at 313 : (1993) 2 Cur. C.C. 747 : (1993) 2 Civ. LJ 936 : (1993) 50 DLT 84 : (1993) 2 Ren CR 56 : (1993) 1 Rent LR 705.

is only a licence pure and simple or a licence coupled with a grant of an interest in immovable property or an easement or a transfer of an interest in immovable property and the solution of this question is not always easy but is attended generally with considerable difficulty.

It is proposed to discuss these distinctive features of a licence by comparison with those of the other rights enumerated above.

Distinction between an easement and a license

(1) An easement right is appurtenant to some dominant tenement, a license is not appurtenant to any land but it is a personal right to do on the land of the grantor something which without such license would be unlawful.

(2) A license is not transferable except in circumstances mentioned in Section 56. An easement right follows the dominant tenement.

(3) The transferee of the land over which the license is available is not bound by the license, but the transferee of the servient tenement takes the tenement subject to the easement right.

(4) An easement right may be positive or negative in character (a right to do or prevent something being done in or upon the servient tenement) but a license is always bound to be of a positive nature, because a license is a right to do or continue to do something in or upon the land of the grantor which would, in the absence of such right, be unlawful.

(5) A license can be revoked at the will of the grantor except in two cases mentioned in Section 60, but an easement cannot be revoked at the will of the servient owner.

(6) A mere licensee cannot maintain an action in his own name for infringement against a stranger. He can only do it after getting the permission of the licensor and that too in the name of the licensor.

Distinction between a license and a lease

The main test for deciding whether a person is a licensee of a property or a lessee is that of *exclusive possession.* If the right granted conveys to the grantee an exclusive right of possession, though subject to certain reservations, it is a lease.

But where the grantee can only use the property in a certain way and on certain terms while the property remains in the possession and control of the owner, the right granted is a license.

(1) A lease gives an exclusive interest in property, whereas a licence does not.

(2) A lease can be assigned to a third person, while a license being a personal right cannot be so assigned.

(3) A lessee can bring an action for trespass in his own name, but a licensee cannot do so. He must do so in the name of the licensor after obtaining his permission.

(4) A lease is not revocable, a license is revocable except in two cases mentioned in Section 60.

Recently the Supreme Court in the case of *B.M. Lall* v. *M/s. Dunlop Rubber Co.,*[1] have drawn a distinction between a lease and a license in the following words :—

> A lease is the transfer of a right to enjoy the premises, whereas a license is a privilege to do something on the premises which otherwise would be unlawful. If the agreement is in writing, it is a question of construction of the agreement having regard to its terms and where its language is ambiguous, having regard to its object, and the circumstances under which it was executed whether the rights of the occupier are those of a lessee or a licensee. The transaction is a lease if it grants an interest in the land; it is a license if it gives a personal privilege with no interest in the land. The question is not of words but of substance and the label which the parties choose to put upon the transaction though relevant, is not, decisive. The test of exclusive possession is not conclusive though it is a very important indication in favour of tenancy.

Whether a deed is a lease or a licence depends on the intention of the parties. If an interest in immovable property entitling the transferee to employment is created, it is a lease, if permission to use land without right to exclusive possession alone is granted, it is a licence.[2]

Right of suit of licensee.—An easement right is carved out in favour of a dominant heritage and is imposed on a servient heritage. In every case the right is exercised *qua*

1. AIR 1968 SC 175.
2. *Quadrat Ullah* v. *Bareilly Municipality*, AIR 1974 SC 396.

owner or occupier of a dominant heritage and falls as a burden on the owner or occupier of a servient heritage. It is for the owner and not for the licensees to resist by suit the right claimed by the person claiming easement right.[1]

Licence and gift—Distinction between.—In the case of *State of Uttar Pradesh* v. *Sayed Abdul Jalil*,[2] the facts were that the Government of Rampur had given a house to the plaintiff on 23rd June, 1945. It appears that after the merger of Rampur State in Uttar Pradesh in 1949, when Rampur became a District of Uttar Pradesh this house was given by the Government of Uttar Pradesh to the Municipal Board of Rampur, which demanded rent from the plaintiff by notice. On the plaintiff's refusal to pay, the house was attached on 23rd February, 1955. The plaintiff deposited a sum of Rupees 100 under protest, and filed a suit for declaration that he is the owner in possession of the house and in the alternative, that he is a 'licensee' entitled to remain in possession of the house for life without payment of any rent.

Exclusive licence, meaning of.—An exclusive licence is leave to do a thing coupled with a contract not to give leave to anybody else to do the same thing.[3] Such a right should be conferred by means of clear and explicit language[4] in the absence of which it cannot be presumed or inferred from a mere leave to do a thing.[5] So a grant of liberty to work mines is not the grant of an exclusive right to work them.[6] So a right given to one of them in a partition deed between two bothers to use a well which fell to the share of the other brother was *held* to be not an exclusive licence so as to prevent the use of the well by servants or agents.[7] The incidents of an exclusive grant in no way differ from those of an ordinary licence except that the violation of the contract not to give leave to anybody else to do the same thing, would give the licensee a right of action against the licensor.[8]

1. *S.C. Mukerjee* v. *Smt. Gangabhai*, 1957 MPC 168 : AIR 1957 MP 44.
2. AIR 1972 SC 1290.
3. *Per* Fry, L.J., *Heap* v. *Horley*, 42 Ch D 461.
4. *Duke of Sutherland* v. *Heathcote*, (1892) 1 Ch 475.
5. *Lord Mountjoy's* case, 1 Andh 307; *Chetham* v. *Williamson*, 4 East. 469; *Doe d. Hanley* v. *Wood*, 21 R 469; *Carr* v. *Benson*, LR 3 Ch App 524; *Duke of Sutherland* v. *Heathcote*, (1892) 1 Ch 475.
6. *Lord Mountjoy's* case, 1 Andh 307.
7. *Janardan* v. *Ramchandra*, AIR 1927 Bom 240. See *Kuruppiah Pillai* v. *Narayana Mudaliar*, (1967) 1 MLJ 91 : 79 Mad LW 632 (a case of wall).
8. *Heap* v. *Hortley*, 42 Ch D 461.

Relationship between the licensor and the licensee.—To understand the true nature of the relationship between the licensor and the licensee, the decisive consideration is the intention of the parties.[1] Where there is no formal document embodying the terms of the agreement, the intention is to be inferred from surrounding circumstances and the conduct of the parties.[2] In another case of the Supreme Court, i.e., *Associated Hotels of India Ltd.* v. *R.N. Kapoor*,[3] their Lordships of the Supreme Court *held* likewise and further said that a party getting exclusive possession under a document is prima facie considered a tenant. In both the aforesaid cases,[4] the Supreme Court considered the terms of a written agreement to find out if they created a tenancy or lease or a mere licence. The crucial circumstance, in such cases, is the nature of grant of exclusive possession. This is a consideration of the first importance, but the test of exclusive possession is by no means decisive of existence of a tenancy or a licence.[5] A grant conferring exclusive possession may, in very many cases, operate as a mere licence.

Adverse possession by licensee.—The possession of a licensee is in its inception permissive. Therefore, his possession can never be deemed to be adverse until he does some overt act which shows that he claims adversely to the licensor and such overt act comes to the knowledge of the licensor.[6] But when the subject matter of the licence changes hands either by a transfer by the licensee or by his death, the possession of the transferee or the heir as the case may be is adverse to the grantor and time begins to run against him from the time of the transfer by or death of the licensee.[7] Where, on the other hand, under a licence granted to a person to live in a

1. *Biswanath Panda* v. *Gadadhar Panda*, AIR 1971 Orissa 115 at 117.
2. *M.N. Clubwala* v. *Fida Hussain Saheb*, AIR 1965 SC 610 : (1964) 6 SCR 642.
3. AIR 1959 SC 1262 : (1960) 1 SCR 368. *See* also *Brahm Raj* v. *Vidyawati*, AIR 1991 P & H 188.
4. *M.N. Clubwala* v. *Fida Hussain Saheb*, AIR 1965 SC 610 : (1964) 6 SCR 642 and *Associated Hotels of India Ltd.* v. *R.N. Kapoor*, AIR 1959 SC 1262 : (1960) 1 SCR 368.
5. *M.N. Clubwala* v. *Fida Hussain Saheb*, AIR 1965 SC 610 : (1964) 6 SCR 642; *P. Narayanan* v. *M.D. Kerala Health Research & Welfare Society*, AIR 1991 Ker 306.
6. *Narsingdas* v. *Ratan Lal*, 34 IC 471 (Nag); *Bhojraj* v. *Hardeva*, AIR 1923 All 140.
7. *Chinnan* v. *Ranjithammal*, AIR 1931 Mad 216 : 131 IC 175 : 1930 MWN 1242 : 60 MLJ 709 : 33 MLW 455.

certain house, the licensee lives in it along with his sons and other members of his family and the licensor has full knowledge of it and raises no objection to the residence of such persons, in the house, a presumption of implied licence arises in their favour. In such cases the possession of the members of the licensee's family being permissive in nature, they are in no better position than the licensee himself, and no question of adverse possession does arise.[1] The petitioners being licensees with liberty to occupy and use the kiosk for a period of 11 months in the first instance could not be said to be in legal possession of the premises, the legal possession all along remained with the Corporation. On revocation of the licence they ceased to enjoy the liberty to continue to occupy the kiosk so as to drive the Corporation to evict them in due course of law, nor could the petitioners' possession be said to be "settled possession".

In *Ganpat Govind Shigvan* v. *Preeti Paresh Shah*,[2] it was held that the courts are not justified in protecting the possession of a caretaker, servant or any person who was allowed to live in the premises for sometime either as a friend, relative, caretaker or as a servant. The court held that Trial Court has not committed error in exercise of the jurisdiction and therefore no interference is called for in the impugned order. Petition dismissed.

Lease or licence.—This fact alone may not convert licence into lease that deceased licensor did not initiate any proceeding against licence holder during his lifetime for obtaining possession.[3]

Licensee not trespasser.—The person inducted on to the premises initially as a licensee and his licence coming to be terminated later on, such licensee could not be treated as a trespasser.[4]

No vesting of right in contractual matter.—The land was given on licence by Municipal Corporation for hotel construction. Held, that the matter involved the rights of the parties under a contract which had been arrived at by the parties consciously with eyes wide open. Any right which the party claimed against the other had to flow from the agreement between them. The licensee had made a

1. *Nand Gopal* v. *Brijmohan Lal*, 1966 All LJ 166.
2. W.P. No 7237 of 2022 Bom.
3. *Smt. Ranuben Bhimji* v. *Padmabai*, AIR 1991 Bom 85.
4. *Ramesh Dwarkadas Mehra* v. *Indrawati Dwarkadas Mehra*, AIR 2001 Bom 470.

representation to the NDMC to reduce the licence fee since it was quite burdensome and not viable for running hotel. The Lt. Governor put a note on the file that a committee be constituted to examine the issue and make recommendations. It was a mere noting on the file and was an opinion of the Lt. Governor which could not be binding between the parties in contractual matter.[1]

Determination of lease or license depends upon intention of parties.—Where it was shown by circumstance and conduct of parties that occupier was granted personal privilege with no interest in land. Held, that occupier was licensee and there was no question of permanent tenancy which could have arisen under Section 106 of Kerala Land Reforms Act, 1964.[2]

Licence.—A license is a right granted by one party to another in respect of immovable property of grantor which in absence of such a right would be unlawful and which would not amount to an easement or an interest in property. The intention of the parties to consent terms has to be determined from nature of the contract.[3]

Where the licensor expressed his intention to get the plot vacated and also consequences of not vacating the plot were unequivocally expressed and communicated, it could be taken that the licence was determined by such communication.[4]

Scope.—Where the suit could only be brought to enforce the revocation of licence and for that purpose necessarily the Court fee has to be paid only in accordance with law governing relief relating to grant or revocation of licence, the suit relating to easements are to be valued as per the said provisions........The *vinculum juries*, that exists between the plaintiff and defendant is licensor and licensee and as such the relationship is clearly governed under S. 52 of the Act, the suit has to be treated as a suit relating to Easement Act, 1882.[5]

Renewal of license.—The petitioner/firm entered into contract with North Eastern Railways for the display of hoardings on the licence basis. But the letter issued by Manager to petitioner/firm did not hold out any promise for the renewal of contract by depositing renewal fees. Hence,

1. *C.J. International Hotels Pvt. Ltd.* v. *N.D.M.C.*, AIR 2001 Delhi 435.
2. *K.P. Sadanandan Nair* v. *M. Vimala*, AIR 2004 Ker 278.
3. *Mini Peter Philips* v. *Dina J.S. Fanibanda*, 2008 AIHC (NOC) 328 (Bom).
4. *Harishchandra* v. *Santosh*, 2008 (4) Mah. LJ 83.
5. *B. Krishnappa* v. *Chandrika G.*, 2007 (1) Kar. LJ 468.

petitioner/firm did not have right of renewal of contract.[1]

Only the document has not to be considered for determining if a transaction is a lease or license. The surrounding circumstances and relationship between the parties are also very much relevant.[2]

Licensee.—Where it has been revealed that there was no relationship as landlord and tenant between the parties and the appellants were permitted by the respondent to use the premises for keeping the business goods as licensee and such licence was terminated, revoked or cancelled by notice, the appellants were bound to hand over the vacant possession of the premises to the respondent.[3]

A licensee has a limited right to evict an encroacher during the period of licence.[4]

The essential features of a licence.—As a grant generally forms the basis of transfer of an interest in immovable property, of an easement, or of a licence pure and simple, as well as of licence coupled with a grant of an interest in immovable property, in each case where a grant is alleged it is to be seen whether the right granted thereby is only a licence pure and simple or a licence coupled with a grant of an interest in immovable property or an easement or a transfer of an interest in immovable property and the solution of this question is not always easy but is attended generally with considerable difficulty. An employee provided with an accommodation by his employer in order to facilitate the employee to discharge his function is only a licensee *vis-a-vis* this employer as licensor.[5]

Licence and lease distinguished.—It is useful in this context to refer to the decision in *Gajriben* v. *Kantilal Uttamram Chevli*,[6] which in turn quoted the principles extracted from Halsbury's Law of England, also referred to in the above Supreme Court case.

Lease or Licence, determination of.—Where possession and control of a shop remained with the owner and tenure of deed was for 11 months, it might be cancelled in

1. *Rajput Advertising Service* v. *U.O.I.*, 2010 AIHC 476 (479-80) (All) (DB).
2. *Narendra Kumar Jain* v. *Pradeep Kumar Jain*, 2011 AIR CC 2867 (Del).
3. *International Electricals* v. *Sunital Jain*, 2008 (2) MPLJ 118.
4. *Rashi Mitra* v. *Ganga Haridas*, AIR 2006 (NOC) 1482 (Gau).
5. *Madan Mohan Kukreti* v. *Geeta Bhawan*, 2007 (3) ALJ 632 (Uttranchal HC); *Shailendra Nath Mishra* v. *Union of India*, 2003 (50) ALR 400.
6. AIR 2007 Guj. 18.

case of violation of any condition, the deed would be licence and not lease.[1]

If a particular sum is deducted from the salary of an employee in lieu of accommodation provided to him by the employer, then only on this ground it cannot be said that the transaction of giving such facility for period of service was lease not licence.[2]

Where nature of a transaction and status of the parties thereto have to be ascertained, one cannot go by mere nomenclature of the document. In order to ascertain the substance of the transaction, the purpose and substance of the agreement have to be ascertained. In such cases intention of the parties is the deciding factor.[3]

Where recital in agreement did not show even remotely that exclusive possession was given to defendant, the document was described as deed of lease and licence and the terms of the deed, the surrounding circumstances and the subsequent events showed that the parties intended to create an agreement of leave and licence, it could not be held as lease deed.[4]

Where intention of the parties was to create licence agreement and not lease, and the executor of the document in his own writing accepted the status of licensee and during his life did not change it, any person succeeding him would not get any right, wide or larger than what the deceased had.[5]

Grant vis-a-vis revocation of and various issues involved in licence.—Section 52 of the Indian Easements Act, defines "license" as where one person grants to another, or to a definite number of other persons, a right to do, or continue to do, in or upon the immovable property of the grantor, something which would, in the absence of such right, be unlawful, and such right does not amount to an easement or an interest in the property. It is manifestly clear that every licence originates in a grant made by one person in favour of another or a definite number of other persons. By implication a license cannot be granted to a fluctuating body of persons who will not be answering the expression of definite number

1. *Mahesh Kumar* v. *Kamlesh Kumar*, AIR 2008 (NOC) 2445 (P & H). See also *G. Krishna Murthy* v. *Government of A.P.*, AIR 2008 (NOC) 2440 (AP).
2. *Madan Mohan Kukreti* v. *Geeta Bhawan*, AIR 2007 Utr. 32.
3. *Achintya Kr. Saha* v. *Nanee Printers*, (2004) 12 SCC 368 (373). See also *Maria Mannela Piedale* v. *Vassant Shet Shirodkar*, 2006 (5) Bom CR 38.
4. *Bento de Souza* v. *Yvette Alvazes Colaco*, 2006 AIHC (NOC) 263 (Bom).
5. *Gajriben* v. *Kantilal Uttamram Chevli*, AIR 2007 Guj. 18.

of other persons. Most importantly, what has been granted was only to do something which would in the absence of such grant be unlawful to be done by the other persons. Equally important to notice is the fact that the person to whom the grant is made, does not acquire any right whatsoever, including easementary right or any interest in the property. It can, therefore, be deduced that a grant, which is called license merely authorized the person or persons to whom the grant is made.[1]

Grantor or the licensor.—In law, grantor or the licensor is always liable to be treated to be in possession of the land in question all through the subsistence of the licensee and hence, it would be open to the licensor to re-enter the premises and reinstate himself once the period of license granted by him expires. This power to re-enter or to reinstate himself is conditioned by not using more force than is actually necessary.[2]

Licence on the basis of family settlement.—This was a case relating to licence based on family settlement. It was argued in this case that the family settlement which gives right to some of the owners introduces new owners or takes away the rights of ownership of some of the co-owners, should necessarily be registered. That legal proposition has rightly been settled by the Hon'ble Apex Court by a Full Bench in the case of *Kale* v. *D.D.C.*,[3] and *Lakshman Das* v. *Ramdas*.[4] This legal proposition is not at all relevant and the thrust of the learned counsel for the appellants on this issue is nothing but a camouflage to delay the disposal of controversy finally, which shall result in nothing less than perpetuity in occupation of the defendants, who are mere licensees and their license has been terminated through written notice, which has been served upon them.

The High Court ultimately held that a licensee has no right to challenge that it is not registered and that suit in absence thereof cannot be maintained.[5]

Rights of Mitakshra father.—In *R.N. Giri* v. *Krishnawati Devi*,[6] it was held that the suit properties were self-acquired properties of the father of the plaintiff, and in such circumstances, it was open for the father of the plaintiffs

1. *Jasti Venkateswara Rao* v. *South Central Railway*, 2012 (110) AIC 577 (AP).
2. *Jasti Venkateswara Rao* v. *South Central Railway*, 2012 (110) AIC 577 (AP).
3. AIR 1976 SC 807.
4. AIR 1989 SC 1923.
5. *Smt. Meeta Gajwani* v. *Hari Ram Achharia*, 2013 (127) AIC 310 (Alld).
6. AIR 2022 (Sikk) 10.

to execute the gift deed in favour of the defendant.

Permission for occupying premises whether a licence?—In the case of *Smt. Meeta Gajwani* v. *Hari Ram Achharia*,[1] the defendant occupied premises on the basis of permission granted by the owners. Trial Court held that the decree granted by the Civil Judge was a nullity, as it was based on unregistered document. Second appeal was preferred and the High Court held that admittedly, defendants are not the owners of the disputed property. It is also admitted that the disputed property was purchased by the two real brothers of defendant No. 1 and remaining defendants are sons and daughter of defendant No. 1. It is also not disputed that the defendants are occupying the disputed premises on the basis of permission granted by its owners, who are the real brothers or their legal representatives, without any condition to pay any rent. Though, the defendants have specifically denied any lease or licence, yet their possession is nothing more than either lessee or licensee. Since there is no lease nor any rent deed, as admitted between the parties, it is nothing more than a licence, which means to give a licence or permit a person to occupy the land and to do work or perform an act on the land owner's property. The visitor has a licence to enter into the property. This kind of licence need not be written, signed and registered. It may be oral or it may be implied by the relationship or actions of the parties.

Licence as defined under Section 52 is obviously different with a lease as defined under Section 105 of Transfer of Property Act. This plea was not seriously placed before the two Courts below, nor it has been impressed upon this Court either in the memorandum of appeal or during the course of argument.[2]

53. Who may grant licence?—A licence may be granted by any one in the circumstances and to the extent in and to which he may transfer his interests in the property affected by the licence.

NOTES

A person having a transferable interest in property can grant license to the extent to his power of transfer. Section 8, which provides 'who may impose easements', is similarly worded.

---

1. 2013 (127) AIC 310 (Alld).
2. *Smt. Meeta Gajwani* v. *Hari Achharia*, 2013 (127) AIC 310 (All).

A co-sharer in an Abadi cannot grant a licence to a third person to build on the site wihout the consent of the other co-sharers.[1]

54. Grant may be express or implied.—The grant of a licence may be express or implied from the conduct of the grantor, and an agreement which purports to create an easement, but is ineffectual for that purpose, may operate to create a licence.

NOTES

A license may be granted orally or in writing.

Licence by implication.—Where the husband of defendant was living in the suit premises as licensee and after the death of this licensee the defendant continued to live in the same premises, she would be licensee by implication.[2]

Modes of granting licence.—As per Section 54 of the Easements Act, the grant of a licence may be express or implied from the conduct of the grantor, and Section 60 of the said Act sets out the circumstances when a license can be revoked and Section 61 sets out that such a revocation can be express or even implied. Section 62 listed out nine circumstances when a licence is deemed to be revoked. Of them, clause (c) clearly discloses that a licence is deemed to be revoked when it has been granted for a limited period and the period expired. Thus, it becomes evident that a licence granted for a limited period is deemed to have been revoked upon expiry of the period of grant.[3]

55. Accessory licences annexed by law.—All licences necessary for the enjoyment of any interest, or the exercise of any right, are implied in the constitution of such interest or right. Such licences are called accessory licences.

Illustration

A sells the trees growing on his land to *B*. *B* is entitled to go on the land and take away the trees.

56. Licence when transferable.—Unless a different intention is expressed or necessarily implied, a licence to attend a place of public entertainment may be transferred by the licensee; but, save as

1. *Manbanhal Rai* v. *Ram Ghulam Pandey*, AIR 1927 All 633.
2. *Surjeet Kaur* v. *Balwinder Kaur*, AIR 2006 P & H 23.
3. *Gorti Venkateswara Rao* v. *South Central Railway*, 2012 (110) AIC 577 (AP).

aforesaid, a licence cannot be transferred by the licensee or exercised by his servants or agents.

Illustrations

(a) *A* grants *B* a right to walk over *A*'s field whenever he pleases. The right is not annexed to any immovable property of *B*. The right cannot be transferred.

(b) The Government grants *B* a licence to erect and use temporary grain sheds on Government land. In the absence of express provisions to the contrary, *B*'s servants may enter on the land for the purpose of erecting sheds, erect the same, deposit grain therein and remove grain therefrom.

NOTES

A licence cannot be transferred by the licensee or exercised by his servants or agents. The only exception has been made in the case of a license to attend a place of a public entertainment. In this case the license may be transferred unless a different intention appears.

The words "save as aforesaid" in Section 56 are important and they must be read with the opening words of the section unless a different intention is expressed or necessarily implied. So interpreting, the section mean that unless a different intention is expressed or necessarily implied, a licence other than a licence to attend a place of public entertainment cannot be transferred by the licensee or by his servants or agents.[1]

Licence implied from the conduct of the grantor.—A licence may be implied from the conduct of the licensor where by acquiescence or encouragement, he allows something to be done on his own land by another person who believes the land to be his own.

Licence is purely a contract between the licensor and licensee. It creates no right in land and lapses with the death of the licensor or licensee. Where, however, licence is given to a person to live in a house but the other members of the family of the licensee live along with him without any objection from the licensor, implied licence may be presumed. The death of the licensee does not terminate the implied licence in favour

1. *Ram Bharose* v. *Bishwanath Prasad*, AIR 1934 Allahabad 336 *See* also *Smt. Aqlnina Bibi* v. *Shiv Shanker*, AIR 1982 Allahabad 158.

of other members.[1]

To say the same thing in different words, a plea of an implied licence on which may be based the right of equity to intervene, must have for its foundation either a contract or the existence of some fact which the legal owner is estopped from denying.[2]

Transfer of licence.—In this case there was licence in respect of property which was descendible and heritable. *Held*, that the transfer could not be effected in absence of legal heirship certificate and no objection from other legal heirs. Therefore, order passed by authorities calling for said documents was perfectly valid in the eye of law.[3]

57. Grantor's duty to disclose defects.—The grantor of a licence is bound to disclose to the licensee any defect in the property affected by the licence likely to be dangerous to the person or property of the licensee, of which the grantor is, and licensee is not aware.

NOTES

A licensor is under a duty to disclose any defect in the property likely to be dangerous to the licensee of which the licensor is, but the licensee is not, aware. If the licensor fails in his duty and does not disclose any hidden risk in use of the subject of license and if any loss is caused due to such non-disclosure, the licensor is liable for damages.

58. Grantor's duty not to render property unsafe.—The grantor of a licence is bound not to do anything likely to render the property affected by the licence dangerous to the person or property of the licensee.

NOTES

A licensor cannot be allowed to injure his licensee wilfully and deliberately. Therefore if a licensor places an obstruction on his land which is likely to cause injury to the licensee, he may be responsible. But a mere omission to keep the way in repairs and to warn the licensee of its unrepaired condition is not sufficient to make the licensor responsible for the injury caused to the licensee.

1. *Nand Gopal* v. *Brij Mohanlal*, 1966 ALJ 166.
2. *Canadian Pacific Railway Co.* v. *King*, AIR 1932 P.C. 108 : 138 IC 292; *see* also *Beni Ram* v. *Kundan Lall*, 21 All 496 (PC) : 26 IA 58.
3. *Y. Doraisamy* v. *Commissioner, Corporation of Chennai*, AIR 2002 Mad 276.

59. Grantor's transferee not bound by licence.—When the grantor of the licence transfers property affected thereby, the transferee is not as such bound by the licence.

NOTES

If the license has become irrevocable in the time of the licensor, the mere fact that he transfers his interest in the land would not extinguish the license.[1]

60. Licence when revocable.—A licence may be revoked by the grantor, unless—

(a) it is coupled with a transfer of property and such transfer is in force;

(b) the licensee, acting upon the licence, has executed a work of a permanent character and incurred expenses in the execution.

NOTES

A license is revocable at the will of the grantor except in two cases mentioned in clauses (a) and (b) of Section 60. The fact that the license was granted for a valuale consideration or for an agreed term cannot affect the revoability of a bare license. In such cases the licensee can claim compensation for breach of contract.

Revocation of licence granted by co-sharers

A license granted by all the co-sharers can be revoked by all of them and not by one of them alone. However, one of the co-sharers may revoke the licence if he acts for himself and for all others.[2]

The prohibition against the revocation of a licence as contained in Section 60 becomes applicable when a licensee "acting upon the licence" makes constructions. This means that where the licence is granted for building purposes, where constructions are made for purposes necessary for the enjoyment of the licence, the license becomes irrevocable when constructions are made in pursuance thereof. But this does not mean that if a person is permitted to visit a particular place just to learn wrestling, he can put up a building and claim that his licence which was confined to his visiting the place

1. *Mathuri* v. *Bhola Nath*, AIR 1934 All 517 & *Deep Chand Sao* v. *Smt. Kasturi Devi*, AIR 1975 Pat 17.
2. *Hafiz Ali Khan* v. *Mohd. Ishaq*, AIR 1977 Allah 469.

for wrestling, entitled him to make constructions thereon and has become irrevocable.[1]

It may be assumed as a proposition of law that a sub-lessee would be bound by a decree for possession obtained by the lessor against the lessee, no matter whether the sub-lease was created before or after the suit, provided the eviction is based an a ground which determines the sub-lease also. Where the sub-lessees fail to establish that they have raised any construction out of their own funds, no question of an irrevocable licence under Section 60 arises.[2]

Licence coupled with transfer of property

A bare licence is something different from a license coupled with a transfer of property and when such a license (i.e., a license coupled with a transfer of property) exists in a valid form, it operates as a contract, or a gift or a grant and becomes irrevocable. Where an ancestral house was partitioned between two brothers and one of them got a portion of the house with a well and the other a portion of the house without a well, and it was provided in the partition deed that the brother who got the house without a well would be allowed to take water from the well out of brotherly affection but subsequently the brother (owning the well) erected a wall near the well to prevent the other brother from taking water. Held that the right acquired by the second brother (brother taking the portion without a well) under the deed was a license and as license was granted as part of a partition which granted certain property to the brother, it was a license coupled with a transfer of property and as such irrevocable.

A person allows another person to come to his park to hunt there and to take away the game. If the owner of the park merely allowed another person to enter the park and to do something there, namely, to hunt in the park, it would be a case of bare license. If he allowed him not only to hunt in the park but also to take away the game then it cannot be said to be a case of bare license. The license in such a case would be coupled with a transfer of property, *viz.*, the game hunted. This would be a complex right which in law would be termed as a license coupled with a grant or license with a *profit a prendre.*[3]

1. *Govind* v. *Mst. Kishai*, 1956 ALJ 527.
2. *Lucy George and others* v. *Nagpur Roman Catholic Diocesan Corporation (P.) Ltd. and another*, AIR 1986 Madhya Pradesh 27.
3. *Ghissu* v. *Hashim Ali*, 1954 ALJ 295.

A person took possession of a plot of land on a monthly rent of Rs. 15/-. He raised pucca petrol pump and shop on the plot at a considerable expense in the knowledge of the landlord but no express permission of the landlord was obtained to do so indepdently of the monthly tenancy. It was held that the transaction was a lease from month to month and not a permanent licence and Section 60 was not applicable to the transaction.[1]

Sub-section (b).—A person would be "acting upon the license" within Section 60(b) only when he executes a work of a permanent character upon the land of the licensor and not when he executes a work of a permanent character on his own land.[2]

Section 60(b): Irrevocable Licenses

In *Smt. Leela Joshi & Ors.* v. *Smt. Kusum Bhatt*,[3] Uttarakhand High Court applied Section 60(b) strictly to protect a licensee. It held that since the defendant had constructed permanent structures on the land (Nazool land) acting upon the plaintiff's permission, the license had become irrevocable, and the plaintiff was barred from evicting them at will.

In *Indian Oil Corporation* v. *The District Collector*,[4] Madras High Court distinguished between a "bare license" (revocable under Section 52) and a "license coupled with interest" (irrevocable). The Court noted that significant investment in infrastructure (like a petrol pump) often triggers the protection of irrevocability under Section 60.

Work of permanent character

The expression "work of permanent character" is intended to denote some work which is not merely of a temporary nature.[5]

1. Erection of an upper wall at a cost of Rs. 25 is a work of a permanent character and license regarding the same cannot be revoked.

---

1. *Swaran Singh and others* v. *Lakhi Prasad Musaddi and others*, AIR 1983 Allah 322.
2. *Deep Chand Sao* v. *Smt. Kasturi Devi*, AIR 1975 Pat 17 Also AIR 1936 PC 77.
3. 2025:UHC:6995.
4. W.P(MD)Nos.31321 & 31329 of 2023.
5. *Narsingh Das* v. *Mian Safiullah*, AIR 1954 All 773 and *P.M. Zacob* v. *The Executive Officer, Mulanthuruty Panchayai*, AIR 1981 Ker 233.

2. A residential house is a work of a permanent character in spite of its having a tiled roof which requires to be renewed from time to time.

3. The building of walls in the process of putting up a building is a work of permanent character and simply because the building is incomplete it cannot be said that it is not a work of permanent character.[1]

It is not necessary to prove that a large sum of money was spent on the construction; even a mud house or kucha house may be a work of a permanent character.

Where the license is to construct a mere shed and not to execute any work of permanent nature, the license is revocable.[2]

The notice under Section 106 of the Transfer of Property Act is a necessity for the revocation of licence.[3]

It is established on record that the respondent herein incurred the complete costs for construction on the plot, got electricity and water connections in her name and also has paid all the charges to the local authorities with respect to the subject property. Clearly therefore Section 60 of the Act applies.[4]

Where licensee had raised *kachcha* construction on suit property and his succession-in-interest raised *pacca* construction, after the death of licensee, license would come to an end as it was not annexed to property in respect to which it was to be enjoyed and was also not transferable or heritable. The successors being total strangers to suit property, license in their favour would be revocable.[5]

If a person who has purchased the property has permitted someone to use the staircase that can only be treated to be a permission like license and it can be revoked by the person concerned.[6]

Where the defendants have raised the construction of a house which is permanent in character and the licensor had not raised any objection, in these circumstances, the license has become irrevocable.[7]

1. AIR 1975 Pat 17 and AIR 1951 Oudh 364.
2. *Sorab* v. *Vishwanath Menon*, AIR 1975 Kerala 99.
3. *Nanhku* v. *Brij Nath*, 2011 AIR CC 146 (148) (All).
4. *Hari Mohan* v. *Maya Devi*, AIR 2012 Del 24.
5. *Om Prakash* v. *Umed Singh*, AIR 2010 P & H 146 (150).
6. *Ashok Kumar Saxena* v. *Naresh Kumar Gupta*, 2011 AIR CC 2694 (All).
7. *Mansho* v. *Sancho Devi*, AIR 2010 H.P. 21.

Plea of irrevocability of licence whether can be allowed to be raised in appeal or second appeal

In the instant case, the appellant had mainly relied on the plea that he had been granted a licence and that acting upon the licence he had executed a work of a permanent character and incurred expenses in the execution thereof, and therefore, under Section 60(b), which was applicable to the area where the property was situated, the licence was irrevocable. No plea of licence or its irrevocability had been raised but what had been pleaded was the validity of a trust and the said question of licence or its irrevocability had not been discussed in the judgment of the trial Court. It was only in the grounds of appeal to the High Court that the appellant had taken, for the first time, the said ground. Dealing in the case in *Iyyappan's* case,[1] their Lordships of the Supreme Court observed that it is not open to a party to change his case at the appellate stage and that in that particular case since there was no case of licence in the trial court, the appellants were precluded from raising it at the appellate stage.[2]

Licensee's remedy against improper revocation.—As has been already noticed a bare licence may be revoked at the instance of the licensor at any time he likes. And it is true that there is no provision in Sections 60, 61, 63 or 64 for the issue of any notice, as in the case of leases before a licence can be revoked. But the licensee should, in proper cases, have reasonable notice of such revocation and after revocation he must be given reasonable time to quit the land and remove his chattels which he has been licensed to put there.[3] If he is thrust off without such notice or before such reasonable time though he is not entitled to an injunction restraining the licensor from adopting such improper course, yet he may get such damages as may have been caused to him thereby.[4] Similarly, where a licence is granted for valuable consideration and before the licensee has had full enjoyment of it, it is revoked in breach of an express or implied contract, the licensee's remedy lies only in an action for damages for breach

1. AIR 1966 SC 1017.
2. *Mahadeo Tatu Naik* v. *Ramakant Atmarama*, AIR 1985 Bombay 347.
3. *Cornish* v. *Stubbs*, LR 5 C.P. 334; *Mellor* v. *Watkins*, LR 9 QB 400, *see* also Section 63 *post*.
4. *Aldin* v. *Latimer Clark, Muirhead & Co.*, (1894) 2 Ch 437; *Wilson* v. *Tavener*, (1901) 1 Ch 578.

of contract or implied covenant not to revoke.[1] If the obstruction in the enjoyment of a bare licence is laid not by the licensor, but by a third party, the licensee may not sue in his own name for the removal of such obstruction.[2]

A bare licence does not create such an estate or interest in the land as to enable a licensee to maintain an action in his own name against a third person for the infringement of his right. He must obtain permission from the licensor to sue the wrongdoer in his name in such cases.[3] The mere fact that the licence is an exclusive licence makes no difference, unless the wrongdoer has notice of its being exclusive.[4] But if the licence is not a revocable licence, the licensee's remedy against an obstruction is either by injunction restraining such obstruction,[5] or in damages for breach of contract.[6] In the cases of irrevocable licence, the licensee has sufficient possessory title to maintain such action in his own name against a third person.[7]

Revocation of irrevocable licence on payment of compensation.—There is consensus of opinion that in those States of the Union to which the Indian Easements Act applies a licence which is irrevocable under the present section cannot be revoked on payment of compensation.[8] There is, however, difference of opinion whether the same rule holds good in States to which the Act does not apply. It was held by the Calcutta High Court [the Act not being applicable to Bengal] that when a licensee has, acting upon the licence, executed

1. *Wood* v. *Leadbitter*, 13 M & W 838 (855); *Smart* v. *Jones*, 33 LJ CP 154; *Cornish* v. *Stubbs*, LR 5 CP 334; *Mellor* v. *Watkins*, LR 9 QB 400; *Well* v. *Kingstone-upon-Hull Corporation*, LR 10 CP 402; *Butler* v. *Manchester, Sheffield and Lincolnshire Railway*, 21 QBD 207; *Kerrison* v. *Smith*, 2 QB 445; *Prosonna Coomar* v. *Ram Coomar*, 16 Cal 640; *Kesava Pillai* v. *Peddu Reddi*, 1 Mad HC 258; *see* also Section 64, *infra*.
2. *Hill* v. *Tupper*, 8 LT 792; *Heap* v. *Hartley*, 42 Ch D 461.
3. *Hill* v. *Tupper*, 8 LT 792; *Heap* v. *Hartley*, 42 Ch D 461.
4. *Heap* v. *Hartley*, 42 Ch D 461.
5. *Philips* v. *Treeby*, 8 Jur NS 711.
6. *Smart* v. *Jones*, 33 LJCP 154; *Kerrison* v. *Smith*, 2 QB 445.
7. *Northam* v. *Bowden*, 11 Exch. 70; *Fitzgerald* v. *Firbank*, (1897) 2 Ch 96.
8. *Shyamlal* v. *Munne*, 8 Luck. 278 : AIR 1933 Oudh 69 at 70 : 140 IC 889 : 90 OWN 986; *Mathuri* v. *Bholanath*, 56 All 975 : AIR 1934 All 517 : 149 IC 389 : 1934 ALJ 698; *Daya Ram* v. *Deo Rao*, AIR 1926 Nag. 376 : 94 IC 923; *Hafiz Manzoor Ahmad* v. *Mohammad Abdul Jamil*, 56 All 207 : AIR 1933 All 842 : 145 IC 948 : 1933 ALJ 1422; *Bhukhan Singh* v. *Jogerdeo Koeri*, AIR 1927 All 197 : 98 IC 814.

works of a permanent character, the licence may be revoked on payment of compensation.[1] The Lahore High Court differs from the Calcutta High Court even though the Act is also not applicable to the Punjab. That Court distinguishing the English authorities relied upon by the Calcutta High Court has laid down that where a licence has become irrevocable by construction of structure of a permanent character it cannot be revoked on payment of compensation.[2] As correctly pointed out by Sulaiman, C.J. revocation of an irrevocable licence on payment of compensation is a contradiction in terms.[3] It should be remembered that once a licence has become irrevocable it is not competent to the licensor to recover from the licensee damages for use and occupation of the land.[4]

Where a licensee has raised *pucca* construction on the land under licence, the licensor if evicts the licensee from the land, the latter is entitled to compensation for the construction left by him.[5]

Termination of licence.—In the present matter, the land over which the shops in dispute are situated are urgently required for developing the sports complex and petitioners are only licensees and not lessees over the land in question. It is well settled that a licence can be terminated at any time vide Section 60 of the Easements Act.[6]

Irrevocable licence.—A licence is irrevocable only if the licensee has executed some work of permanent character with permission of licensor.[7]

Validity of cancellation of licence to run canteen and P.C.O. in Government hospital.—The licence of petitioner was not coupled with transfer of interest in property nor licensee was permitted to execute work of permanent character by licensor. *Held*, that such licence could be revoked by grantor at any time and that hearing to licensee before

1. *Surnomoyee* v. *Chandra Kumar*, 12 CLJ 443 : 8 IC 793; *See* also *Motilal* v. *Kalu Mandar*, 19 CLJ 321 : 19 IC 853.
2. *Jagat Singh* v. *District Board, Amritsar*, AIR 1940 Lah. 509 confirming on L.P.A. case reported as *Jagat Singh* v. *District Board, Amritsar*, AIR 1940 Lah. 18 : 186 IC 890.
3. *Hafiz Manzoor Ahmad* v. *Mohammad Abdul Jamil*, AIR 1933 All 842.
4. *Ram Dayal* v. *Nisar Hussain Khan*, 91 IC 1031.
5. *Dropadibai* v. *Laxmi Narayan*, 1993 M.PLJ 338 at 342 (MP).
6. *Mawana Stand Vyapar Samiti and another* v. *State of U.P.*, 2004 (56) ALR 502.
7. *Suraj Prakash* v. *Union of India*, AIR 1998 Del. 236.

cancelling licence was not necessary.[1]

Irrevocable licence—Whether injunction of removal of pump-house could be granted. No.—Where in a suit for mandatory injunction commanding removal of pump-house from property of plaintiffs/purchaser three facts *viz.*, (i) that defendant had obtained permission to use water from well from plaintiff's vendor; and (ii) for this purpose pump-set was installed and pump-house was constructed; and (iii) continued use of such water even after the plaintiff purchased the property, were clearly asserted by the defendant in the written statement in support of his claim of irrevocable licence, such a pleading means that defendant acted on the licence and erected a permanent structure. The actual words used by the draftsman of the written statement may be different from the words used in clause (b) of Section 60. It is enough if the defendant through the written statement conveys the nexus between such installation of water-pipes and the licence to use water from well. The words "for this purpose" in the written statement mean "for the purpose of drawing water in accordance with the licence granted by the owners" and in the context they convey the same meaning as the words "acting upon the licence" used in clause (b) of Section 60. Therefore, written statement has adequately set out the material facts necessary to make out a case of irrevocable licence under clause (b) of Section 60.[2]

Licensee.—It was held that the right conferred on the plaintiffs was in the nature of easement, which did not become to be absolute having been perfected by a statutory prescription. Therefore, in respect of the said right they cannot be considered as licensees.[3]

Protection to licensee in eviction suit.—The claim of defendant that he had constructed house on suit-land and remained there as licensee was accepted. There was no material on record to conclude that he had constructed rooms acting on licence or within the terms of licence. *Held*, that due to non-availability of such material, he could not claim any

1. *Purnima Pandey* v. *Chief Medical Superintendent*, (SSPG), Hospital, AIR 2003 All 57.
2. *Thayyil Kanissante Valappil Saraswathi* v. *M/s. Bharatha Textiles, Cannur*, AIR 1992 Ker 219.
3. *Mrs. Sudha S. Alva, wife of K. Sadashiva Alva* v. *Mrs. Sanjeevi R. Shetty, wife of late Ramayya Shetty, since deceased by her Legal Representative*, AIR 1996 Kant. 5 at 7.

protection under Section 60(b) of the Easements Act.[1]

Claim for licence in suit for possession.—The plaintiff had granted permission to defendant to stay in suit property temporarily. Defendant had claimed that he was licensee since he had raised the construction on suit property and therefore was entitled to benefit of Section 60 of the Easement Act. However, no such pleading was made by him before trial Court. Defendant had raised inconsistent pleas before trial Court and pleaded that he was owner in possession. He had subsequently taken the plea that he had purchased suit property. In written statement he denied that he was licensee. Held, that there was no question for trial Court holding that defendant was licensee and that licence was irrevocable.[2]

Validity of refusal to renew revocable licence.—Plaintiff was tenant of first floor or premises. He was permitted to use roof top and garden but not as part of her tenancy right. Intention of parties was never to create irrevocable licence in favour of plaintiff. Permission granted would be revocable. Owners of land would have right to make construction over suit property. Injunction restraining owner from taking construction could not be granted.[3]

Revocation of licence on death of licensee.—The licence would automatically come to an end, the plaintiffs would not be entitled to inherit the same, considering that the licence could not be said to be heritable. As referred to above, a licence is personal to the person in whose favour the licence has been granted. It is not heritable and as such on the death of licensee, the LR's would not be entitled to inherit the same. It was held, the plaintiff would not be entitled to seek the possession of the disputed property from the defendants, on the ground that they had inherited the suit property on the death of the licensee.[4]

Exception to revocability of license.—License was granted to construct VIP Welcome Arch at the entrance of aerodrome. License was for fixed period and was terminable in terms of agreement. Construction of permanent nature by spending money will not make licence irrevocable. Section 60(b) was not sacrosanct. Plea of licensee that it was orally agreed to treat license as irrevocable one was not tenable since

1. *Subal Baliar Singh* v. *Chanchala Bewa*, AIR 2003 NOC 560 (Ori).
2. *Rajinder Parshad Verma* v. *Pushpa Verma*, AIR 2004 Del 308.
3. *Madhulata Kankani* v. *Hemant Bangur*, AIR 2005 Cal 268.
4. *Sunder Lal* v. *Sita Bali*, AIR 2003 P & H 277.

Sections 91, 92 of Evidence Act exclude oral evidence.[1]

Order passed for vacation of licensee of premises/or shops not invalid.—There was a Sports Stadium in Meerut city and certain shops were allotted to the members of petitioner No. 1 in that stadium and certain open land was also allotted. District Magistrate, Meerut, had asked the members of petitioners society to vacate the premises/shops forthwith. It is well settled that a licence could be terminated at any time vide Section 60 of the Easement Act. The writ petition was dismissed and the interim order, if any, of High Court was vacated. No further time was granted for vacation as petitioners were already in continued occupation of the shops and land even after ten years of the eviction notice which was served upon them in the year 1994.[2]

Unauthorized occupant had no right of possession.—Where licensee was occupying land post expiry of license. He had an unauthorized occupant and has no right vide Section 60 of the Act.[3]

Licence creates rights.—The grant of licence create some rights in the favour of licensee. Where the licensor says that it was secured by misrepresentation, a show cause notice should be issued and opportunity of hearing should also be given.[4]

Contract.—It is well settled that a licence is irrevocable only if the three conditions are fulfilled : namely : (i) licensee executed work of permanent character; (ii) he did so acting upon the licence; (iii) he incurred expenses on doing so and *onus* of pleading and proving these facts in always on the defendant who pleads irrevocable licence.[5]

Licence, not coupled with grant.—An exclusive possession for any length of time does not, *ipso facto*, prove that it was a licence coupled with a grant.[6]

Licensee, protection to.—A licence cannot be revoked and the licensee evicted unless expenses incurred or investment made on permanent character of work remain

1. *Skylines Advertising (P) Ltd.* v. *National Airport Authority, New Delhi*, AIR 2005 NOC 431 (Kant).
2. *Mawana Stand Vyapar Samiti* v. *State of U.P.*, AIR 2004 All 394.
3. *A. Thayal Nayagi* v. *Union of India*, AIR 2005 NOC 305 (Mad).
4. *Baraka Overseas Traders* v. *Director General of Foreign Trade*, 2006 (8) SCC 103.
5. *Ramesh Raghunath* v. *Pandurangrao A. Ratnalikar*, 2006 (4) Bom CR 910.
6. *Duijendra Lal Roy* v. *Dipta Rani Chaudhury*, 2007 (1) CLJ (Cal) 493.

unrecovered. The licensor can, however, always revoke a licence after expenses made by the licensee are paid to him.[1]

Licence, revocability of.—Where intention of the parties was never to create irrevocable licence in the favour of plaintiff, the permission granted to him to use roof top and garden but not as tenancy rights could be revocable.[2]

A licence becomes irrevocable if it is coupled with a transfer of property and the transfer is enforced and thereafter the licensee has executed a work of permanent character incurring expenses thereon, under Section 60 of the Act.[3]

Under Section 60 of the Act, a license becomes irrevocable when it is coupled with a Transfer of Property Act and the transfer is enforced and when the licensee has executed a work of permanent character and incurred expenses in such execution.[4]

Where a licence coupled with the grant of interest in the nature of property and it could be inferred from the conduct of the parties that the licence was not given for temporary occupation it would be irrevocable one.[5]

Absence or termination of clause or specific period of licence is not itself sufficient to convert a revocable licence to irrevocable one.[6]

Acting upon the licence.—A licence can be revoked if the licensee could not produce any evidence showing permanent nature of construction and spending of huge sum on it. He would not get benefit of Section 60(b) of the Act.[7]

61. Revocation express or implied.—The revocation of a licence may be express or implied.

Illustrations

(a) *A*, the owner of a field, grants a licence to *B* to use a path across it. *A*, with intent to revoke the licence, locks a gate across the path. The licence is revoked.

(b) *A*, the owner of a field, grants a licence to *B* to stack hay on the field. *A* lets or sells the field to

1. *Muktal Hussain* v. *Ali Aswab*, AIR 2006 (NOC) 1586 (Gau).
2. *Madhulata Kankani* v. *Homant Bangur*, AIR 2005 Cal 268.
3. *Mini Peter Philipi* v. *Dina J.S. Fanibenda*, 2008 AIHC (NOC) 328 (Bom).
4. *Mini Peter Philips* v. *Dina J.S. Fanibanda*, 2007 (4) Bom CR 526.
5. *R.P. Srivastava* v. *Sheela Devi*, 2007 (4) MPLJ 102.
6. *Thomas Cook (India) Ltd.* v. *Hotel Imperial*, AIR 2007 (NOC) 169 (Del).
7. *Ram Gopal* v. *Idol of Radha Krishna Mandir*, AIR 2007 (NOC) 900 (Raj).

C. The licence is revoked.

NOTES

A licence may be revoked either by words of mouth or by conduct. The words or conduct must show an unequivocal intention on the part of the licensor to extinguish the right.

62. Licence when deemed revoked.—A licence is deemed to be revoked—

(a) when, from a cause preceding the grant of it, the grantor ceases to have any interest in the property, affected by the licence;

(b) when the licensee releases it, expressly or impliedly to the grantor or his representative;

(c) where it has been granted for a limited period, or acquired on condition that it shall become void on the performance or non-performance of a specified act, and the period expires or the condition is fulfilled;

(d) where the property affected by the licence is destroyed or by superior force so permanently altered that the licensee can no longer exercise his right;

(e) where the licensee becomes entitled to the absolute ownership of the property affected by the licence;

(f) where the licence is granted for a specified purpose and the purpose is attained, or abandoned, or becomes impracticable;

(g) where the licence is granted to the licensee as holding a particular office, employment or character, and such office, employment or character ceases to exist;

(h) where the licence totally ceases to be used as such for an unbroken period of twenty years, and such cessation is not in pursuance of a contract between the grantor and the licensee;

(i) in the case of an accessory licence, when the interest or right to which it is accessory ceases to exist.

NOTES

Section 60 is not the only section under which a licence is revoked. This section deals with a case when the licence is revoked at the will of the licensor. Section 62 enumerates the circumstances on the happening of any one of which, a license is revoked by operation of law. Each clause of Section 62 is independent of the other. If a licensor can prove that his case falls under any one clause, the licence stands revoked even if the remaining clauses do not apply. Where the land was given to the appellants so that they may make a house and live in the village, the moment they abandoned the residence of the village the purpose is abandoned and clause (f) applies and the license stands revoked.[1]

Where A was constructing a building on his own land and B allowed his land to be used by A as passage for the limited purpose of carrying bricks and other material to the construction site, the license granted by B to A for using his land as passage must be deemed to have been revoked with the completion of the work of construction.[2]

Lease and Licence.—While it is true that the essence of a licence is that it is revocable at the will of the grantor the provision in the licence that the licensee would be entitled to a notice before being required to vacat is not inconsistent with a licence. Thus the mere necessity of giving a notice to a licensee requiring him to vacate the licensed premises would not indicate that the transaction was a lease, whether an agreement creates between the parties the relationship of landlord and tenant or merely that of licensor and licensee, the decisive consideration is the intention of the parties. This intention has to be ascertained on a consideration of all the relevant provisions in the agreement. In the absence, however, of a formal document, the intention of the parties must be inferred from the circumstances and conduct of the parties. Where the terms of the document evidencing the agreement between the parties are not clear, the surrounding circumstances and the conduct of the parties have also to be borne in mind for ascertaining the real relationship between the parties.[3]

Principle and scope of the section.—A licence may be revoked by an act of a party or by operation of law. Section

1. *Bhaga* v. *Girwar*, 1953 ALJ 164.
2. *Deep Chand Sao* v. *Smt. Kasturi Devi*, AIR 1975 Pat 17.
3. *Mrs. M.M. Clubwala* v. *Fida Hussein Saheb*, AIR 1965 SC 610.

61 deals with revocation by the licensor either expressly or by implication. Section 62 is confined to revocation by operation of law or by an act of the licensee. In cases where a licence is revoked by operation of law, an act on the part of the licensor revoking such licence is not necessary. Clause (b) deals with the acts of the licensee while the rest of the clauses relate to revocation by operation of law. Section 62 is not confined to mere licences which are revocable at the instance of the licensor, but covers a wider field including the licences which are not revocable.[1] A licence, unlike lease cannot be revoked by a denial of licensor's title.[2]

Clause (a)—When the grantor's interest ceases.—A person having a life interest in the property cannot grant any licence whether revocable or irrevocable so as to last after his death or after the ceasing of the life-interest. Section 62 (a) of the Easements Act is not controlled by Section 60 of the same Act. Even if a licence has become irrevocable under the provisions of Section 60, it shall be deemed to be revoked if from a cause preceding the grant of it, the grantor ceases to have any interest in the property.[3] It is only contractual tenant who can create a valid licence and not the statutory tenant and as such a licence granted by a statutory tenant prior to his determination of contractual tenancy stands revoked under clause (a) of Section 62 of the Act.[4]

As has been already noticed, a grantor's power to grant a licence is coeval with his power of disposition. He cannot grant a licence which will affect interests beyond his own, if he has no power to dispose of property affecting such interests. For instance, a person who has only a life-interest in a property cannot grant a licence which will continue after the ceasing of his life-interest. Hence, if he grants licence it will continue only so long as he lives and will cease by operation of law as soon as the grantor dies. But the cause by which the grantor ceases to have any interest in the property affected by the licence must precede the grant of such licence. If it is only of a date subsequent to the grant of the licence, the licence may or may not be revoked, as it is revocable or not

1. *Bhaga* v. *Girwar*, AIR 1953 All 439 : 1953 ALJ 164 : 1953 AWR (HC) 306.
2. *See* Section 60, Note 13 *ante*.
3. *Kapoorchand* v. *Lalchand*, AIR 1975 Raj 178, 181 (S.N. Modi. J.).
4. *S.J. Pande* v. *P.K. Balakrishnan*, 1994 Bom Rent Cases 190 at 195 (SC) : (1993) 3 SCC 297.

at the instance of the grantor. If it is revocable at the will of the grantor, any subsequent cause, depriving him of his interest, may operate as implied revocation.[1] If it is not so revocable, it is not affected by the grantor ceasing to have any interest in the property affected by the licence due to such subsequent cause.[2]

Licence stands revoked on the expiry of the period thereof. If the licensee makes default in payment of licence fee, no notice for ejectment need be given.[3]

Clause (b)—Express or implied release by the licensee.—A licensee can release a licence at any time he pleases. Such release may be express or it may be implied from certain acts, which are indicative of his intention to release either by being inconsistent with the continued exercise thereof or otherwise. But a mere denial of the title of the licensor does not imply such release.[4]

Clause (c)—Grant for a limited period or subject to a condition.—Clause (c) of Section 62 will be attracted where provisions of Sections 59 and 61 of this Act are not applicable.[5] Where a licence is granted only for a limited period,[6] or on condition that it shall become void on the performance or non-performance of a specified act, it shall be deemed to be revoked when the period expires or the condition is fulfilled. If the licence is for a limited period only or subject to a condition, the fact that the licensee acting upon such licence has executed work of a permanent character and has incurred expenses thereon, does not affect its revocability on the expiry of such period or on the fulfilment of such condition.[7]

Where a licence to run book stalls at a Railway Station expires and is terminated after expiry, no opportunity of hearing need be given before termination.[8]

The law does not permit a licensee whose licence had

1. *Wallis* v. *Harrison*, 4 M & W 538 (544).
2. Cf. Section 37, *ante*.
3. *Municipal Committee, Ambala* v. *Lal Chand*, 1969 Cur. LJ 589 (Punjab).
4. *Dharam Kunwar* v. *Fakira*, 1901 AWN 157; *Amjad Khan* v. *Shafiuddin*, AIR 1925 All 203.
5. *Sahab Ram* v. *Banarsi*, AIR 1997 All 222 (224).
6. *Gulab Chandra* v. *Harbhagat*, 136 IC 884 : AIR 1932 Nag. 36.
7. *Liggings* v. *Inge*, 7 Bing. 682 (694); *see* also Commentary on Section 60, clause (b), *ante*.
8. *M. Gulab Singh & Sons* v. *Union of India*, AIR 1988 NOC 34 (Delhi) : (1987) 13 I.J. Rep. 530 (S. Ranganathan & H.C. Goel, JJ.).

been validly revoked to exercise his licence any longer. If he does so, he does something wrong. He will be only a trespasser after he had lost his right under the licence and the owner of the land is entitled to deal with him as a trespasser.[1]

Conditions of defeasance should be expressed in clear and unequivocal terms in order to be operative; if they are vague they cannot be given effect to as being void for uncertainty. They should be construed strictly. Courts also lean in favour of strict construction.

If under an oral agreement between debtor and creditor, the creditor remains in possession of debtor's land in lieu of interest, the creditor is not a mortgagee or sub-tenant but a mere licensee.[2] The parties agreed that on the debtor paying the creditor the principal and interest, the debtor would be entitled to take back possession of the land. Therefore, the licence could be revoked by the debtor at any time either by instituting a suit for possession or by making a demand for possession on payment of money and the refusal of the creditor to deliver back the possession.[3]

Where in such a case the grantor had reserved to himself unlimited power to terminate it at any time for reasons which he considered to be sufficient or adequate, the power is not in conformity with Section 62(c) and the grantor is not invested with the general power to revoke and grant before the expiry of the period stipulated. The power in question does not constitute a defeasance of the grant.[4]

If there is a condition in the licence that the licensee would be entitled to a notice before being required to vacate and the condition is fulfilled, the licence will be deemed to be revoked; such a condition is not inconsistent with a licence.[5]

A licensee in possession of his debtor's land in lieu of interest is not an *adhivasi* under the U.P. Zamindari Abolition and Land Reforms Act, 1950. To do so would be to give him a better status than that of a mortgagee.[6]

1. *Bant Singh* v. *Cantonment Executive Officer, Jammu*, AIR 1960 J. & K. 83.
2. *Mahabal Singh* v. *Ramraj*, 1950 ALJ 713 : AIR 1950 All 604.
3. *Hansu Koeri* v. *Jang Bahadur Rai*, 1963 ALJ 456.
4. *Mammunhi* v. *Kunhibi*, ILR 1960 Ker 115 : 1959 Ker LJ 1349 : 1960 Ker LT 1343 : AIR 1961 Ker 147.
5. *M.N. Clubwala* v. *Fida Hussain Saheb*, (1964) 1 SCWR 750 : (1964) 2 SCJ 448 : (1964) 2 MLJ (SC) 83 : (1964) 2 Andh WR (SC) 83 : AIR 1965 SC 610; *P. Narayanan* v. *M.D. Kerala Health Research & Welfare Society*, AIR 1991 Ker 306.
6. *Hansu Koeri* v. *Jang Bahadur*, 1963 All LJ 456, 458, para 7-9.

Clause (d)—Where property affected by licence is destroyed or permanently altered by superior force.—A licence ceases to exist when the property on which it is exercised is destroyed or by superior force so permanently altered as to render its exercise impossible. When the alteration is only temporary, the licence may remain suspended until the property is again restored to a condition fit for its exercise. If such alteration is not due to some superior force but due to an act of the licensor, the licence may be revoked by implication, if it is revocable at the instance of the licensor.[1] If it is not so revocable, the licensee may sue the licensor for an injunction—mandatory or otherwise— restraining him from such further acts and ordering him to restore the property in the condition fit for its exercise.[2] If such permanent alteration is due to an act of the licensee, it may amount to an implied release under clause (b). As to what constitutes superior force commentaries on Section 44 can be seen.[3]

Clause (e)—Where licensee becomes absolute owner.—A licence ceases to be enjoyed as a licence when the property in the land on which it is exercised becomes vested in absolute ownership of the licensee. Its exercise, thereafter, is not as a licence but as an ordinary right of property. The licence thenceforth, ceases to exist and is deemed to be revoked. But this clause will apply only when the licensee becomes the absolute owner of the property affected by the licence. If he acquires only a limited interest, the licence will not be revoked, though in certain cases it may be suspended for the time such interest subsists. If the licence, due to such a cause, ceases to be exercised as a licence for a full period of twenty years it may be deemed to be revoked.[4]

Clause (f)—When the purpose for which the licence was granted is attained or abandoned or becomes impracticable.—A licence may be granted for a specified purpose. In such cases it ceases to exist when such purpose is attained or is abandoned or is no longer capable of being attained by the licence. For instance, where a *zamindar* grants a right of residence to a tenant to enable him to live in the village and till his fields, the licence comes to an end if the tenancy terminates or is abandoned or the tenant dies

1. *See* Section 61, Illustration (a); *see* also *Aldin* v. *Latimar Clark Muirhead & Co.*, (1894) 2 Ch 437; *Hyde* v. *Graham*, 1 H & C 593.
2. *Phillips* v. *Treeby*, 8 Jur. N.S. 699.
3. *See* Commentaries on Section 44, *ante*.
4. *See* Clause (h), *infra*.

heirless.[1] The defendant had allowed his land to be used as a passage for the purpose of carrying bricks and other materials to the construction site of the plaintiff. Thus the term of the licence was limited to the use of the passage only for the specified purpose mentioned above and did not grant a perpetual licence. It will appear from Section 62(f) of the Act that "where the licence is granted for a special purpose and the purpose is attained the licence is deemed to be revoked." In fact, it must be deemed to have been revoked with the termination of the work of construction,[2] for in view of provisions of Section 61, revocation of licence need not be express.[3]

In *Suraj Baksh Singh* v. *Bhagga* cited above, the plaintiff, a *taluqdar* filed a suit on the allegation that he was the sole proprietor of the village and that the defendant was his *raiyat* and was in occupation of the house in suit in his capacity as a tenant and had therefore no right to mortgage it. The Courts below held that the transferor had the power of transfer. The plaintiff went to the Chief Court in second appeal. The Chief Court held that the house was appurtenant to the tenancy that it belonged to the *zamindar* and that it was non-transferable. It was also pointed out in the judgment that as the specified purpose for which the house was given was abandoned, the licence must be deemed to have been revoked.

If the owner of a house grants a licence to another for the purpose of residence therein, such a licence stands revoked on the sale of the house to a third person as in consequence of the sale, the purpose becomes impracticable.[4]

Unless it is shown that the house was given for a specified purpose that is residence, the licence cannot be revoked merely because it has been converted into a temple.[5]

Where abandonment is alleged it must be proved

1. See *Fakir Chand* v. *Kewal Ram*, 10 ALJR 118; *Shohrat Singh* v. *Jhagru*, 13 ALJ 745; *Suraj Baksh Singh* v. *Bhagga*, 8 Luck. 509 : AIR 1933 Oudh 302 : 144 IC 776 (20 All 248 relied); *Iqbal Hussain* v. *Shanker Dayal*, AIR 1942 Oudh 427; *Mohd. Usman* v. *Babu*, 9 IC 314; *see* also 11 IC 285; 47 IC 645; *Bhaga* v. *Girwar*, AIR 1953 All 439 : 1953 ALJ 164 : 1953 AWR (HC) 306.
2. *Deep Chand Sao* v. *Kasturi Devi*, AIR 1975 Pat 17, 19 (Madan Mohan Prasad, J.).
3. *Mulakh Raj* v. *Sewa Samiti*, (1993) 1 Punj LR 177 at 181 (P & H).
4. *Balak Ram* v. *Surat Ram*, AIR 1958 Him Pra 5.
5. *Mir Iqbal Hussain* v. *Shankar Dayal*, AIR 1942 Oudh 427; *Kanhaya Lal* v. *Hamid Ali*, AIR 1930 Oudh 235.

affirmatively by unimpeachable evidence.[1] Abandonment is essentially a question of fact and cannot be allowed to be raised in second appeal particularly when it was not raised in the lower appellate Court.[2]

If the purpose for which a licence was granted was presumably the construction of a thatch and though the thatch fell down and no attempt was made to re-build it or to construct another on the site within a reasonable period (in the instant case it exceeded twelve years), the purpose can be said to have been abandoned. The licensor's act of preventing the licensees from constructing a house on the land itself, after the licence was deemed to be revoked as aforesaid, can be treated as an implied revocation of the licence (the licensees in the circumstances were trespassers).[3]

Clause (g)—Where the licence is granted to the licensee as holding a particular office, employment or character.—Where a licence is granted to a person as holding a particular office, employment or character, it is deemed to be revoked as soon as such office, employment or character ceases to exist inasmuch as a right which is granted to a person as occupying a particular position can no longer be claimed by him after he ceases to occupy that position. So, when land was allotted to the ancestors of the defendants to erect a house and reside therein while they were in the service of the plaintiff and his ancestors as *patwari* and *karinda*, it was held that after the defendant ceased to act as such, he became a tenant-at-will and was liable to be ejected notwithstanding the fact that he had erected a *pucca* house thereon.[4]

Clause (h)—Where the licence totally ceases to be used as such for an unbroken period of twenty years.—Like easements, a licence is also extinguished by mere non-user for a period of twenty years. Thus, where a site in respect of which a licence to build upon is granted remains vacant for a period of twenty years or more, the licence will be deemed to have been revoked.[5] House built by licensee fell

1. *Mahinder Singh* v. *Nihal Kaur*, 66 Punj LR 1174 : AIR 1965 Punj 119 (a case of alleged abandonment of allotted plot by allottee of evacuee property).
2. *Yarlagedda China Rattaya* v. *Dondapudi Venkataramayya*, AIR 1959 Andh Pra 551.
3. *Raghubir Saran* v. *Param Kirti Saran*, 1962 ALJ 297 : 1962 AWR (HC) 264 : AIR 1962 All 444.
4. *Budh Singh* v. *Parbati*, 4 ALJR 556.
5. *Chhaganlal* v. *Nathu Singh*, ILR 1938 Nag. 326 : AIR 1937 Nag. 338.

down and he did not rebuild it for more that 20 years. The licence thereby stood revoked.[1] But where in exercise of the right under a licence a house has actually been built, the mere fact that it has fallen into disrepair will not attract the application of Section 60 (f) so as to curtail the licensee's rights under Section 60 (h),[2] though the position would be different if in such a case the house is wholly abandoned by the licensee.

The use of the words "as such" is very significant. It shows that in order to keep a licence alive, it should be used as licence. Any other user will not suffice. For instance, if the licensee acquires a life interest in the property affected by the licence, his enjoyment of the licence is no longer as a licensee but only as life-owner of the property and if such ownership continues for twenty years, it will extinguish the right altogether. The right of the licensee remains suspended in such cases during the period the licensee is in possession of property as owner or holding such limited interest and comes to an end, if the user is not resumed as such, on the expiry of twenty years. The use of the word "totally" should also be carefully noticed. A partial enjoyment is sufficient to keep the right alive and a partial non-user does not affect it.

Such cessation is not in pursuance of a contract between the grantor and the licensee.—If the cessation of user is due to an agreement between the parties, the right is not extinguished for mere non-user, though if such agreement amounts to release or revocation it may come to an end under other provisions of the Act. Parties are always at liberty to suspend the enjoyment of a right for any period by agreement and such suspension will not affect the right itself.

Clause (i)—Accessory licences ceases with the interest or right to which they are accessory.—As accessory licences come into existence by sheer necessity, they naturally come to an end when such necessity ceases. So when the interest or right, in the constitution whereof they are licensees, are implied and for the enjoyment or exercise whereof they are necessary, ceases to exist, such licences themselves cease to exist and are deemed to have been revoked. As they are created by implication of law so they cease by a similar implication. For instance, if a *zamindar* grants a lease of a plot of land, for agricultural purpose and the land is irrigated from a tank in his *zamindari*, the tenant

1. *St. Narayan Lal* v. *Bansh Bahadur*, 1979 All LJ 441.
2. *Hashmat Jahan* v. *Sheo Dularey*, AIR 1924 Oudh 180.

has an implied licence from him to irrigate the plot from the water of the tank. This licence continues only so long as the tenant cultivates the plot as such tenant and will cease to exist when the tenancy comes to an end. *See* commentary on Section 55.

Revocation of licence when permissible.—The licensee had taken the plea that specified purpose for which licence was granted had been abandoned and became impracticable but the said unilateral act was not supported by any evidence. *Held*, that the licensee could not invoke provisions of Section 62(b) or (f) to contend that licence stood revoked. Even otherwise licence was irrevocable for the period of three years as per agreement between parties. Therefore, such licence would not stand revoked due to circumstances contemplated under S. 62(b) or (f).[1]

Deemed revocation of licence on expiry of period.—There was finding of fact that licence was not limited to period of three years. Only stipulation in licence deed was that it could not be terminated for a period of three years and it could be terminated at any time thereafter giving notice to guarantee. *Held*, that in such case Section 62(C) would not be attracted and plea that licence stood revoked was not tenable.[2]

Irrevocable licence.—An argument not raised before trial Court as well as lower appellate Court. The same cannot be entertained by the High Court.[3]

Section 63 recognized that, where a licence is revoked, the licensee is entitled to a reasonable time to leave the property affected thereby and to remove any goods which he has been allowed to place on such property. What would be the reasonable time required for achieving these objectives is therefore dependent upon the facts and circumstances prevailing in each case. No hard and fast rule can be prescribed in this regard. Section 64 recognized the right of the licensee, when he was evicted without any fault of his by the grantor before he has fully enjoyed, under the licence, the right which he was granted, to recover compensation from the grantor, for the breach of the grant.[4]

---

1. *Indian Molasses Co. Ltd.* v. *Kerala State Civil Supplies Corporation Ltd.*, AIR 2003 Ker 383.
2. *Francis* v. *Sarda*, AIR 2004 Ker 187.
3. *Sahab Ram* v. *Banarsi*, AIR 1997 All 2222.
4. *Jasti Venkateswara Rao* v. *South Central Railway*, 2012 (110) AIC 577 (AP).

63. Licensee's rights on revocation.—Where a licence is revoked, the licensee is entitled to a reasonable time to leave the property affected thereby, and to remove any goods which he has been allowed to place on such property.

NOTES

Right to licensee.—In order to keep the premises in good repairs, certain repairs are needed. Even under the Rent Control Act a tenant is entitled to allowance of one month's rent in a year for effecting the repairs. In Court's opinion the licensee should also be entitled to such allowance. So court held that the defendant would be entitled to deduct the amount calculated at one month's licence fee in a year provided it is shown that the defendant actually carried the repairs and spent the amount. The defendant will have to furnish the proof of the amount so spent and thereafter he would be entitled to deduct the amount not exceeding one month's licence fee in a year. The local Commissioner will also go into this aspect as to how much amount the defendant is entitled to on account of this deduction.[1]

Applicability.—Where the licence was not renewed after the expiry of stipulated period the licensee became a trespasser and had no right to retain possession of the plot beyond the period of licence.[2]

Licence revoked, no revival.—A licence once revoked by operation of law, or act of parties does not get revived simply because the licence fee is survived after such revocation.[3]

64. Licensee's rights on eviction.—Where a licence has been granted for a consideration, and the licensee, without any fault of his own, is evicted by the grantor before he has fully enjoyed, under the licence, the right for which he contracted, he is entitled to recover compensation from the grantor.

---

1. *M/s. Hind Trading & Manufacturing Co.* v. *M/s. Didi Modes Pvt. Ltd.*, AIR 1993 Del. 301.
2. *Midi Extrusions Ltd.* v. *U.P. State I.D. Corpn.*, 2007 (69) ALR 95. See also *Joseph Severance* v. *Benny Mathew*, 2005 (7) SCC 667.
3. *Regional Manager, A.P.S.R.T.C.* v. *H.S. Sudhindra Aras*, AIR 2006 AP 207 (209).

NOTES

Non-permissibility of forceful eviction of licensee.—Under Section 64 even if a licensee is evicted, though grounds for revocation of licence do not exist, or is forcefully evicted, his only remedy is to recover compensation from grantor and not to resume occupation which undoubtedly would never mean that a licensee can be forcefully evicted by the grantor without taking recourse to the provisions of law.[1]

Applicability.—The provision under Section 64 of the Act does not expressly prohibit a contract to the contrary quo Sections 59 and 60 of the Act. Section 64 applies to a case where a licensee is evicted without any fault of his own.[2]

---

1. *Corporation of Calicut* v. *K. Sreenivasan*, AIR 2002 SC 2051.
2. *Sunnikim Bussan* v. *Manharlal T. Mody*, 2006 (4) Bom CR 131.